LANGUAGE AND LITERACY S

Dorothy S. Strickland, FOUNDING ED

Celia Genishi and Donna E. Alvermann, se

D0469872

* Volumes with an asterisk following the title are a part of the NCRLL set: Approaches to Language and Literacy Research, edited by JoBeth Allen and Donna E. Alvermann.

(Continued)

TEACHING THE

New Writing

Technology, Change, and Assessment in the 21st-Century Classroom

ANNE HERRINGTON
KEVIN HODGSON
CHARLES MORAN
EDITORS

Foreword by Elyse Eidman-Aadahl

TEACHERS COLLEGE PRESS

NW**P**

Teachers College, Columbia University
New York and London

The National Writing Project
Berkeley, CA

Published simultaneously by Teachers College Press, 1234 Amsterdam Avenue, New York, NY 10027 and the National Writing Project, 2105 Bancroft Way, Berkeley, CA 94720-1042.

The National Writing Project (NWP) is a network of more than 200 university-based sites that serve teachers of writing at all grade levels and in all subjects. The mission of the NWP is to improve student achievement by improving the teaching of writing and improving learning in the nation's schools.

"Advice from the Experts" by Bill Knott (2008) originally appeared in *Laugh at the End of the World: Collected Comic Poems 1969–1999*, BOA Editions, 2000. Reprinted with permission.

Library of Congress Cataloging-in-Publication Data
Teaching the new writing : technology, change, and assessment in the 21st-century classroom / Anne Herrington, Kevin Hodgson, and Charles Moran, editors.
    p. cm. — (Language and literacy series)
    Includes bibliographical references and index.
    ISBN 978-0-8077-4964-7 (pbk. : alk. paper)—ISBN 978-0-8077-4965-4 (hardcover : alk. paper)
    1. English language—Composition and exercises—Study and teaching—Computer-assisted instruction.   2. Creative writing—Computer-assisted instruction.   3. Educational technology.   I. Herrington, Anne, 1948–   II. Hodgson, Kevin Thomas.   III. Moran, Charles.
    LB1576.7.T45 2009
    808'.0420285—dc22

                                                                                    2008050120

ISBN: 978-0-8077-4964-7 (paperback)
ISBN: 978-0-8077-4965-4 (hardcover)

Printed on acid-free paper
Manufactured in the United States of America
16   15   14   13   12   11   10   8   7   6   5   4   3

Contents

Foreword

As technology continues to alter societies and cultures, it has fostered and supported an unprecedented expansion of human communication. In 2005, 172,000 new books were published in the United States alone. One hundred million Web sites now exist worldwide. One hundred and seventy-one billion e-mail messages are sent daily. To write in this world is to engage in a millennia-old act that is reinventing and regenerating itself in the modern age. (Writing Framework for the 2011 National Assessment of Educational Progress, p. 1)

While educators collected in this book were working at the intersections of writing and technology in their classrooms, another group of educators and public representatives were hard at work on a new Writing Framework for the 2011 National Assessment of Educational Progress.

A new NAEP Framework is no small thing. Congressionally mandated as "the Nation's Report Card," NAEP provides a nationally representative and continuing look at what students know and are able to do across subject areas at grades 4, 8, and 12. The Frameworks that govern NAEP assessments constitute major statements on the very nature of the field to be assessed. In March 2008, to the surprise of many, the National Assessment Governing Board announced that the new NAEP Framework in Writing would take the unprecedented step of requiring students to compose on computers. By 2011, mass assessment in writing would need to accommodate new digital tools.

As a member of the Planning Committee for that Framework, I witnessed the strong commitment to this change that developed among the committee's educators, business leaders, and civic representatives. As a committee, of course, we wrestle with some of the challenges that mass assessment must address as it moves in this direction: challenges of implementation, concerns about equity and the "digital divide," contradictions between standardized assessment contexts and digital tools built to offer maximum customization. We also wondered about the diverse impacts of such a change on students at the 4th, 8th, and 12th grade levels. But we agreed: by 2011 it would be hard to argue for the validity of an assessment in writing that did not provide for digital composing.

For all our efforts, however, we barely touched on the questions that motivate the teachers in this book: What does *writing* mean in a digital age? What happens when writers can routinely and easily blend image, audio, text, and movement in their compositions? How can teaching, learning, and assessment even begin to address the acceleration of writing, the new affordances of diverse tools and environments, the creation of new forms and genre that characterize communication today?

These questions belong to all of us, and in this volume they are taken up by teachers of students in grades three through college. These teachers, many from the National Writing Project and other teacher networks, demonstrate that changes catalyzed by the new digital tools and Web-enabled environments demand a whole revisioning of how we teach and assess writing at all levels. We benefit from seeing the spectrum of their work and their students' achievements gathered together.

At the National Writing Project, we see this as an extraordinary time for our discipline. The millennia-old act of writing is reinventing and regenerating itself in the modern age, and teachers and their students are at the forefront of creating new knowledge in the teaching of writing. The 16 educators collected here point toward the changes we must embrace if we are to realize the vision of 2011.

—*Elyse Eidman–Aadahl*, Director, National Programs and
Site Development for the National Writing Project

REFERENCE

Writing Framework for the 2011 National Assessment of Educational Progress. (n.d.) (unpublished working draft). National Assessment of Educational Progress, Washington, DC.

Preface

The conversations that led to this book began in 2005 at a conference titled "Writing, Teaching, and Technology, K–College." The conference pursued questions that increasingly engage educators at all levels: What has technology done to the concept and activity of writing? What am I to teach when I teach *writing*? What are effective ways to incorporate existing and emerging technologies into writing instruction to serve specific teaching ends?

The chapters in this book pursue these same questions in the context of goals for learning and assessment. The teachers who are the contributing authors ask their students to compose using words, images, and sound to create digital stories, Web sites, PowerPoint presentations, and blog texts that look and read quite differently from alphabetic texts. But what are the goals of these teachers for their students' learning? And how do they assess these multimodal texts? Further, in a time of mandated high stakes, standardized assessments, how do these teachers view these multimodal projects in relation to the demands of these assessments and the pressure to prepare students for them? In writing toward answers to these questions, we have encouraged the authors to include samples of their students' work. Some of these students are named directly in the text, and some are given pseudonyms, depending upon the nature of the materials used, the students' own preference, and the circumstances of the research.

Our intention with this book is to prompt teachers, elementary through postsecondary, to reflect on their own conceptions of writing and related teaching practice. To this end, in the chapters that follow we provide models of teachers who have engaged the new writing in their classrooms, identifying learning objectives and assessment criteria for their e-writing projects. For teachers, curriculum developers, policymakers, and students in graduate seminars in composition and language arts, we hope the collection will further reflection on the relations between multimodal and alphabetic writing and the nexus between classroom practice and state curriculum frameworks and assessments.

As the biographical sketches at the back of the book show, we coeditors and the contributing authors are all teachers, ranging from second grade through university and college teaching. The elementary, middle, and high school teacher-authors are located in states with a range of curriculum standards and approaches to statewide assessment, including standardized tests as well as portfolio assessments. Public and independent schools are represented, as well as rural, urban, and suburban schools, and a range of student populations in terms of ethnicity and class. Among the contributors are participants in the National Writing Project and the Bread Loaf School of English, two of the programs recommended as "Resources for Best Practice" by the National Commission on Writing. Both programs are also nationally known for fostering innovative work on writing and new technologies.

In these chapters, teachers ask their students to write for a range of purposes, including the interpretation of poetry, the presentation of research findings, the creation of scientific texts, and interpersonal communication and, as they do so, either implicitly or explicitly learning to compose with various media. The authors consider how they view the student creations—a digital story with audio and animation, a Web site with words and images, a poetry video—in relation to the traditional print-based, essayist conception of writing and the challenges these new texts pose for assessment. They also reflect on how their conceptions of writing and the writing process have changed, as well as ways in which their teaching practices have accommodated these changes. Tracing through all of the chapters is the teachers' belief that new media projects heighten the composers' sense of the presence of audience, their understanding of the social basis of literacy, and their willingness and ability to collaborate with their peers in the composing process.

In Chapter 1, Anne Herrington and Charles Moran set the context for the interwoven concerns of this collection: the evolution of computers and composition and the rise in high stakes standardized assessment. Chapters 2–11 are grouped into three parts according to grade level. The chapters in Part I focus on elementary and middle school classrooms; the chapters in Part II focus on high school classrooms; and the chapters in Part III are based on college-level classrooms. In the closing chapter, "Technology, Change, and Assessment: What We Have Learned," we coeditors reflect on our own reading of these chapters, pointing to what we found that was anticipated and what was unexpected and surprising in terms of expanded conceptions of writing, teaching and assessment practices, and classroom practices in relation to state curriculum standards and assessments.

Though we have organized the collection by grade level, we encourage readers to explore beyond their own familiar territories. As teacher-consultants with the National Writing Project we realize again each year, with every multi-grade Summer Institute, how much we learn from teachers at levels other than our own.

As you read these chapters, because we are publishing a traditional alphabetic text about electronic multimodal texts, you will be unable to click on a link to view students' multimodal compositions directly. To compensate, we include still images of some compositions, and a few of the authors provide the URLs for Web sites where you will find examples of some students' work. Because some of the terminology may be as new to you as it has been to some of us, we include a Glossary of Terms at the end of the book. And although Web sites are not permanent, we have included a list of useful Web resources for teaching the new writing.

The authors in these print pages provide thorough explanations of their goals for multimodal projects and their reflections on changes these projects entail for conceptions of writing, teaching practices, and assessment. We thank them for making this book possible.

We want to acknowledge as well others who supported this project and the work of the contributing authors. Grants from the University of Massachusetts President's Office and from Lee Edwards, the former Dean of the College of Humanities and Fine Arts, UMass Amherst, supported the conference that prompted us to consider this collection. We and many of the contributors to this book have also been supported by the teacher networks of the National Writing Project and the Bread Loaf Teacher Network. These and other informal networks in our schools and professional organizations provide sounding boards for sharing ideas, receiving formative feedback on our work, and encouraging us to take the risk to try new things, including new technologies.

We have been supported, as well, by the editorial staff of Teachers College Press, and in particular by Meg Lemke, Acquisitions Editor, and Susan Liddicoat, Development Editor, whose editing greatly improved our manuscript. Finally, we acknowledge our students whom we teach and from whom we learn, particularly about the world of multimodal composing.

—*Anne Herrington, Kevin Hodgson, and Charles Moran*

CHAPTER 1

Challenges for Writing Teachers

Evolving Technologies and Standardized Assessment

ANNE HERRINGTON
CHARLES MORAN

TECHNOLOGY AND THE EVOLUTION
OF WRITING, 1980–2008

There is a general consensus among teachers and researchers that reading and writing are changing, driven by the pressures of emerging technologies. Newspapers are in decline nationally, as advertising revenues migrate to the internet. Even the *New York Times* asks, on its own pages, "How much longer will the newspaper itself exist?" as citizen-reporter blogs routinely beat print media to breaking news (Dunlap, 2007, p. 5). And a range of studies documents the ways in which teenage literacy has changed, no longer exclusively the private book world of the print reader, but now the more social worlds of e-mail, cell phone text messaging, and on-line gaming (Anstey, 2002; Cruikshank, 2004; Ware & Warschauer, 2005). Scholars argue that the visual is returning to the page (Kress, 2003), that the page is losing ground to the screen (Snyder, 1997), and that new venues for writing, including e-mail, texting, and blogging, ask for new composing skills and mindsets. As an indicator of the rate of change in this entity we call writing, the words *texting* and *blogging*, not yet in our word processor's dictionary, appear today on our screens underscored with squiggly red lines. These words and the writing activities they represent are more recent than the latest iteration of the program's dictionary.

Teachers, schools, and colleges find themselves challenged to respond to this rapidly changing environment in responsible and constructive ways. Political rhetoric has, since the Clinton-Gore Administration, carried the assumption that simply bringing technology into our classrooms will help keep the United States competitive in the global economy (Selfe, 1999). Further, schools, colleges, parents, and students have been subjected to heavy duty marketing from hardware and software suppliers—beginning with the Apples in the Schools campaign in the 1980s, and continuing today with manufacturers of tablet PCs and designers of software that claims to grade and respond to student writing. Parents and students are regularly told that computer literacy is a prerequisite to success in the new economy. Responding to the voices of scholars and politicians and to marketing pressures from the technology industry, state and federal Departments of Education, and professional societies such as the College Composition and Communication Conference and the National Council of Teachers of English, have adopted statements that urge schools and colleges to embrace technology in their teaching.

Writing teachers have inevitably felt pressured to change from the forces we have listed above. But more important, teachers, and in particular those who have contributed to this book, have felt the world of writing shifting under them and have wanted to account for this change in their teaching. These teachers are embracing technology in their teaching, to support not only the learning of traditional essay texts but also new electronic text types—what Colin Lankshear and Michele Knobel (2006) call "post-typographic forms of texts" (p. 23). These new electronic texts—a Web site with words and images, blogs where multiple readers and writers contribute—challenge our basic notion of written texts as linear, verbal, single-authored texts.

At the same time that new forms of writing—and thus literacy—are emerging in our culture and in our classrooms, forces of assessment and standardization exert a counter-pressure, asking us to prepare students to produce conventional, formulaic print texts in scripted ways. Paradoxically, technology is also being harnessed for these purposes by educational publishers and testing companies, taking the form of machine-scoring and responding to student writing. So it is that technology seems to be leading us forward to new forms of writing, but, as used by standardized testing programs, backward to the five-paragraph theme.

Teachers are caught in this conflict, for their students' sake wanting to respond to the changes taking place in this thing we call writing, and at the same time wanting their students to do well in the 19th-century school essay called for on standardized tests. All of the contributors to this book have in some degree resolved this conflict, as they describe an e-writing project they have developed and taught, the learning objectives they had for this project, and their criteria for assessing the writing that resulted from the project. Taken together, the chapters support grounded generalizations about how our understandings of writing are changing and how this broader conception of writing—and the skills it draws on—aligns, or does not align, with current standardized testing. Equally, if not more important, the collection provides guidance and support to teachers generally, giving them models of teachers who have, despite pressures to do otherwise, engaged the new writing in their classrooms, identifying learning objectives and assessment criteria for their e-writing projects.

EVOLUTION OF COMPUTERS AND OUR (RELATED) UNDERSTANDINGS OF WRITING

The changes in this entity we call writing have, since the early 1980s, presented teachers with both challenges and opportunities.

Introduction of Computers to the Classroom

Writing teachers' first serious connection with emerging technologies dates from the early 1980s introduction of the microcomputer. With the Apple II and then the IBM PC, everyday writers who could afford the $2,000 price tag (and another $400 for the dot-matrix printer) could for the first time compose on the computer—a task that had been previously possible but difficult, requiring access to a mainframe computer, stacks of punch cards, and long waits at the print window. With the microcomputer, a writer could compose on-screen and easily revise without retyping the full draft. Not surprisingly, writing teachers at this time saw the microcomputer as a writer's tool, a really fancy typewriter that enabled writers to produce the traditional print forms with greater efficiency. In contrast to educators like Seymour Papert (1980), who saw computers more broadly as machines to think with, writing teachers initially saw the computer narrowly—as a writer's aid.

This focus on print text, which now seems so retrograde, was inevitable, given the writing process pedagogy then widely in place, with its focus on the single writer and on the production of text, and given that the microcomputer was at that point a limited, stand-alone machine. Word processing programs used (and still use) print-technology vocabularies, including such words as *page* and *indent* and *margin*, much as the early automobile was called the horseless carriage. The focus of teachers and researchers was on the relative virtues of early word-processing programs like *Bank Street Writer* and *Applewriter*, and later, on program suites like William Wresch's *Writer's Helper* that included, as future, more complex word processing programs would, grammar- and spelling-checkers. Typically in schools stand-alone computers were set up in labs—where students were scheduled, often for math courses or computer literacy sessions. In these labs, keyboarding, as an aspect of computer literacy, was taught by the teachers who formerly had taught typing or business communication.

Moving Beyond Print-Text

By the late 1980s it became clear to many that even though the new technology was good at producing traditional print texts, the text that it produced was different in subtle but important ways. Given the possibility of infinite and rapid revision, the text could seem always unfinished, always awaiting closure. And given the writer's new ability to change fonts and type sizes, the page increasingly was becoming visual, something to look at, as well as something transparent, to read through, for meaning (Lanham, 1989, p. 265).

Advances in processing speed and memory drove software development that made these changes widely evident. The first commercially available desktop publishing program, Aldus Pagemaker for the Macintosh, was introduced in 1985, as was the HP LaserWriter, the first PostScript printer. Expensive at first, these technologies gradually moved into homes and schools, making page design—not just type font and sizes, but the introduction of complex graphics and photographs—an aspect of the composing process and expanding our everyday sense of what writing might include.

Kress and Van Leeuwen (1996) were among the most cogent of those who argued that we must include the visual in our understanding of writing. Their *Reading Images: Grammar of Visual Design* brought the term "multimodal text" into popular use. Less than a decade later, in *Literacy in the New Media Age* (2003) Kress could invoke new technologies as an ally. In the opening paragraph of his book he argued, "It is no longer possible to think about literacy in isolation from a vast array of social, technological and economic factors" (p. 1). Of these factors he highlighted two: "the broad move from the now centuries-long dominance of writing to the new dominance of the image and, on the other hand, the move from the dominance of the medium of the book to the dominance of the medium of the screen." Kress (1999, 2003) maintains that in this screen-based and visual present we need to think of student writers not as producers of print text but as designers, composers who are able to use all available resources to make the meanings they need to make.

Writing as a Social Process

As the move from page to screen expanded our sense of what writing included, advances in communications technologies began to make it possible for teachers to work with the new writing as a social, as well as an individual, process. Packet-switching protocols developed in the early 1980s made it possible to connect multiple computers into a network; and as computing power continued to increase, classroom-based chat programs, running on local area networks, became a feature of some computer-equipped writing classrooms and labs. In a parallel development, home and classroom computers could be connected by telephone lines to wide area networks such as Bitnet; and on these networks electronic mail, or e-mail, became available as a form of written communication.

By the late 1980s, writing teachers were aware of the potential of networks for their student writers. As Judy Rickard, a primary teacher in Halifax, Nova Scotia, said, "Computers are useful for writing but something is still missing. Writing for classmates is a first step toward making writing a collaborative enterprise. Electronic mail takes writing even further. It brings our students' voices to the rest of the world." (Newman, 1989, p. 797). But this writing that Rickard referred to was not quite the same as page-based, classroom writing. It was quick and immediate, composed online, on the fly, without revision. Linguists had argued in the early days of electronic mail and bulletin boards that online writing was syntactically different from paper-based writing, an "electronic English" (Collot & Belmore, 1996). Somewhat later, scholars in composition studies called for a new rhetoric of e-mail (Hawisher & Moran, 1997).

As school computer labs began to be networked, and chat programs such as Interchange were designed for these networked classrooms, oral in-class discussions moved online, as students could now write directly to one another. This was yet another new form of writing: the written discussion. Writing teachers saw the online discussion as an advantage, because what had been oral was now written: there was more writing going on. Further, at the end of the chat session there was a transcript of the discussion, which itself could become the subject of further analysis and discussion. It was hoped that chat programs would erase the differences among a diverse group of students; that the voices of women and minority students, or students who were for one reason or another reluctant to speak out in class, would make themselves heard online in ways that they did not in face-to-face classroom discussions (Faigley, 1992).

Given that this new writing was social, not the relatively private writing composed and revised on a word processor, writing teachers confronted for the first time issues of online behavior. Online exchanges called *flaming*, or the use of hurtful language, took place—not in the relative privacy of the traditional student-teacher exchange of writing—but now in the full public forum enabled by the classroom network. The generally accepted explanation for this online behavior was twofold: that online writing was quick and immediate, and that online writing took place absent the usual social constraints imposed by the physical presence of the listener in face-to-face discussions.

Using the Hyperlink

A final development that changed writing forever was the hyperlink, first commercially available in 1987 as Apple's Hypercard, and later to become the warp and weft of the World Wide Web. The hyperlink radically changed text from linear to linked, distributed—what scholars and practitioners termed *rhizomatic*—that is, like a grass that propagates by its spreading roots, a shallow but broad, vast, and connected single organism. The hyperlink made it possible for the reader/viewer to go from one page or screen to another with the click of a mouse. Whereas the writer of print text could lead the reader along a line from the first sentence to the last, the writer of hypertext/hypermedia lost this control. The reader of print text had always been able to skip and scan. Extreme forms of print text, like Cortazar's (1967) *Hopscotch* or Sterne's (1760–1767) *Tristram Shandy*, had pushed at the limits of the printed page. But even in these experimental novels, the text was still there, linear, with a beginning and an end. With the advent of the hyperlink, the writer wrote with no certain knowledge of where the reader had been or where the reader would go next. Indeed, different readers would now almost certainly create their own paths through the hypertext/hypermedia composition. Writing for this linked medium brought new challenges for the writer, who now had to make decisions about not only voice, structure, syntax and vocabulary, but also what in the text to link to what, and for what purposes (Burbules, 1997).

Implications for Writing Classrooms

These changes in writing—the inclusion of the visual and the aural, the immediacy of online written communication, and the ability to link a word, sound, or image to other words, sounds, and images—have become widespread in the past decade as a result of the ever-increasing power of computers and the increasing availability of broadband Internet connections. Richard Lanham argued in 1989 that digitizing would blur the distinctions among the arts, because they now all had "digital equivalency" (p. 274). This blurring of distinctions is happening in homes, libraries, and classrooms, as emerging technologies make multimedia composition widely accessible. Indeed, multimedia is altering the way young people interact with our traditional spheres of literacy, and educators are just now beginning to consider the impact of these developments on their classrooms.

Young people are certainly active participants with technology, as the 2007 report of the Pew Internet and American Life Project, "Teens and Social

Media," amply demonstrates. The Report tells us that "93 percent of teens use the internet"; and, more important for our argument, that "64 percent of online teens ages 12–17 have participated in one or more among a wide range of content-creating activities on the internet" (Lenhart, Macgill, Madden, & Smith, 2007, p. i). According to the report, "39% of online teens share their own artistic creations online," "33% create or work on webpages or blogs," and "26% remix content they find online into their own creations" (p. i). Given these statistics, it is clear that something substantial is happening in the world of our students' literacy.

Teachers, because they are working closely with young people, often see changes taking place in society before the rest of us. Though they may want to adapt their classroom practice to these changes, they may find adaptation difficult because of the nature of the school and classroom or because change is, for all of us, often difficult. Change may be particularly difficult for teachers who are still relative newcomers to the world of multimedia. Lankshear and Knobel (2006) have argued that in reference to posttypographic forms of texts people have one of two mindsets: that of the "insider" and that of the "newcomer" (p. 34). All of us born before 1970 or thereabouts are newcomers, and as such have had to learn to read and compose posttypographic text forms; those of us born after 1970 or thereabouts are insiders, and find posttypographic forms of texts natural. So it is that outside of the classroom, the convergence of audio and video with reading and writing is normal literacy practice for many young people today, as they easily toggle among the various modes. Some teenagers, as the Pew report indicates, even compose with these new tools in mind, adding hyperlinks to connect ideas together in different ways or enhancing written text with moving images and sounds.

Kathleen Blake Yancey (2005) calls this use of the new media "textured literacy": "the ability to comfortably use and combine print, spoken, visual and digital processes in composing a piece of writing" (p. 38). She argues that writing can be improved through implementation of new technology if the technology is complementary to the curriculum. "Writers use digital technologies to write many new kinds of text, such as Web logs, hypertexts, and electronic portfolios. Helping writers develop fluency and competence in a variety of technologies is a key part of teaching writing in this century" (p. 38).

STANDARDS, STANDARDIZATION, AND THE TESTING ESTABLISHMENT

Whether we speak, as Yancey does, of a textured literacy or as Lankshear and Knobel do, of "posttypographic forms of texts" (2006, p. 25), it is clear that our understanding of what writing is has expanded. And yet state- or federally mandated standardized testing has had the effect of reducing the definition of what good writing entails.

Emphasis on Testing

The current era of accountability and standardized assessment began in the 1970s and has been gaining steam ever since (Gallagher, 2007; Hillocks, 2002). The *Newsweek* article "Why Johnny Can't Write" (Shiels, 1975), is emblematic of the 1970s Back to Basics discourse that used a decline in SAT test scores as one reason for more emphasis on teaching conventions and grammar. In 1983, President Reagan's Commission on Excellence in Education issued its report, *A Nation at Risk*, which decried low educational standards and called for standardized achievement tests as one means to increase rigor and improve education. These accountability provisions were enacted in many states and traced through various presidential initiatives, including those of George H.W. Bush and Bill Clinton, culminating in the *No Child Left Behind* (NCLB) legislation, signed into law in January of 2002.

A U.S. Department of Education (2004) Web site, entitled "Stronger Accountability: Testing for Results" addresses what it identifies as myths about testing, one being that "Testing narrows the curriculum by rewarding test-taking skills." According to the site, "the Reality" is as follows:

> Surely a quality education reaches far beyond the confines of any specific test. But annual testing is important. It establishes benchmarks of student knowledge. Tests keyed to rigorous state academic standards provide a measure of student knowledge and skills. If the academic standards are truly rigorous, student learning will be as well.

A Study of State Writing Assessments

While rigor is important, the content of a test is more important in relation to curricula and student learning. As George Hillocks' (2002) research has shown, high stakes statewide assessments can narrow curricula, depending on the standards they target and the type of literacy privileged by the test design and rubrics. In *The Testing Trap: How State Writing Assessments Control Learning*, Hillocks reports on his study of K–12 statewide assessment programs in five states: Illinois, Kentucky, New York, Oregon, and Texas. These five states provide a range in population, test design, and nature of the stakes for the assessments. For the study, he analyzed mandating legislation, test design, rubrics, and sample papers; he also interviewed state department of education officials as well as teachers and administrators in six school districts in each state: two large urban districts, two suburban districts (one middle class, one working class), one small town district, and one rural school district.

Hillocks' findings show the most dramatic contrast in test design between Kentucky, on the one hand, and Texas and Illinois on the other. Kentucky's Commonwealth Accountability Testing System (CATS) for writing, using a portfolio, is closest to sound assessment principles and includes the broadest range of writing. Unfortunately, few other states equal Kentucky in this regard. The Kentucky writing assessment includes an on-demand writing assessment and a portfolio writing assessment, with the portfolio carrying more weight than the on-demand writing. The portfolio for each grade level includes four pieces of student-selected writing in a range of genres. For example, for grade four, students are to include one example of reflective, personal, literary, and transactional writing, with at least one coming from a study area other than English language arts. For grade 12, one piece is to be reflective, one to be Personal, Expressive, or Literary Writing; one to be Transactional Writing in a genre of choice, and another Transactional Writing with an analytical or technical focus various authentic genres (forms). At least one piece must come from a content area other than English (Kentucky Department of Education, 2007).

In contrast, the writing assessments for Illinois and Texas are on-demand tests that require either one or two samples of narrative or persuasive writing. For example, the Texas assessment for grade 7 calls for one sample of narrative writing; the exit level assessment calls for one sample of persuasive writing (Texas Education Agency, 2006). In Illinois, the grade eight assessment calls for one narrative composition and one persuasive one (Illinois State Board of Education, 2007).

These assessments, like those of many other states across the country, favor traditional print-based writing. Further, while it seems not to have been the intention of those designing the tests, these tests also tend to elicit formulaic writing. In this regard, it is worth noting that on the Illinois Web site, which includes the scoring rubric and sample essays for persuasive writing, all five of the top-rated essays are five paragraphs long.

For all of these assessments—even Kentucky's—only traditional print-based writings are assessed. Further, for the states that assess only on-demand writing, the universe of writing is reduced even further to one mode at the high school level. The criteria for assessment are frequently variations on the traditional ones of focus, development, organization, and conventions. On the basis of his study of the five states, Hillocks (2002) concludes:

> If state assessments have the following characteristics for expository and persuasive writing, it is predictable that they will engender formulaic writing and the thinking that goes with it: (1) prompts providing a specific topic and subject

matter with no or highly limited accompanying data, (2) one limited session for writing, and (3) criteria that call only for 'developing ideas' without specifying the nature of development much beyond a request for detail. (p. 201)

Hillocks is describing conditions that obtain in far too many states.

The impact of these K–12 assessments obviously extends to higher education as well as students move from high school into college. Assessments that invite and reward formulaic writing work at cross purposes with efforts to improve articulation between high school and college, and teach rhetorical and composing skills identified as valuable by most high school and college teachers. See, for example, the Council of Writing Program Administrators (2007), Outcomes Statement for First Year Composition. It identifies as outcomes a range of rhetorical skills (including ability to "respond to the needs of different audiences" and "write in several genres") and writing process skills (including ability to "use a variety of technologies to address a range of audiences"). Comments by high school teachers in *What is 'College-Level' Writing?* (Sullivan & Tinberg, 2006) reflect similar values. Higher education is also being pressured to adopt standardized tests for assessment of broad learning outcomes, including for writing. (See, for example, American Association of State Colleges and Universities, 2006; Commission on the Future of Higher Education, 2006; National Center on Education and the Economy, 2006).

Implications for Curriculum

Hillocks' (2002) study documents what we know from myriad sources: tests, particularly when high stakes, drive curriculum. If persuasive writing is what is assessed in a timed writing, then that is what is going to be privileged in instruction, particularly in two situations: when a school has been identified as underperforming, and when teachers do not have adequate education about writing theory and pedagogy. As Hillocks concludes, "Few teachers had the special training in composition and rhetoric that might enable them to conduct a detailed critique of the assessments. Indeed, it is much more common for the state assessment to become the theory of writing upon which teachers base their teaching" (p. 198). In other words, even though state curriculum standards are often more theoretically sound and broad based, it is the high-stakes tests and the limited standards that they define and target that guide practice.

For this reason, state standards regarding technology or media do not carry the weight that the test-targeted writing standards carry. Further, some states do not even include standards for technology. If we add our home state, Massachusetts, to the five states Hillocks studied, only three of these six states have standards related to technology or media: Kentucky, Massachusetts, and

Texas. All three of these include media production or communication, but none use the words writing or composing. The Massachusetts Media Production standard (Massachusetts Department of Education, 2007), however, invokes criteria consistent with criteria for writing, suggesting some connection between the two:

> Students will design and create coherent media productions (audio, video, television, multimedia, Internet, emerging technologies) with a clear controlling idea, adequate detail, and appropriate consideration of audience, purpose, and medium. (p. 96)

Further, this standard is linked explicitly with a writing strand for research, but only the research strand. For the most part, however, these standards are distinct from writing standards, although as we write in 2008, a committee convened by the state Department of Education is recommending that the media standards be integrated with writing, research, and reading standards.

Electronic Assessment of Writing

Ironically, as electronic technologies create new possibilities for writing, educational publishing companies are using technology to teach a reductive construction of writing. Consider three such products that are being marketed for use in elementary through college classrooms: *Criterion*, available from ETS; *Writing RoadMap*, from McGraw-Hill; and *MY Access*, from Vantage Learning. All three use automated scoring programs to assess writing, providing feedback to student writers and assessment scores for teachers and administrators. All are marketed by invoking the language of accountability and large-scale assessment, promising to evaluate students in relation to a benchmark corpus of texts and to provide tracking data for teachers and administrators.

While the three automated scoring programs differ in some features, all focus on traditional print-based essays written with a word processor. Each program operates by providing a bank of essay topics for teachers to use for writing assignments. *Criterion* also enables teachers to create their own prompts, following the model of the prompts in their essay banks. These prompts are similar to those for on-demand writing assessments, tailored to writing from observation without other inquiry or research. Most high school prompts are for expository or persuasive writing. For persuasive writing, the formulaic prompt of arguing for one of two alternatives is favored. These programs are touted for providing speedy and consistent feedback, and, on the basis of testimonials on their Web site, for improving student writing. On the basis of our own review of these programs and that of others (Cheville, 2004; Rothermel, 2006), we know that the automated scoring programs distort the nature of writing as a human activity, a dialogue between writer and reader, even as they invoke the language of process writing. The holistic feedback these programs give is generic, reading much like scoring rubrics, and thus not tailored to a specific writing. Further, given that a machine program cannot actually read as a person, it responds to what it can count—structure, sentence length, word frequency—and not to rhetorical factors such as voice or to the substantive nature of writing.

Although the scoring rubrics imply that depth of thinking can be assessed, from our experience using one of these programs, *Criterion*, we have found that it identifies not depth and complexity, but length; number but not quality of examples; and traditional, explicitly marked structure but not more complex or implicit structure. It also errs in identification of errors. (Herrington, 2007; Moran & Herrington, 2006). For example, for an essay written for *Criterion* that received a score of 4 initially, we were able to raise the score to the top rating of 6 by providing an additional superficial example, creating five paragraphs instead of the original three, and adding a clearly marked facsimile of a thesis statement. The rubric for a 6 includes the following explanation:

> You have put together a convincing argument. Here are some of the strengths evident in your writing:
> Your essay:
>
> • Looks at the topic from a number of angles and responds to all aspects of what you were asked to do
> • Responds thoughtfully and insightfully to the issues in the topic

Despite the invocation of a human reader, *Criterion*'s e-rater cannot read as a human and is incapable of deciding on whether an essay is "thoughtful" or "insightful." In fact, for an essay such as we entered into the program, it provides a mistaken and misleading judgment, praising a rather limited revision as thoughtful when it did not differ substantially from the 4-rated first draft (Herrington, 2007). In short, *Criterion* and its cousins, *Writing Roadmap* and *MY Access*, reinforce the reductive definition of writing instantiated in most statewide tests of writing.

While there have been few studies of the uses of automated programs for instructional purposes, in his study of schools where all students had laptops, Mark Warschauer (2006) notes that of the 10 schools he studied, three were using *MY Access*. He reports that in those schools, 51% of students agreed that *MY Access* helped improve their writing, as compared to 16% who disagreed and 33% who indicated either "don't know" or "neutral" (pp. 73–74). What is noteworthy, though, is that he observed that students focused on mechanical aspects and tended to ignore "the more generic feedback offered by *MY*

Access on style, organization, and development" (p. 74). Warschauer also reports that automatic evaluation "tended to reinforce formulaic writing as students dropped colloquial language or nontraditional structures to try to get a high score" (p. 74). He concludes, though, that this type of writing is what the schools value, so automated assessment isn't the cause of it. Also of note, he mentions the difficulty of "low-SES students" with poor language skills: "working independently with automated essay feedback was difficult for students who could not comprehend the meaning of the feedback or understand the grammatical terms used" (p. 149).

Integrating Technology and Writing

Fortunately, there are a few voices resisting the use of technology in these limited ways and resisting the focus on standardized assessment. These voices are reflected in the second report of the National Commission on Writing (2006), *Writing and School Reform*. While reinforcing the recommendations of the Commission's first report, *The Neglected "R,"* in a number of ways, *Writing and School Reform* differs on key points related to technology and assessment. Some background: The Commission is notable among national education commissions in that it included reasonable representation of teachers, instead of being solely composed of business executives and senior educational administrators. Its first report, *The Neglected "R,"* makes a persuasive case that more resources need to be devoted to improving writing and professional development for teachers of writing. For our purposes, two other recommendations are of note: one is that assessment be "fair and authentic" (p. 67). The second regards technology: that "the private sector work with curriculum specialists, assessment experts, and state and local educational agencies to apply emerging technologies to the teaching, development, grading, and assessment of writing" (p. 68). The elaboration for this point focused almost exclusively on assessment, including programs for "technologically based corrections and commentary on students' papers" (p. 69). (The hand of the College Board, which sponsored the Commission, may be evident in this recommendation that favors technology for assessment, given its links to the Educational Testing Service ETS.)

After the publication of *The Neglected "R,"* in a move exceptional for national educational commissions, the Commission held hearings across the country at which hundreds testified, most of them elementary through college teachers of writing. According to *Writing and School Reform,* one of the clear messages from those hearings was that assessment has gone awry:

> Standardization and scripting of instruction threaten to undermine writing instruction. (p. 9)

> Existing state standards and assessment systems frequently constrain schools and teachers from best practice in writing. (p. 19)

Further, while the consensus of those testifying supported "fair and authentic assessment," they did not support recommendations that money be invested in developing technologies for grading and assessment. Instead of the first report's heavy emphasis on using technology for assessment and error correction, those testifying supported using technology as a tool for writers and learners. Specifically, this was the reasoning of those testifying:

> *The Neglected "R"* seemed to consider technology largely as a tool for advancing traditional writing and assessment instead of understanding that video and multimedia projects enabled students to find new ways not only to communicate with their audiences but to understand the world around them. (p. 22)

Those testifying also strongly endorsed recommendations in *The Neglected "R"* for more professional development for teachers, not just to deliver curricula but to develop it.

Perhaps the American public is coming to realize the limitations of the current apparatus of standardized assessment as well, and its costs—both financial and educational. According to a national survey, *Learning to Write*, conducted by Belden, Russonello, and Stewart (2007), "by a margin of two to one, the public prefers putting more resources into helping teachers teach writing, rather than putting those resources into testing students to see how well they are learning to write." Those surveyed also recognize the importance of learning to write, as over 80 percent said that students should "learn to write well as a requirement for high school graduation" and believed that writing is important to success in college and success in work, "regardless of what type of job it is."

The teachers in this collection build on the views expressed in *Writing and School Reform*, as they develop curricula that teach students to use new media to compose, communicate with others for a range of purposes, and understand and act in the world around them. In doing so, these teachers help us all understand how teachers and their students can negotiate between two apparently distinct worlds, the world of standardized writing assessments that privilege linear, essayist literacy, and the world of contemporary society where the ability to compose nonlinear, multimodal, and sometimes interactive texts is becoming increasingly valued. More positively, these chapters should help educators address the integration of technology and writing in both practice and in the curriculum standards that guide practice. The teachers who have authored the chapters that follow embody in their practice the words of Sandholtz, Ringstaff, and Dwyer (1997), authors of *Teaching with Technology*.

The benefits of technology integration are best realized when learning is not just the process of transferring facts from one person to another, but when the teacher's goal is to empower students as thinkers and problem solvers. Technology provides an excellent platform—a conceptual environment—where children can collect information in multiple formats and then organize, visualize, link and discover relationships among facts and events. Students can use the same technologies to communicate their ideas to others, to argue and critique their perspectives, to persuade and teach others, and to add greater levels of understanding to their growing knowledge. (p. 176)

REFERENCES

American Association of State Colleges and Universities. (2006). Value-added assessment: Accountability's new frontier. *Perspectives*. Retrieved January 24, 2008, from http://www.aascu.org/pdf/06_perspectives.pdf

Anstey, M. (2002). It's not all black and white: Postmodern picture books and technology. *Journal of Adolescent and Adult Literacy, 45,* 444–457.

Belden, Russonello, and Stewart Research and Communications. (2007). *Learning to write*. Survey conducted for the National Writing Project. Retrieved May 31, 2007, from http://www.writingproject.org/cs/nwpp/download/nwp_file/8614/NWP_2007_Survey_Report—Writing.doc?x-r=pcfile_d

Burbules, N. C. (1997). Rhetorics of the web: Hyperreading and critical literacy. In I. Snyder (Ed.), *From page to screen: Taking literacy into the electronic era,* (pp. 102–122). St. Leonards, Australia: Allen and Unwin.

Cheville, J. (2004). Automated scoring technologies and the rising influence of error. *English Journal, 93*(4), 47–52.

Collot, M., & Belmore, N. (1996). Electronic language: A new variety of English. In S. C. Herring (Ed.), *Computer-mediated communication: Linguistic, social, and cross-cultural perspectives,* pp. 13–28. Amsterdam: Benjamins.

Commission on Excellence in Education. (1983). *A Nation at Risk*. Retrieved April 18, 2007, from http://www.ed.gov/pubs/NatAtRisk/risk.html

Commission on the Future of Higher Education, United States Department of Education. (2006). *A test of leadership: Charting the future of U.S. higher education*. Washington, DC: U.S. Department of Education.

Cortazar, J. (1967). *Hopscotch*. (G. Rabassa, Trans.) London: Collins, Harville Press.

Council of Writing Program Administrators. (2007). Outcomes statement for first-year composition. Retrieved June 8, 2007, from http://www.wpacouncil.org/positions/outcomes.html

Cruikshank, K. (2004). Literacy in multilingual contexts: Change in teenagers' reading and writing. *Language and Education, 18*(6), 459–473.

Educational Testing Service. (2007). *Criterion* Online Writing Evaluation. Retrieved April 18, 2007, from http://www.ets.org/portal/site/ets/menuitem.435c0b

5cc7bd0ae7015d9510c3921509/?vgnextoid=b47d253b164f4010VgnVCM
10000022f95190RCRD

Dunlap, David W. (2007, June 10). Copy! *The New York Times*, section 4, p. 5.

Faigley, L. (1992). *Fragments of rationality: Postmodernity and the subject of composition*. Pittsburgh, PA: University of Pittsburgh Press.

Gallagher, C. (2007). *Reclaiming assessment: A better alternative to the accountability agenda*. Portsmouth, NH: Heinemann.

Hawisher, G., & Moran, C. (1997). The rhetorics and languages of electronic mail. In I. Snyder (Ed.), *From page to screen: Taking literacy into the electronic era*, (pp. 80–101). Sydney, Australia: Allen and Unwin.

Herrington, A. (2007, April 21). *Brave new world: Writing, assessment, and new technologies*. Paper presented at the annual conference of the State University of New York Council on Writing, University of Albany, SUNY. Albany, NY.

Hillocks, George, Jr. (2002). *The testing trap: How state writing assessments control learning*. New York: Teachers College Press, 2002.

Illinois State Board of Education. (2007). Student Assessment: Writing. Retrieved April 26, 2007, from http://www.isbe.state.il.us/assessment/writing.htm

Kentucky Department of Education. (2007). Core Content for Writing Assessment. Retrieved April 24, 2007, from http://education.ky.gov/oapd/curric/textbook/cd_revised/CurrDocs/CCwrite.PDF

Kress. G. R. (1999). Genre and the changing contexts for English language arts. *Language Arts*, *32*(2), 185–96.

Kress, G. R. (2003). *Literacy in the new media age*. London: Rutledge.

Kress, G. R., & van Leuwen, T. (1996). *Reading images: The grammar of visual design*. London: Routledge.

Lanham, R. A. (1989). The electronic word: Literary study and the digital revolution. *New Literary History*, *20*(2), 265–290.

Lankshear, C., & Knobel, M. (2006). *New literacies: Everyday practices and classroom learning*, 2nd ed. Maidenhead, UK: Open University Press.

Lenhart, A., Macgill, A. R., Madden, M., & Smith, A. (2007). Teens and social media. Pew Internet and American Life Project. Retrieved August 13, 2008, from http://www.pewinternet.org/pdfs/PIP_Teens_Social_Media_Final.pdf

Massachusetts Department of Education. Massachusetts English Language Arts Curriculum Framework June 2001. Retrieved March 29, 2007, from http://www.doe.mass.edu/frameworks/ela/0601.pdf

McGraw-Hill Education. (2007). *Writing RoadMap 2.0*. Retrieved April 18, 2007, from http://www.ctb.com/products/product_summary.jsp?FOLDER%3C%3Efolder_id=1408474395292760&CONTENT%3C%3Ecnt_id=10134198673325234&bmUID=1176919523404

Moran, C., & Herrington, A. (2006). *Writing Across the Curriculum: The Power of An Idea*. Keynote Address for the 8th International Writing across the Curriculum Conference. Clemson, SC. Retrieved April 18, 2007, from http://wac.colostate.edu/proceedings/wac2006/keynote.cfm

National Center on Education and the Economy. (2006). *Tough choices or tough times: The report of the new commission on the skills of the American workforce*. San Francisco, CA: Jossey-Bass.

National Commission on Writing for America's Families, Schools, and Colleges. (2006, May). *Writing and school reform including the neglected "R"*. College Board. Retrieved March 12, 2007, from http://www.writingcommission.org/

Newman, J. M. (1989). Online: From far away. *Language Arts, 66*(7), 791–797.

Papert, S. (1980). *Mindstorms: Children, computers, and powerful ideas.* New York: Basic Books.

Rothermel, B. (2006). Automated writing instruction: Computer-assisted or computer-driven pedagogies. In P. Ericsson & R. Haswell (Eds.), *Machine scoring of student essays,* pp. 199–210. Logan: Utah State University Press.

Sandholtz, J. H., Ringstaff, C., & Dwyer, D. C. (1997). *Teaching with technology: Creating student-centered classrooms.* New York: Teachers College Press.

Selfe, C. L. (1999). *Technology and literacy in the twenty-first century.* Urbana, IL: National Council of Teachers of English.

Shiels, M. (1975, December 8). Why Johnny Can't Write. *Newsweek, 92,* 58–65.

Snyder, I. (Ed.). (1997). *From page to screen: Taking literacy into the electronic era.* Sydney, Australia: Allen and Unwin.

Sterne, L. (1760–1767). *The life and opinions of Tristram Shandy.* York: John Hinxman.

Sullivan, P., & Tinberg, H. (2006). *What is 'college-level' writing?* Urbana, IL: National Council of Teachers of English.

Texas Education Agency.(2006, Spring). *Texas assessment of knowledge and skills, Grade 7 written composition scoring guide.* Retrieved April 22, 2007, from http://www.tea.state.tx.us/student.assessment/resources/release/taks/2006/g7sg.pdf

United States Department of Education. (2004, September 16). *Stronger Accountability: Testing for results.* Retrieved April 17, 2007, from http://www.ed.gov/nclb/accountability/ayp/testingforresults.html

Vantage Learning. (2007). *MY Access!* Retrieved April 18, 2007, from http://www.vantagelearning.com/myaccess/

Ware, P., & Warschauer, M. (2005). Hybrid literacy texts and practices in technology-intensive environments. *International Journal of Educational Research, 43*(7, 8), 432–445.

Warschauer, M. (2006). *Laptops and literacy: Learning in the wireless classroom.* New York: Teachers College Press.

Yancey, K. B. (2005). Using multiple technologies to teach writing. *Educational Leadership, 62,* 38–40.

PART I

Beginning in Elementary and Middle School

In this part, Marva Solomon and Glen Bledsoe, both elementary school teachers, and Kevin Hodgson, a middle-school teacher, focus on impacts on composing processes and writing workshop. In Chapter 2, Solomon examines the creation of Web sites by second-grade students who are struggling readers and writers, showing us how the project introduces them to new, nonlinear genres and the composing process while also foregrounding the social nature of writing. In Chapter 3, Bledsoe describes how a project-based multimodal assignment provides an occasion for collaboration and engagement of students in the writing process—particularly planning and revising in ways that would be difficult without technology. In Chapter 4, Hodgson investigates how sixth graders tap into digital tools through the process of composing and publishing their own multimodal picture books that are intended explain scientific concepts to younger students.

CHAPTER 2

True Adventures of Students Writing Online

Mummies, Vampires, and Schnauzers, Oh My!

MARVA SOLOMON

This chapter chronicles the events and findings of a digitally enhanced summer tutoring session that took a small group of struggling primary readers to the Internet for a writing workshop. As the teacher for this project, I had a pretty exciting ride. I was treated to a small and intimate group of students who were highly engaged by the computer and its capabilities. And it is not often one gets to participate in downright serious conversations about mummies, vampires, and Schnauzers—some of the topics the students decided to write about—all in the same half hour. And beyond these teacher perks, I felt as if I were a part of something big. This project provided opportunities for children to create texts with Internet, digital, and multimodal elements, giving them an insider's (Lankshear & Knobel, 2003) knowledge of how such communication works, a valuable skill for comprehending the digital messages of others.

For all the newness and excitement of using the multimedia capabilities of computers to create their writing projects, however, the moment when these students were most enthusiastic about their writing came when their Web pages were printed out on plain white paper. Then, they had something to grasp, wave in the air, and spontaneously hold up proudly to the video camera, singing, "Check this out, check this out."

THE PROJECT

The premise of this project was not to replace the traditional writing workshop as it exists in thousands of primary classrooms today, but rather to expand student writers' vistas to a new genre relevant to the lives they lead by creating their own online content. Writing instruction must continue to evolve to fit the electronic buzz and zap of the high tech social worlds of children. This project was a first step for me in discovering how writing workshop can and will change when we give students the opportunity to use the multimodal communication tools available through computers and the Internet.

Of particular interest to me was how the online nature of the writing might affect the social nature of young writers' process. Literacy researcher Anne Haas Dyson (1989) told us that young children do important social work while writing. How will online writing and the use of computers reflect or change what we already know about writing workshop?

This project took place during the summer, in an all but empty suburban/rural elementary school, in a classroom ringed with desks and chairs still stacked and pushed together for the summer. The students' 3-hours-a-day regimen occurred over 3 weeks in June and encompassed 13 days of classes. In this chapter, I focus on the participation of Mario, Kevin, and Krystal, (all pseudonyms), three of my former second graders whom I and a colleague offered to tutor due to their status as struggling readers and writers. They were all headed to third grade next year, and I felt they would greatly benefit from more time spent reading and writing in a formal setting. Other students also participated in the tutoring sessions.

Each day, the tutoring sessions started with a joke to start us off laughing and enjoying language. Next, there was a children's book read-aloud, and then a think-aloud centered upon a reading strategy that provided these students a head start on preparing for third grade's standardized tests. Then, students were given the opportunity to practice the targeted reading strategy that was modeled during that day's read-aloud. Tutoring also included a small period of free-choice reading, memory and structural analysis word games with second and third grade words identified as nonnegotiable in the local district's curriculum guide, and very important—snack time.

The last 45 minutes of each tutoring session were dedicated to online writing workshop. I defined online writing workshop as a time when the students became Kimber & Wyatt-Smith's (2006, p. 30) "students-as-designers"; they were engaged in researching, planning, and composing, all with the tool of wireless-capable computers. We were blessed with access to the elementary school's cart of aging Apple iBook laptops, which we eagerly unlocked, pulled out, and turned on each day.

I assigned students to three tasks during the online writing workshop, tasks that were designed to give them meaningful ways to practice the traditional literacy skills of speaking, reading, writing, and listening. The first task was to create a beginning page that served as an All About Me page. It wasn't long before they were given a second task: to create a page about something they enjoyed writing about. Here, John Cena met Baptista in a coffin match (or some such violent action) as one of the students wrote about wrestlers. The only girl in the group launched the soon to be infamous Girl's Only page that featured a few of her favorite singers.

These first two tasks were complete by the beginning of the second week of tutoring. The third and final task required students to create an Expert Page, a page where they presented knowledge on a topic that they had researched using Internet resources and compiled as an aesthetically pleasing Web page. The third task held the high expectations that the children would take on the role of students-as-designers and meet the 21st century challenge of juggling technology, literacy, and information learning.

When the children were asked what they liked to write about, Mario said wrestlers, and Krystal said singers. Kevin was not present for the initial interview. Not surprisingly, the first topics Mario and Krystal chose to write about during online writing workshop were wrestling and singing stars, respectively.

Neither Kevin nor Krystal had working computers in their homes at the time of the study. Kevin mentioned that the computer in his home did not work because the "Internet was broken." When asked what adults used computers for, Kevin had no answer, but Krystal mentioned that her mom, whom she did not live with, would sometimes download music. Both Krystal and Kevin were hard pressed to come up with their own ideas for how adults might possibly use computers for work.

In contrast, Mario was a fount of information regarding computers. He regularly used his computer at home to look up wrestlers and wrestling sites. When he wasn't looking up wrestling sites, he claimed he was playing his poker games. He was fairly certain that most adults used computers for shopping and playing games. Mario was the most confident computer user throughout the study. Krystal required a lot of handholding and often called out for technical help, and it was not uncommon for Kevin to exclaim at the "crazy" things that his computer would do unexpectedly.

My students used the Web-based software, Think.com, to create their Web pages. Think.com is an educational endeavor from the Oracle Education Foundation (2006). On the home page, they describe their site as "an online community for learning."

Think.com is a very restricted community where only educational organizations can enroll and gain access. The user name and password system is very complicated, which made it hard to use with second graders, but also made the environment very secure. If the school chooses, exposure to children from other schools can be limited, or the school can be open to interact with the entire world wide Think.com community. Students often reached out to strangers and friends alike with "stickies,"—a way for people within the online environment to leave notes for each other—asking others to visit their site. The site is patrolled by the participating teachers who have the power to flag and delete content that is deemed inappropriate. Also, teachers are e-mailed a reminder if pictures have been posted by their students longer than 15 days without teacher review. Admittedly, things can slip through, as evidenced by my missing an offending graphic from Mario until he showed it to me during tutoring. Think.com has more interactive and collaborative tools than were used by the students in this particular study.

Search engines Yahooligans, KidsClick, and Nettrekker were used when students were gathering information and I, as their teacher, searched for links they might be interested in as well. Music clips came from Amazon.com, as copyright laws allow up to 15 seconds to be used for educational purposes. Last, the educational film database, United Streaming, was used to access films appropriate for the topics that interested the students.

As mentioned previously, students used Apple iBook G3s computers from a mobile cart for this study. The carts were designed to provide a lab on wheels for classroom use. The G3s, most likely typical of elementary school hardware everywhere, were out of date, slow, quirky, and poorly maintained. Krystal's laptop was missing the G key which caused her some consternation, but also some pleasure as she repeatedly pressed the "funny-feeling" rubbery knob that usually resides hidden underneath the keys. The computers had wireless cards and were also connected wirelessly to a laser printer that was included with the cart.

Since my students were struggling readers and English Language Learners (ELL), my goal for their online writing was to provide them with authentic and meaningful experiences with language. Often, instruction for students with their special needs is focused heavily on skills in isolation and word drills disconnected from real texts. Yet most teachers know that children with language issues benefit greatly from the meaning supports that real texts offer, and benefit greatly from creating and reading their own texts.

TEACHING CONSIDERATIONS AND ASSESSMENT

During the body of this project, I was interested in my students' invented spellings and conventions. Editing and revising were done in later sessions.

One reason for this was that, in my experience, struggling readers who are focused on correct spelling and grammar often spend less time focused on gaining meaning from the texts they read and write. Also, I preferred to see what progress they have made by evaluating what they are able to produce on their own.

As I perused my students' online writing, I found Krystal to be the strongest speller but the least likely to take a risk and include a more interesting or specialized word in her writing. Mario was able to take highly complicated information about mummies from video and higher level Web sites and synthesize the ideas into his own words. During this process, his spelling suffered, but for this project, I would definitely trade the thinking skills for the conventions.

Figure 2.1 is a passage from Mario's Web page. He is telling his version of the complicated story of Hatshepsut, female pharaoh of Egypt. To produce this text, he used an educational United Streaming video to first gather his information. To organize his thoughts before writing, he retold the story to Kevin and then to me. Both Kevin and I questioned him when we didn't understand what he was saying, and his ideas became more organized. Mario struggled greatly to produce this text, but he was highly motivated to complete it, I believe, due to the digital nature of the task.

Kevin, an identified English Language Learner, also synthesized information from high level, multimodal Internet texts. Much of his digital writing, like his paper and pencil writing, embodied typical spelling patterns for an ELL.

To make sure this project met the curricular goals of my school district, I created a checklist based on the literacy skills in the third grade Essential Knowledges and Skills, the Texas State Standards (Texas Education Agency, 2007). The checklist can be found in Figure 2.2.

Figure 2.1. Mario's Mummies Page

mummies

Story | 6.28.2006
hacifes

hacifes was a great leadr but he was a she becuause her dad died. she wuted to be a fero so she put on a fakn berd. so they puta girl as a boy. so she had a son. so he wanted to be ferro so he be came a soldier leader so she die her son be cam a ferro so he read of hacifes as ferro an he rewrot the histre then her son ruled the wold for 25 years.

Figure 2.2. Texas Essential Knowledges and Skills Checklist

---

(7) Reading/variety of texts. The student reads widely for different purposes in varied sources. The student is expected to:

___ (B) read from a variety of genres for pleasure and to acquire information from both print and electronic sources.

___ (C) read to accomplish various purposes, both assigned and self-selected.

(9) Reading/comprehension. The student uses a variety of strategies to comprehend selections read aloud and selections read independently. The student is expected to:

___ (H) produce summaries of text selections.

___ (I) represent text information in different ways, including story maps, graphs, and charts.

(12) Reading/inquiry/research. The student generates questions and conducts research using information from various sources. The student is expected to:

___ (D) use multiple sources, including print such as an encyclopedia, technology, and experts, to locate information that addresses questions.

(20) Writing/inquiry/research. The student uses writing as a tool for learning and research. The student is expected to:

___ (A) write or dictate questions for investigating.

___ (B) record his/her own knowledge of a topic in a variety of ways such as by drawing pictures, making lists, and showing connections among ideas.

___ (C) take simple notes from relevant sources such as classroom guests, books, and media sources.

___ (D) compile notes into outlines, reports, summaries, or other written efforts using available technology.

Note: Checklist compiled from Texas Education Agency. *Texas Essential Knowledges and Skills*. Retrieved August 25, 2008 from http://www.tea.state.tx.us/teks/.

I also used the rubric found in Table 2.1 to measure their progress toward traditional literacy skills as well as their progress toward becoming fluent users and creators of digital content.

THREE QUESTIONS

When I began the tutoring sessions, I kept in mind three questions about young children and online writing:

- How does the online aspect of the writing affect the social nature of primary students' writing process?

Table 2.1. Online Writing Workshop Rubric

	4 To a great extent	3 Adequately	2 Very Little	0 Not at all
Gathers information across multiple electronic sources and synthesizes the information into Web page test.				
Combines multiple digital texts, images, and multimedia resources to create a coherent message.				
Makes decisions about their digital writing based on self interests and audience considerations.				

- How do students, and their teacher, negotiate ownership of online materials?
- How will online writing and the use of computers reflect or change what I already know about writing workshop and primary writers?

The following three sections describe the adventure my students and I took in pursuit of the answers to these questions.

Which Me Will the World See?

Many teachers I have talked with hold to the notion that young children and their writing are egocentric and that they don't consider their audience until after they get the chance to share their work with others. Dyson (1992), who has spent many hours observing young children from culturally diverse backgrounds as they participate in writing workshop, found that the term egocentric did not jive with what she saw in real classrooms. Instead, the children she observed wrote with a social purpose in mind. They wrote in anticipation of how their audience might react. "Children's writing is not made socially sensitive by the response of others; it is itself, a social act, a way of interacting with each other" (p. 6). Dyson went on to challenge writing teachers to replace the notion of socializing the egocentric with one of making children's written tasks relevant to the sociocentric.

Figure 2.3. Krystal's All About Me Page

Article | 6.14.2006
Al about me
I am a nice girl and funny and 9 years old.
I am ~~dumbing~~ and i live in ~~austin~~.
And how are you and how old are you.
whih state do you live in.
Are you funny and are you nice to your friends.

I observed that my students definitely had a sociocentric sense of audience and a purpose for their online writing. For example, Krystal created the All about Me page, found in Figure 2.3.

Krystal is certainly writing to an audience in this page. Also on the page was a photo I took of her (wearing sunglasses to hide her true identity—an attempt by me to teach Internet safety). She said several times to the other students in the room that the picture "looked funny." So of course she had to tell her audience waiting in cyberspace the same thing by adding a caption underneath the picture.

Evidence of a sense of audience was also present in Mario's front page, found in Figure 2.4, as he both reports information and asks questions. On his wrestling page, found in Figure 2.5, Mario tells his audience when wrestling is on television.

The writing the students did had a personal feel to it, as if they are in intimate conversation with their audience, a common occurrence in Web writing such as blogs, according to Burnett and Marshal (2003). While I expected the students to title their beginning pages with their names, they chose instead iconic titles, heavy with meaning. Krystal chose the name of a singing group whose name is similar to her own. Kevin chose a gender power statement: "Boys Rock and Rule." Mario decided to use his title to declare to the World Wide Web in big bold letters that he was Indian (see Figure 2.6).

Figure 2.4. Mario's Front Page

mario
i like cars i like wwe to watca t.v. to run

stuf i like
i like cars do you

Figure 2.5. Mario's Wrestling Page

Story | 6.16.2006
All About Wrestling
This page is so cool because it has cool pictures of wwe. it is so cool to watch on channel 66 or 23 on monday and friday.

Having just spent a year with Mario, I recognized this game. He told me in September that he was Lebanese, and then in February told the boys at his table that he was French. (On his permanent school folder, he is officially identified as Latino.) During our year together, he constantly pointed out the race or ethnicity of others in our multicultural class, and most often referred to himself as a Mexican. I called him on his title the minute I read his page, reminding him that he had said he was French, Lebanese, and Mexican in the past. With wide, serious, poker player's eyes, he answered, "Well I'm all those things. I'm Indian too."

Mario in real life is a shuckster, a chameleon, a comedian, a mere shadow to his true soul. He spends most of his time trying to impress other boys or shock and amaze adults with the facts of his Lebanese (French?) heritage, or the unusual things he knows, or a well placed "Go to H–ll." His Web page reflected a version of that same identity for his Internet audience. His pages are a collection of the coolest stuff he could find: a dancing banana; an animated gif of a wrestling match, complete with slams to the mat; pictures of a coffin match; and, from his Expert Page, a description of how mummies are made (see Figure 2.7).

Mario complained bitterly when I made him remove the Kitty Snipper—his pronunciation—an image of a kitten with an assault rifle (see Figure 2.8). Since he could not have the picture on his Web page, he took what satisfaction he could at telling me about it.

Mario: Why can't I have the kitty snipper?
Teacher: Sniper, not snipper. And because I said, no guns.
Mario: But he's a kitty. And he snipes. See? Kitty Sniper.

Figure 2.6. Mario's Title

i,m a indan

Figure 2.7. Mario's Expert Page

Story | 6.22.2006
Mummies, the unliving dead
I watched a movie and it showed me that to make a mummy, you have to cut all
the organs out and get everything out. Then they put wine on them and it made
the body smooth.
then thay put toilet paper on the body they put seshal gule os it will stik it then
thay put hem in the cofin

Like Mario, Kevin had the beginnings of a cool stuff collection going on
his pages, but the following conversation occurred in Kevin's first day of tutoring. Before his arrival, only Krystal and Mario were in the online writing
workshop focus group. Here, Mario got his anticipated reaction from his target audience, another boy, while he ignored the attention of Kyrstal, who visited his page uninvited.

> *Krystal:* You already wrote that? Why do you keep writing that?
>   (Mario wrote "stuff I like" twice on his first page.)
> *Mario (to Kevin):* Hey Dude, go on my Web site.
> *Kevin:* I'm going to. . . . All right. . . . Yep it's working.
> *Teacher:* These computers are real slow.
> *Mario:* Go to WWE. (He invites Kevin to the wrestling page he just
>   finished.)

Figure 2.8. Removed from Mario's Site: Kitty Sniper
(from http://www.flickr.com/photos/24947988@N00/4583867)

Krystal (Still critiquing Mario's Web pages): Mario, your picture looks
   funny.
Kevin: You better have some wrestling on here. You have wrestling.
   Awesome! Awesome it's a movie! That's so awesome! A movie!
   (Actually, Mario's praiseworthy image is not a movie, but an
   animated gif that repeats a loop of motion.)

Mario manages to ignore Krystal's comments about his page, while direct-
ing his target audience, other boys such as Kevin, to see his cool stuff collection.
   Krystal's Web page writing also did social work, though she had a very
different purpose than Mario. She was all about connecting with me, her former
second-grade teacher and fellow female. Her effort to connect with me started
early as she began a page themed with her favorite singers. She included pictures and a song from the singing group Black-Eyed Peas because she knew
that was a group we'd both enjoyed during the school year. She even asked to
make sure, ("You like them, right, Ms. Solomon?")
   For the final task the students were asked to pick a topic that they could
use Internet resources to research and create an Expert Page with all the facts,
pictures, and multimedia they could collect. Mario instantly picked Mummies,
and Kevin decided on Vampires. Krystal was stumped at first.

Krystal: mmmmmmm. Singers! Singers! Singers!
Teacher: Something new. You already have a singers page.
Krystal: I don't know. (*Long silence.*) I want to write about you,
   Ms. Solomon.
Teacher (laughs): No, Something you can research and find out more about.
Krystal (long silence): Schnauzers. Schnauzers. Schnauzers!
Teacher: You want to write about dogs? That's a good one.
Krystal: No, Schnauzers, like your cute little dog Madison.

Krystal sought a special connection with me and she achieved it. Everyone with
a dog knows that those treasured little companions—not food—are the way
to one's heart. Krystal's purpose for writing was not egocentric, nor was she
waiting passively for an audience before her writing became a part of the communication chain. Instead her ideas were sociocentric from the conception,
her powerful text imbued with life and meaning by their social goal. A page
from Krystal's Web page about Schnauzers can be found in Figure 2.9.

Yours, Mine, and Ours

This project did not take on the larger issues of copyright, yet the ideas
of ownership and controlling one's text was a recurring theme in the study.

Figure 2.9. Krystal's Page About Schnauzers

Text | 6.26.2006
Schnauzer Dogs
Schnauzers are salt and pepper, black and silver and all black. There are three types. A minature, standard, and giant. The giant one is a police dog. The standard keeps rats out of the farm. The minature is friendly. It loves his owner. If someone comes in side your house it will bark. if you welcome the person in, your the dog will stop barking,

Pictures | 6.27.2006
this my teachers dog,

To find the "kitty snipper" image to include in this chapter, I used Google to search for the picture. In the search image results, I got more than 10 identical copies of the graphic from 10 different sites. Those 10 don't include the versions of the image that have been altered with speech bubbles or other additions. If I was going to cite where I got the picture, which site would I credit?

Copyright and authorship rights are a huge issue when dealing with the Internet. Most people agree that copying and pasting text is plagiarism, and visits to sites like BuyPapers.com and ResearchPapers.com are done furtively. The Napster story was prominent enough to remind all that music clips for education purposes should be kept to 15 seconds. Yet compelling graphic images and film clips spread from site to site and from e-mail to e-mail and become cultural icons.

In a traditional writing workshop, there is a share time, or author's chair that students anticipate and prepare for. Generally only finished works are shared and teachers usually allow students to choose when and if they wish to share a piece that they wrote. With online writing, choosing to share or not share is really out of the hands of the writer. The moment the students pushed "save" or "upload," their writing was available for anyone and everyone to see. Thus the online writing workshop generated strategies for controlling one's own text that were not necessary in traditional writing workshop.

Krystal came up with the idea of creating a Girls Only page. Her second page, in response to the task that asked her to create a page about anything she wished, can be found in Figure 2.10.

Her efforts are seen in the Girls Only title in big red letters and the warning in the first sentence of what would happen to a boy who might foolishly seek to read the page. But Krystal was concerned that these prohibitions were not enough. Conversations throughout the tutoring weeks were riddled with her reminding the boys that this page featuring her favorite singers was for girls only. In a traditional writing workshop, perhaps Krystal would merely walk around the room sharing her text with the girls. If a boy passed by looking even remotely interested, she might cross her arms across the text and hold it hidden against her heart. In online writing workshop she had to find other strategies to control her audience.

Mario was more subtle in his attempts to control access to his space. He spoke several times about protecting his password, and even cautioned me not to leave the card with his password laying around for others "to get." One time he asked me if I still remembered his password. When I answered no, he was obviously relieved. He wanted to be assured of sole control of his Web pages. He did not want anyone else to have access to his cool stuff collection.

Controlling his Web page was also an issue for Kevin. He got into an argument with Krystal over visiting Web sites after he innocently asked if he could get a printed copy of all the students' pages.

> *Krystal:* You mean of my page? Nooooo. Can't you see? It's girls only. Boys not allowed.
> *Kevin (defiantly):* Yesterday I went to your Web site.
> *Krystal:* Oh . . . today, I'm going to go to yours. I'm going to get you, Kevin. (*singing*) I'm going to go to Kevin's Web site. (*goes to his Web site*) Kevin, look what I'm on.

Figure 2.10. Krystal Girls-Only Page

Kevin: That's not the one. (*She is on his first page, not his vampire page.*)

Krystal (*going to his vampire page*): Vampires! I don't get it, Kevin. You still believe in vampires? I think they are fake.

Kevin: You didn't see the movie I saw. Vampires are real. Used to be real. (*He is referring here to a United Streaming movie he watched for his research.*)

Krystal: New pictures. Can I go to Kevin's new picture? (*This question is directed at me, the teacher.*)

Kevin: If you put a picture on mine, I'm going to put a clown in yours.

Krystal: You can't go to my page, Ms. Solomon said. They can only get to the first one. Not the one about girl's only and the schnauzer dogs. See my rules? No boys allowed.

Kevin: You can't do nothing. You can't do nothing here. Everything you write on me I'm going to delete.

I assured Kevin that no one could put any pictures on his page without his password. But the incident was important to him because later in his post-tutoring interview, he mentioned that online writing workshop was different from traditional writing workshop because, "No one could change your stuff but you." When I asked him to elaborate, he said, "Well like if what you write is paper, someone could grab it and write on it or color on it. But no one can change your Web site but you."

The students didn't seem to have any qualms about taking pictures from search engines such as Google, Yahooligans, or KidsClick. They downloaded and then uploaded those jpegs and gifs without a second thought. Figure 2.11 shows a section of Kevin's Web site featuring images he retrieved from Yahooligans. He chose these images to illustrate what he'd learned about vampires and vampire bats.

Taking an image or idea from one of their second grade classmates who was not in tutoring but who had created a Web page during the regular school year in the same closed network of Think.com, or from a stranger's Web page within the community, was acceptable practice, but always accompanied by guilty giggles, furtive mouse clicks, and was considered stealing. Taking an image or idea from a classmate *present* in the room was completely taboo. The following occurred the first day of online writing workshop when Mario laid down the law about taking images and ideas from his Web page. I was giving Krystal some examples of how she might title her first page. Back in the spring, Mario had originally titled his first page with the handle, "weiney dog" before changing to "I'm an Indian" during the first week of summer tutoring.

Figure 2.11. Kevin's Vampire Bats Page

Pictures | 6.28.2006
The face of evil

Isn't this scary?

Click to see the picture better.

 Multimedia | 6.26.2006
The Sucker!

It's about vampire bats! And there's different kinds of bats like rhinoceros bats and big bats.

File Type: **video/x-ms-asf: 155 B**

[Download File]

 Article | 6.28.2006
Dracula and Other Vampires

Dracula first Vampire man. they were more vampiers. they were nise but Dracula wus not. these other vampiers invited people to go to their houses. and there were one man live he wus bad man. that whay people tray to kill Dracula. he told people but they did not Sorvive!!!

Teacher: Like Mario named his page weiney dog.
Krystal: Can I put weiney dog too?
Mario: Nooo! That's called stealing! That's called jacking.
Teacher (*quipping*): Intellectual thievery.

Ownership and property issues continue to be a big concern on the Internet. It is fitting that such real-life issues would also play a large part in the online writing life of primary youngsters.

The Evolution of the Writing Workshop

Online writing workshop as organized in this project was meant as an extension of the traditional writing workshop. The intention was never to replace writing workshop, but merely to supplement it with a digital genre that is highly motivating for children, and gives them an insider's look at what it means to be literate in the 21st century. However, online writing may provide evolutionary elements to what it means to teach writing. I identified what I termed the Three Cs of Online Writing that seem to all out challenge elements of the traditional workshop: composing, computers, and commotion.

Composing. What makes a good Web page has a lot in common with traditional student writing, but there are differences as well. Traditional writing might be considered well written if it takes on a linear form and has pictures that work with the text to make meaning. Online writing at its fullest capacity is multimodal and semiotic, taking on all the different sorts of things that can take on meaning such as sounds, graphs, images, animations, and movies (Gee, 2003).

When asked in his posttutoring interview what makes a good Web page, Mario said, "Pictures and words and movies all about the same thing." Instead of a linear story model, Mario's ideal Web page used a variety of different modes all communicating around a central theme. His wrestling page communicated that he liked wrestling with photos of wrestlers, title belts, and coffin matches; animated gifs; and the descriptions and captions he wrote. His picture, movie, and word choice are distinctive enough to give his page what traditional writing workshop calls *voice*. Writing a topic sentence such as "I like wrestling" would be unnecessary.

Computers. The added element of computers dramatically changed the type of talk in the writing workshop. Very little time is spent talking about pencils and crayons in the traditional writing workshop; if a student's pencil breaks, generally he sharpens it or borrows another one without much ado. However, computers, a mere tool in the process, played a prominent role in the online writing workshop. Over the 3 weeks, students became immersed in the language of computers—search, save, upload, download, windows, online, text box, drag, and click. Computer talk was more common than that of traditional process writing—edit, draft, revise, and publish.

Unfortunately, computers often appear to have minds of their own and are sometimes suspected of having secret agendas. Krystal explained the phenomenon of the computer responding to my keystroke commands quickly after rejecting several of her own attempts, as the computer "liking" me more than her. ("That computer just likes you, Ms. Solomon.") Kevin could often be heard exclaiming in amazement at what "crazy" thing his "weird" computer had done to separate him and his work. A teacher who decided to take on this kind of writing would need to be accepting of the almost physical persona computers exert into the workshop. On a comforting note, Mario had very little trouble controlling his computer, so time and experience with the little electronic beasts did seem to tame them.

Commotion. Online writing is not quiet. In fact, the introduction of multimodal elements such as photos, music clips, animated graphics, and movies seemed to heighten the physical reactions of the students. Krystal would exclaim, snap her fingers, and burst into song when her search successfully pulled up a photo of Ciara or 50 Cent. ("Ooooh! It goes like this: 'I'm so cool, I'm so fly'—It goes like that!") Krystal wasn't the only one who sang: Mario sang, worked his neck, and moved rhythmically in his chair as he placed a picture of the wrestler, John Cena, on his page. ("He's my favorite wrestler. He's a rapper. I'm trying to get his album.") Mario and Kevin sang together in joyous chorus to the beat of a little animated banana that was the prize image of Mario's site. ("Peanut Butter Jelly Time! Peanut Butter Jelly Time!")

All the children had strong physical reactions to the multimedia elements they added to their pages. The intensity of their reactions is hard to communicate fully under the limits of print, but their responses to the multimedia they were placing on their Web sites were so powerful that they seemed to mark events radical enough to be included with composing and computers as evolutionary elements within online writing workshop.

FINAL THOUGHTS

Recently, I read a warning from literacy researchers Labbo and Reinking (1999) that "researchers who fail to acknowledge issues of technology in their work may have to face the reality that their findings . . . may seem outdated, incomplete, or irrelevant" (p. 486). I took their words as a call to teachers as well. Today's kids are digital kids with digital lives bombarded by digital messages. If I don't learn to incorporate the digital into my classroom, I am also in danger of presenting a curriculum that is incomplete. The lessons I learned from the project described in this chapter reassure me that I can respond to the changing nature of my students' lives and offer my students support for traditional literacies that are tested on the statewide assessments and new literacies that reflect their real lives.

Yet, for all the excitement over photos of famous singers and wrestlers, over animated gifs of wrestling smack downs, and clips of rap music, that spontaneous moment when Kevin raised his printed pages to the camera with pride, speaks clearly through the digital milieu. The concreteness, the tactile pleasure, the *realness*, the ability to hug a printed page that you've created close to your heart, is a sensation that won't easily be replaced.

REFERENCES

Burnett, R., & Marshall, P. D. (2003). *Web theory: An introduction*. London: Routledge.

Dyson, A. H. (1989). *Multiple worlds of child writers: Friends learning to write*. New York: Teachers College Press.

Dyson, A. H. (1992). *Whistle for Willie, lost puppies, and cartoon dogs: The sociocultural dimensions of young children's composing or toward unmelting pedagogical pots*. Retrieved August, 2006, from http://www.writingproject.org/cs/04am/print/nwpr/684

Gee, J. P. (2003). *What video games have to teach us about learning and literacy*. New York: Palgrave Macmillan.

Kimber, K., & Wyatt-Smith, C. (2006). Using and creating knowledge with new technologies: a case for students-as-designers. *Learning, Media and Technology, 31*(1), 19–34.

Labbo, L. D., & Reinking, D. (1999). Negotiating the multiple realities of technology in literacy research and instruction. *Theory and Research into Practice, 34*(4), 478–492.

Lankshear, C., & Knobel, M. (2003). *New literacies: Changing knowledge and classroom learning*. Buckingham, UK: Open University Press.

Oracle Education Foundation. (2006). *More than a Blog . . . and Safer Too!* Retrieved November 7, 2006, from http://www.think.com/en_us

Texas Education Agency. Texas essential skills and knowledge (2007). Retrieved September 7, 2008, from http://www.tea.state.tx.us/teks/

CHAPTER 3

Collaborative Digital Writing

The Art of Writing Together Using Technology

GLEN L. BLEDSOE

The room is dark. I'm balancing my MacBook Pro on my lap. Everyone's attention is focused on the rectangle of light thrown by the projector on the screen at the front of the room. The class and I pause, thinking of how to continue the piece we've been working on for several weeks. Without raising her hand someone says, "I don't think that Joey is going to go outside when it's dark. He's not that brave." Another student adds, "Well, he might go out if he has his dog with him. *And* his flashlight." A third student says, "What if he goes out with his dog and it runs away? Then when he starts yelling for his dog, his flashlight goes out."

"Yeah," several students answer in unison. "Cool." The class rustles appreciatively. They can visualize the situation as if it were happening to them.

"Okay," I say, "that sounds great to me. So how do we put what you've just described into the dialog of the characters?"

"Well, first," the first student says, "Joey's got to say he hears a noise outside the house."

My fourth grade class and I are writing a story. It could be just a text story written with a word processor. It could also be repurposed as an audio podcast. Adding photos and sound, we could turn it into a digital story. The choice of medium doesn't matter very much to me, given my goals for students' learning. What does matter is the process we're using to write the story.

The process is one I've been developing with students over the last 10 or so years. I call it Collaborative Digital Writing.

Collaborative Digital Writing is (at least in the first phase) a whole class writing activity. Collaborative Digital Writing projects are complex projects that typically take weeks of relatively short but frequent periods to complete. The end result can be published traditionally (print), distributed by digital means, or be presented in a style similar to project-based learning demonstrations.

Technology plays a big part in making collaborative digital writing effective. It provides a shared user interface for the class to see and work on the writing. A computer projector or Smartboard is used to project the writing on a screen located where everyone can see it. I recommend that the teacher do the actual keyboarding. In an elementary setting, once students have sufficient typing skills, they may take a turn at it, although I seldom let students do this for the following reasons.

Students may believe that they can type as well as the teacher (if more slowly), but they may not know about such techniques as setting paragraph indentations, centering titles, spell checking, or dragging and dropping words, phrases, sentences, and paragraphs to rearrangement them. In Collaborative Digital Writing, the teacher models not only the use of these techniques, but coaches students through neglected but important parts of the writing process.

What software is used? Any word processor will do, but when my students and I are writing fiction in the form of an audio play, we've discovered outliners to be very helpful. Specifically we've been using OmniOutliner to create scripts with pop-up menus displaying a list of the characters' names for speaking parts, automatic line numbering, and check boxes (useful in recording podcast plays). Please see Figure 3.1.

Collaborative Digital Writing can be as simple as students collaborating on a word processing document, but the additional steps of turning these documents into podcasts, digital stories, digital graphic writing, or video increases the opportunities for students to recognize the need for revision. Collaborative digital writing projects provide many opportunities for students to see revision modeled and to participate in the process.

Revision is one of the most difficult things for a teacher to get across to students. Students believe that revising means to correct misspelled words and supply missing punctuation. Individually and on paper they are far more reluctant to change the order of paragraphs, rewrite awkward sentences, regroup sentences into different paragraphs, or ultimately rethink how their reader is going to react to their writing. One obstruction to revision is that students dread the labor of recopying their writing by hand. Elementary students especially are likely not to want to rewrite their sloppy copy. Many turn in work which has been extensively erased with words crammed into tiny spaces. The

Figure 3.1. The Collaborative Script, in Process

Characters	What they say
• □ 1. Narrator	One afternoon the sky drew dark and rain began to fall.
• □ 2. Matty	I wonder if school will be closed.
• □ 3. Marge	Remember the floods we had last year?
• □	Yeah, we had to use our canoe to get food.
• □	We had to sleep over at our grandma's house.
• □	I hope the rain stops soon.
• □	You guess just have no sense of adventure.
• □	I hope the rain stops. I just bought tons of sun tanning products.
• □	Very funny.
• □ 1(	The principle voice is heard over the school intercom.
• □ 1	Attention, students. I have an announcement to make. Because of the rain school is closing early today. We'll have a quick lunch and then the busses will pick you up and take you home.
• □ 12. Oliver	Whoopee!
• □ 13. Matty	Great! Now what about my birthday party?
• □ 14. Bea	Don't worry. You'll still be able to have your friends over.
• □ 15. Oliver	Getting out of school is a present.
• □ 16. Blanche	Not like having a birthday party. Besides, we'll have to make up the days later.
• □ 17. Oliver	I didn't think about that.
• □ 18. Bea	Yep that's right Now click on Binary Existence
• □ 19. Jane	I think this is going to be so much fun! I'm so excited!
• □ 20. Bea	Oliver turn off the lights, now there is no talking when we enter Binary Existence. This way we are really in the world.
• □ 21. Matty	But why can't I talk? I like to talk?
• □ 22. Oliver	Well if you can't type fast then you're screwed
• □ 23. Matty	I can't type fast, my index finger is getting sore
• □ 24. Bea	We can go to Typing Island and you can practice
• □ 25. Blanche	I already know how to type, where can I go?
• □ 26. Marge	The possibilities are endless...let's go be in the eye of a tornado
• □ 27. Jane	I've always wondered what that would be like!
• □ 28. Blanche	A tornado can go up to 300 mph and be more than a mile across
• □ 29. Matty	I don't like tornados...my aunt's trailer was picked up by one last year and dropped DEtroit. We never saw her again
• □ 30. Jane	Maybe she's in OZ and took out a witch and saved all the munchkins!
• □ 31. Oliver	I'm scared of the flying monkeys

The dropdown overlay lists: Oliver, Jane, Matty, ✓ Blanche, Marge, Bea, Narrator, Principal

teacher can refuse the work and insist on the students turning in their best effort, but is likely to be met with complaint or flat out refusal.

Students suffer from what I call the "Clark Kent syndrome." In the Superman television series from the 1950s whenever Reporter Clark Kent was late in writing his story for the next edition of the *Daily Planet* (which was all the time because of his duties as a superhero), he typed it at superspeed, fingers blurring until he ripped the page from the carriage of his typewriter. Clark never had to stop and think what he was going to write next, never reread his writing, never changed anything once it had been typed. Maybe that's what makes Superman super. But we puny earthlings must reread, rethink, and especially, revise.

ELEMENTS OF COLLABORATIVE DIGITAL WRITING

In the first phase of collaborative digital writing the class as a whole is involved. In the second phase, students work asynchronously in small groups. That is, a small group of students work on recording audio, or taping, for example, while the rest of the class works on something else or is in another class, such as library or music. This allows a small group of students to be focused on a specific task. Any writing mode can be addressed, but I've used it primarily for writing scripts in fiction such as digital storytelling or podcasting plays. The following are important elements of collaborative digital writing:

- *Pitching ideas.* When a student has an idea to contribute, she must learn to sell it to the whole group. The idea might be incomplete or undeveloped, but she must persuade enough of her fellow students to incorporate her concept into the body of the work.
- *Engaging in leap frogging.* A dynamic is created when one student makes a suggestion and then another student inspired by the idea builds upon it. The process repeats itself until an endpoint is reached—one that a student working independently would never have achieved. This is a very powerful effect and should not be underrated. The following example based on a real conversation in our class will help illustrate.

> *Student A:* Let's write a story about a model in Alaska.
> *Student B:* Yeah. One of those guys with long hair.
> *Student C:* And he has his photographer with him.
> *Student B:* The model guy gets sunburned though.
> *Student A:* In Alaska?
> *Student B:* Yeah, that's what's so weird. When he goes back to his hotel he stands in front of the mirror and begins to peel away the burnt skin. But it's not burnt skin coming off. He discovers he's wearing a rubber mask.
> (The rest of the class grunts with satisfaction at the twist.)
> *Student B:* What's under the mask?
> *Student A:* That's what we've got to figure out.

Students working independently would unlikely have reached a plot rich with so many twists and turns.

- *Making friendly amendments.* Enthusiasm runs high when students are free to chime in their ideas. I usually don't require students to raise their hands during this phase of the writing. I tell them it's acceptable for them to say (not shout) their suggestion out loud, and I'll hear them. If they keep it short, there's rarely overlapping suggestions. When I hear a suggestion, I'll repeat it aloud and ask students what they think.

They will either approve it or make what I call a "friendly amendment," a suggestion which retains the spirit of the original line, but extends or refines it in some way.

- *Pacing and meeting deadlines.* Collaborative digital writing projects work best with a deadline: a technology night at school, for example, a contest, a presentation for School Night at the Apple Store, or a technology showdown with another school. My experience has been that if there is no deadline, the project has greater chance of not being completed. Giving students a deadline drives them to work harder and smarter. Implicit in a deadline is audience: someone or some group other than the teacher is waiting to see what the students have done.

  Given a deadline, students have to judge what pieces in what order need to be completed by which dates on a timeline. Knowing when to work hard, when to ease off, and how much can be accomplished in a set amount of time are skills that students can't begin to learn early enough. Pacing is a skill that is the trademark of every successful adult.

- *Developing patience.* Collaborative digital writing projects are typically completed over weeks rather than days, and working with that timeframe requires and develops patience in students. They have to be able to visualize the end product and be satisfied with achieving it one step at a time.

- *Polishing the story.* One of the advantages of using technology in education is that students are able to give their finished project a much higher level of polish than they would had technology not been incorporated. Students' ideas often are more developed than their ability to produce them. Technology helps bring their finished project closer to their own vision of the concept. But polish means more than that. Polish also refers to taking care that details have been attended to: all i's dotted and t's crossed.

- *Completing a project.* For students the experience of working through a complex project from beginning to end is a more powerful learning experience than doing a series of disconnected assignments. Students experience a sense of mastery and accomplishment when they collectively direct a work through multiple stages over long periods of time. The accomplishment also draws them closer together as a group, a nice by-product of collaboration.

THE TEACHER'S ROLES

Many artists are leery of being too conscious of how they create for fear of disturbing the process. Teachers, on the other hand, not only focus on the process, but how to pass this process on to their students. The teacher's part in collaborative digital writing is a leadership role which blends elements of theater with the traditional teacher role.

- *Model and encourage revision.* With digital collaborative writing there are many opportunities for students to see revision modeled and to revise the work in progress. Students pick up very quickly that every word is subject to revision. It doesn't make any difference who wrote it or why it was written in the first place. As the story grows, the words will need to change to strengthen the story, to make the students' meaning clearer.

    Revisions are suggested at three points in the process: (1) at the beginning of each new session, as teacher and students reread what they've written thus far; (2) as the teacher types suggestions students are encouraged to make suggestions verbally without raising their hands; and (3) during try-outs, rehearsals, and as we're recording spoken lines on the computer.

- *Provide and model organization.* Collaborative digital writing projects require the management of hundreds of individual sound files, digital photos, and matching lines of dialog. If the project isn't organized from the very beginning, it will grind to a halt. Students will feel frustrated and the teacher will find herself with a great deal of clean-up work.

- *Model rereading.* As the lines of the characters are entered onto the screen, the teacher backs up and rereads aloud what's been written. This is done not only because the teacher will need to be reminded of what's already been written, but more important to model to students that they too must stop, back up, and reread their original writing projects. Telling them to do that won't change that behavior. Modeling that for students will make a change over time.

- *Play Devil's advocate.* At any time during the process the teacher reserves the right to wrinkle his brow and say, "Um, I don't get it. Remind me why your character says that." If the student can't justify the line, she may need to change it until it makes sense.

- *Model word processing formatting.* As I pointed out earlier, in an elementary setting, students aren't typing the text as it's being suggested. The teacher is (in upper grades a student with good keyboarding skill may be selected to take that role). When I write with the class using the overhead, I verbalize each step I'm using in formatting. I will say, for example, "Press return for a new line—shift for a capital J—single space between words," almost as if I were talking out loud to myself. My intent is to teach the basics of word processing, but to slip them in casually.

- *Direct.* A good teacher is like a good director in that both wish to draw the best out of their people. The teacher gives praise and encouragement.

- *Merge ideas.* The teacher takes suggestions that students see as competitive or mutually exclusive and models how the ideas can be combined to make for a richer idea.
- *Establishing the phases of the project.* Sometimes the activities are whole group, sometimes they are small group.
- *Wrap up.* During the assembly of the final product when the students have taken the project as far as they can, some or all of the finishing work may be shouldered by the teacher.

LIBRARY GHOST: AN EXAMPLE

Let me describe an example of a specific project that will help clarify collaborative digital writing in the classroom.

At the end of a hot September school day a half-dozen years ago students waited in casual lines for their buses. One particular bus was late as it nearly always was. The students assigned to that bus looked especially tired and more than a little disgusted. I walked over to them and said with as much gravity as I could muster, "I'm sorry to have to tell you your bus ran off the road. You'll have to spend the night here at school." Everybody at school knows I am an unrepentant tease, so they played along. "Yes!" They threw up their arms and cheered. "That means you'll have to eat McDonalds hamburgers." They didn't take that as the bad news it was meant to be. They cheered again. "The custodian will have to make up beds for you on the library tables," I said, then added in a moment of inspiration: "But please pay no attention to the library ghost. He's nothing more than a rumor anyway."

One more cheer made three in a row. Spending the night at school, eating fast food, sleeping on a hard table, and a visit by a ghost are attractions that fade as we grow older. The next day students who didn't ride the late bus asked, "Can we spend the night with the library ghost, too? And eat hamburgers?" How quickly news travels. "Ghost?" I would say with a false look of innocence. "I'm afraid I don't know what you're talking about." The library ghost was an ongoing joke for the next several years.

Describing the Characters

In September 2005 I decided to take our little joke a step farther. I said to my new set of fourth grade students, "You all know the story of the library ghost?" They grinned. "We get to eat hamburgers," they were quick to add. Hamburgers were a part of the formula not to be forgotten.

I said, "Why don't we write a story about the library ghost? Not just a regular story on paper. We can make it a digital story using photos, words, and sound effects. When we're done, we'll burn it to DVD, you can take a copy home to your parents, and we'll use it in our presentation at the Apple Store."

They loved the idea.

I said, "How many of you want lines? Any student who wants a speaking part will get at least two lines."

A number of hands went up—not all, but nearly so. "Next, let's begin by giving our characters names," I said. "Let's not use our real names."

Students raised their hands and suggested common names, but not of anyone in our class. I could have written the names on the chalk board, but keeping everything digital makes it easy to make changes. I plugged my laptop into an overhead projector and dimmed the lights. At the top of a word processing document I wrote the title "The Library Ghost." Beneath that I typed in the suggested character names. After we reached the necessary number of names, I asked students, "Tell me about the characteristics of these people."

Hands shot up. Someone suggested that one of the female characters was a follower. "She's into fashion, but she doesn't really know what's fashionable and what isn't." I typed that next to the character's name. Other qualities were assigned to other characters: bully, leader, good friend, brave, smart, and so on. Some were more complex like "tough guy, but he's really a chicken" or "she has many friends, but she doesn't tell them about all her feelings." I said, "With this knowledge about our characters, it'll be easier for us to write their lines." That was enough for one day.

Writing the Script

During the days and weeks that followed the class spent about half an hour each day with the lights dimmed and the computer projecting our script onto the screen at the front of the class. Each session began with either me or an impromptu cast rereading what we'd written thus far to refresh our memories and to regain the voice in our heads. As the rereadings took place, students would frequently say, "That line doesn't sound right" or "that doesn't sound like something he would say," and make a suggestion for a revision.

Once we had settled the revision I'd say, "What's the next line?" Without raising his or her hand someone would make a suggestion, and the rest of the class would either murmur their approval, or someone would propose an alternate idea. This open-class discussion was usually harmonious, and students supported one another's ideas in a culture of friendly amendments. Finally the script was complete to everyone's satisfaction, although revisions still could take place during the recording sessions.

Recording the Script

The next step was recording. This is done as part of the second phase of the project, in which small groups of students work together separate from the entire class. Using a microphone connected to the USB port of my computer, students recorded their lines one at a time. It's unrealistic to expect students to read their lines like live radio and not make serious errors. Allowing them to read their lines over and over and picking the best version works well. The lines of the script were numbered and as we recorded the lines we numbered the sound files to match. This is a simple step but extremely important.

Recording spoken lines in a classroom can be tricky. When are students ever completely silent? I worked around the problem of noise several ways. When I wanted students to be completely silent, I counted backwards in a voice loud enough for everyone to hear: Three, Two, One. Students knew they must be completely still until the speaker had completed saying her line. Then students returned to their normal rustlings.

When the class just can't be quiet for whatever reason, I wait for students to go to music or library but ask for small groups of students to stay back in the class and record.

Adding Photos

After the lines are digitally recorded, photos are taken. Usually this is my time to be the director. A student called Scriptboy or Scriptgirl and the director group and coach the principal actors for a given scene. The Scriptboy then reads aloud what line is being said for a given particular photo. The actor then holds herself in such a way as to mime the line. Body language, facial expressions, and camera angles are all very important in conveying meaning. Don't underestimate the power of these three elements in supporting the text of the story. The script always comes first. You can't create a very compelling digital story with a weak script, but with a strong script adding the above characteristics will add a level of polish.

Each photo is for a given line and taken by a third student called the Photographer. The process repeats until all the lines have corresponding photos. Upload the photos to your computer and number the photos to match the lines of the script.

Assembling the Script

With the lines, sound files, and photos all numbered according to the script, assembly of the digital story in the software of your choice is relatively easy. While the sound recording and photography are the most technical parts of the process, they actually take the least amount of time if well organized. Spend most of your time on the writing. I can't emphasize that enough. Lately, the final assembly has fallen onto my shoulders mostly because of deadlines, but in the early years of my experiments with collaborative digital media projects, students were responsible for the final phase as well.

The Ultimate Purpose

There are two kinds of scripts. The first kind is a script that students cobble together, and then as rehearsals and recording proceed, it becomes clear that the finished piece is going to be too long. My students have created digital stories and podcasts which range from about 15 minutes to an hour. Twenty minutes is the target length if you consider your audience. Students trim lines and scenes to tighten the story to the target length. This will involve some students losing a few or perhaps all of their lines. Some classes will elect to do this. The teacher can promise that whoever loses all their lines will be certain to get lines in a different digital story at a later date. The second kind of script is one which students may elect not to eliminate lines. In fact, the second kind of script may need to be padded to be certain to include all interested students in spite of making a product that may be too lengthy for the target audience.

It's a trade-off which the teacher will have to decide. Produce a script edited to a length for the audience? or provide an opportunity for all interested students to participate? I've done it both ways. The example above of "The Library Ghost" was produced to involve the greatest number of students. This digital story may be viewed at <http://www.molallariv.k12.or.us/~mes/podcast/LibraryGhost.mov>. For links to examples of other collaborative digital media projects, please see Figure 3.2.

ASSESSMENT, EVALUATION, AND STANDARDS

I am sometimes asked how I assess students' work on collaborative digital writing projects, and it is my pleasure to explain my thoughts on the subject.

Assessment

While the terms *assessment* and *evaluation* are sometimes used interchangeably, I think of assessment as being what teachers do to guide their instruction. Being a very active part of this collaborative process, the teacher is constantly listening to and combining the thoughts and contributions of individual class members. I may not hear something from a particular student for a length of

Figure 3.2. Examples of Collaborative Digital Stories

Writing and Math:
http://homepage.mac.com/glenbledsoe/winners/Room5web/index.html

Writing and History:
http://homepage.mac.com/glenbledsoe/winners/EgyptWeb/index.html

Creative Writing:
http://homepage.mac.com/glenbledsoe/winners/Triptych
http://homepage.mac.com/glenbledsoe/winners/Case/index.html

Podcasting:
http://youthradio.wordpress.com/2007/02/03/donny-and-the-ghost
http://youthradio.wordpress.com/2007/05/08/donny-ii-the-mummy-and-donny-altman/

Stop Animation:
http://cate.blogs.com/ds_lessons/2006/09/school_train.html

3D Computer Animation:
http://cate.blogs.com/ds_lessons/2006/09/3d_computer_ani.html

Digital Storytelling (Slideshow style):
http://cate.blogs.com/ds_lessons/2006/07/too_many_taras.html

Digital Storytelling (Cartoon style)
http://homepage.mac.com/glenbledsoe/comiclife/The%20Switch/Comic.html

---

time, and if so I'll make it a point to call on this student to either offer ideas, to help me make a decision about how to phrase something, or to make a choice between two mutually exclusive ideas. That's not as hard a process as it might appear. The kind of environment that collaborative digital writing perpetuates promotes creative thinking. There's little emphasis on providing a right answer, but rather to provide the next step in the story line or to revise a line to make it consistent with what's already been written. Sometimes the improvement may be as simple as rephrasing the sentence to make it easier to read aloud.

Evaluation

I'm going to define evaluation as giving value to a body of work. With evaluation the evaluator must always have a target audience in mind. SAT test scores, for example, are primarily for college entrance boards and are expressed in values that they best understand. While parents may look at SAT scores, they don't give them the weight of their students' report cards. Some evaluations only have value for the students themselves. Sometimes the value of the work is so personal to the students that the teacher may not understand its depth or how the students wish to have that value recognized. Here's an example:

During the late 1990s I was beginning to develop the method of working with students collaboratively using digital media. Students in my classes entered in a series of yearly Web site creation contests in Oregon called the Master WEBster Competition. My fifth grade class won the first year's elementary competition handily with an entry called "Our Room in Three Dimensions" and used our $3,000 prize money to buy more hardware and software. We won the next year's middle school competition with "The Lost Museum of Ancient Egypt," with a small subset of the students who were in my winning class the year before. As sixth graders they came after school from their middle school to their old class to work together. The third year of the contest was an entirely new group of students. They were extremely talented and worked well together naturally. They developed an astonishing site called "Triptych" with over 50 Web pages, complete with tutorials on how they achieved some of their complex effects. "Triptych" far exceeded the first two classes. I felt confident that we would easily win, giving me my third year in a row.

I was crushed to discover that not only had we not won, but that we hadn't even placed. The winning Web site, moreover, was a poorly executed set of six pages about bats.

But when I revealed the results to the class, to my astonishment, my students couldn't have cared less about losing. *They* knew the value of their work. They were satisfied with a body of work not just well done, but superior. They knew it was superior because they had made it themselves and knew what the effort had been. They knew who the real winners were.

So giving *value* to a collaborative work can come from the students themselves. The value that the contest committee gave the work of the students in the end meant nothing to them. The intended audience for the value of the students' work was the students themselves. To share their work with family, the students held a reception for parents after school one evening, with sparkling apple cider and—naturally—a cheese ball with crackers. The kids couldn't have been more proud.

If a work was created collaboratively, it doesn't appear to me to make sense to evaluate it individually. Wanting to measure the components comes down to us from Descartes, and it really doesn't serve a useful purpose. The impact of collaborative digital writing projects however, does reveal itself in students' individual writing. The skills that the teacher models during the collaborative writing do change the way students write, and for the better. In the affective domain, the parents of students tell me that their children come home from school every day excited about the project at hand. Parents often tell me that their child hated writing last year, but loves it this year. The change in attitude about writing alone makes the exercise worthwhile.

Additional evaluation is most powerful for students, in my experience, when it doesn't come from the teacher. The teacher is too close to the project.

The best evaluation will come from an outsider. Like any project-based learning effort, collaborative digital writing needs to have an audience. In the 1990s I read about Nicholas Negroponte's Media Lab (Brand, 1988) and adopted Negroponte's motto of "demo or die" as a personal one for my classes. My interpretation of the motto is that it's not enough that my students create collaborative works with digital technology, but they must also demonstrate them to receive the value of the work. It's not practical, of course, to expect students to be able to enter Web page contests for every digital media project they create. Since collaborative digital writing projects take long periods of time to complete, a teacher might plan to demo them once or twice a year by holding a technology reception at school.

As a variation of this my students have participated in School Night at the Apple Store for a number of years. School Night at the Apple Store is an opportunity for students to present their digital media projects in an Apple Store for an hour during an evening. Not only do family members attend, but customers who are complete strangers will stop and watch students pitch their projects. Some of the greatest rewards my students have received have been from Apple Store employees who asked students "How in the world did you do that?"

I have seen video clips of students giving presentations for project-based learning demonstrations and watched them shrug and give a "I dunno" to tough questions put to them by their evaluators. I think it's important for students to not only demonstrate what they've done, but also be able to answer tough questions. Preparing students to answer tough questions is the job of the teacher. When my students prepare for a demonstration, my goal is to have the media of the project complete at least 1 week prior to the demonstration. The final week is spent polishing the presentation itself and trying to anticipate the kinds of questions that our audiences might ask us. This preparation phase is as important as the creation of the digital media.

Several classes who've demonstrated at School Night have so impressed the management of the Apple Store that some of my students were offered jobs. Being only 10 or 11 years old they were unable, of course, to accept them. However, the manager said he would be happy to accept and hold their applications until they turned 18. What better feedback, what greater compliment is there than that? Did the students who participated in School Night at the Apple Store get an important evaluation? I would contend that they received a more important evaluation than I could ever have given them.

Standards

It's not difficult to take a collaborative digital media project and match it against either a given state's technology or language arts standards. The state of Oregon where I teach has educational standards, as do all states. The

Technology Common Curriculum Goals were adopted by the Oregon State Board of Education in March 2002: "Under these standards, students will:

1. Demonstrate proficiency in the use of technological tools and devices.
2. Select and use technology to enhance learning and problem solving.
3. Access, organize and analyze information to make informed decisions, using one or more technologies.
4. Use technology in an ethical and legal manner and understand how technology affects society.
5. Design, prepare and present unique works using technology to communicate information and ideas.
6. Extend communication and collaboration with peers, experts and other audiences using telecommunications. (Oregon Department of Education, 2002).

The only time I've been asked to match the state standards against a collaborative digital media project was for the Web site contests my students entered during the 1990s. While the exercise is not difficult to do, I don't set the standards first and then design the projects around them. I look at the project from an artistic perspective and then find standards that match. That's just the way my mind works. The inspiration comes first. If the idea is powerful enough to move me and my students, then it will have enough substance to engage the standards. Grabbing an idea and following through with it is a real-world task. I believe the purpose of standards is to reflect real-world needs and apply them to student work. If students are creating projects that reflect real-world tasks, then it follows that they will be adhering to standards.

During the late 1990s I spent some time looking over the technology standards of a variety of states. My conclusion was that technology standards were reflections of the jobs of the people who wrote them more than a tool to guide instruction. Most of the standards I saw were focused on word processing, spreadsheets, slideshow presentations, and gleaning information from the Internet. These are just the sort of skills required by education administrators. If we were to ask, say, the folks at Pixar Studios what they thought the standards should be, my guess is that we'd get a very different sort of list, which would include skills in the areas of sound design and videography.

In addition to the technology standards, the writing benchmarks for Oregon 4th, 8th and 10th grade students taken early in each calendar year are also addressed: "Use correct spelling, grammar, punctuation, capitalization, and paragraphing." (Oregon State University School of Education, 1999). Students choose either an imaginative, expository, narrative or (in secondary) persuasive prompt to write about. These are given scores of 1–6 in the following categories: ideas and content, organization, voice, word choice, sentence fluency, and conventions (Oregon Department of Education, 2008).

Obstacles

If students are used to writing in a word processed environment, it only makes sense that when they are tested they should write in the same environment. In the state of Oregon fourth grade students take a writing test in February from a choice of writing prompts provided by the Oregon Department of Education. Generally, however, students hand write their papers, but provisions exist for those who would prefer to incorporate technology. Students may word process their writing so long as *spell checking* and *cut, copy* and *paste* have been disabled. This is to eliminate any advantage in conventions and organization that technology-using students may have over their paper and pencil counterparts. Finding a word processor or text editor without *cut, copy* and *paste* is nearly impossible and so for the most part the restrictions effectively eliminate using technology for students writing. I, however, do a little programming, so I recently wrote a basic text editor that satisfies the state's restrictions.

Using my crippled writer students can't revise their writing as easily as we do when we are writing collaboratively since we can't cut, copy, paste nor presumably drag and drop to reorganize sentence and paragraphs. Nevertheless, students love the idea of being able to make changes and not have to rewrite the entire paper to make a clean copy.

He Said, She Said

Whenever I have a student who is a reluctant writer, I encourage him to concentrate on what his characters are saying. I might, for example, ask a student to write a story about taking his younger sister Christmas shopping and dwell on the ensuing arguments that he gets into with her. That usually opens the floodgate, and the student will write pages of dialog. Students usually have a keen ear for conflict in dialog and have little problem reproducing it. Collaborative digital writing projects are also dialog driven much as a script for a play. Unfortunately, the Oregon Department of Education refuses to score papers with more than a few lines of dialog. The reason given is that they believe it isn't possible to determine if a student can write well if she uses dialog too much. I don't agree with that thinking, but I nevertheless encourage students to avoid dialog in the state writing tests.

The Solitary Occupation

We don't usually write collaboratively, of course. Writing is a solitary occupation. The lessons and skills learned from collaborative digital writing projects, from my experience, carry over into solo writing. Students are more aware of paragraphs and capital letters. They have to consciously press *return* twice to create a new paragraph and hold the shift-key down to make a capital. In spite of the restrictions of cut, copy, paste, students are more willing to revise and do so without prodding from their teacher. It's clear that students are pleased with the cleanness of the finished word processed document. Students read books with set text all the time. When their own writing looks as legible and clean as a published book, they take more pride in the finished product.

CONCLUSION

Students using technology work much of the time in isolation, but that need not be the case. When students are led in collaborative digital writing projects, they will develop not only their technology skills but also improve their interpersonal communication and organizational skills. They will learn how to pitch their ideas and amend and build on the ideas of others. The process of collaborative digital writing also gives the teacher an opportunity to model revision and the organization of complex projects, which is difficult to convey in any other way. Although collaborative digital writing projects aren't going to necessarily eradicate the "online disinhibition effect" (Goleman, 2007), teachers who add this practice of collaboration to their curriculum will help improve their students' abilities to work in teams in a meaningful and creative way.

REFERENCES

Brand, S. (1988). *The media lab: Inventing the future at MIT.* New York: Penguin.
Goleman, D. (2007, February 20). Flame first, think later: New clues to e-Mail misbehavior. *New York Times.* February 20, 2007. Retrieved May 28, 2008, from http://www.nytimes.com/2007/02/20/health/psychology/20essa.html?_r=1&scp=9&sq=goleman%20d&st=cse&oref=slogin
Oregon Department of Education. (2002). Instructional technology common curriculum goals. Retrieved May 28, 2008, from http://ode/state/or/us/teachlearn/edtech/standards/aspx
Oregon Department of Education. (2008). Official scoring guide, writing 2004–05. Retrieved September 7, 2008, from http://www.ode.state.or.us/teachlearn/testing/scoring/guides/2004–05/writingscoringguide0405.pdf
Oregon State University School of Education. Benchmarks from the Oregon writing standards for English. (1999). Retrieved September 5, 2008, from http://oregonstate.edu/instruct/ed416/benchmarks.html

CHAPTER 4

Digital Picture Books

From Flatland to Multimedia

KEVIN HODGSON

The pigs won't stay put, and for readers of the picture book *The Three Pigs* by David Wiesner (2001), that is exactly the way it should be. In this postmodern retelling of the classic fairy tale, the wolf comes knocking on the door with mischievous intent, and the pigs escape by tearing down the walls of the story itself, escaping through holes in the wreckage of the book. At one point, the pigs actually take a page with the picture of the surprised wolf, fold it into a paper airplane, and soar off to another story where they save a dragon from a knight on a quest. The dragon later returns the favor by "taking care" of the wolf when the pigs return to their own story.

Wiesner's *The Three Pigs* and picture books like it inherently hold the possibilities of breaking the rules of the genre. Through a combination of illustrations that don't need to conform to the rules of a conventional story, writing that can reach across many age levels, and writers' play with the canvas of the book, many writers of picture books are finding interesting ways to twist new stories out of the old and draw the reader into the mix as an active participant. This concept is as old as the first pop-up book that required small hands to pull a tab and cause something to spring from the flat page. But technology has added new layers of possibilities.

CONNECTING PICTURE BOOKS AND TECHNOLOGY

Consider the popular Magic School Bus series of science picture books by Johanna Cole and Bruce Degen. These picture books can be read any number of ways. There is a traditional story that deals with some scientific concept, which elementary students come to understand by magically becoming part of the environment, or the experiment, after a ride in the magic bus. In *The Magic School Bus at the Waterworks* (1986), for example, the students and their teacher, the ever inventive Ms. Frizzle, shrink into raindrops and then journey through a water purification plant. On a typical page, there is a traditional narrative (usually written in first person), dialogue clouds above the students and Ms. Frizzle (often containing science-based jokes and banter), and, in text boxes shaped like little student notebooks off to the side of the page, are the facts being discovered by the students on their journey. The books are a cacophony of information, as young readers bounce between reading the book as narrative, comic-style story, or as factual information. One intriguing development in the popularity of the Magic School Bus series is that the books led to a very popular television show, which then led to a series of interactive multimedia CD-ROM games and then to Internet sites, until the series itself became a multimedia franchise of sorts. Perhaps the format of the books, with the many layers of story lines, is a natural fit for the shift into the multiple media world. And many other media have followed this lead, as comics have been developed into movies and movies into online games and online games into books.

Michèle Anstey (2002) seeks to identify the traits of a postmodern picture book with emerging technologies in ways that make sense to me in terms of connecting an old genre (picture books) with a new medium (computers):

> I was concerned that children's literature could be constructed as 'old literacy,' comprising traditional print and visual literacies. If this was the case, then the use of children's literature in which to teach new literacies might be limited, as it would not provide the opportunity for students to practice new literacies. . . . I [later] concluded that literature that exhibits particular characteristics can be most useful in teaching new literacies. One aspect of children's literature that I found particularly suited to teaching new literacies was the postmodern picture book. It is a product of new times and incorporates many of the characteristics of new literacies, requiring the reader to engage in the text in new ways. (p. 2)

Anstey then goes on to articulate some of these characteristics, including a conscious intention to engage the reader on multiple levels, creative use of layout design, contesting discourses between text and illustrations, multiple readings for multiple audiences, and the use of narrative voice in varying ways.

Context for the Project

Although young writers like my own sixth graders are drawn in as readers by these kinds of shifting narratives, it is not so easy for them to make the shift from reader to writer. Through discussions and reflections, however, students can come to grips with the genre of the nontraditional picture book. I believe that technology can help young writers realize that the tools for composing an interactive book with "moving" parts and multimedia can be found on most desktop computers and that the creation of such books makes visible the otherwise invisible structure of a book. For the past 2 years, I have been working with my young authors, using some basic tools of the PC to create math- and science-based picture books that push their conception and writing beyond the traditional boundaries. By integrating video, audio, Internet links, and animation into the creation of their picture book stories, my students have come to realize the ways in which technology can change their writing. By using a curricular theme as the center of their stories, and by designing their work for an audience of younger children, these sixth graders become more informed about the science content explored in their books as they take on the role of teacher.

Over a 6-week period, my students work from a writing process that begins with brainstorming and storyboarding before their fingers ever even hit the keyboards for rough draft writing. From there, the computers become a compositional slate in which any kind of media is a possible tool, as long as it informs the story. What they don't use in creating their books is almost as important as what they do use, although this lesson often becomes one of the hardest to instill, as they would like to throw every cool little trick into their books until each becomes one giant, messy, moving montage of gimmicks. This digital book project requires many minilessons in technology and writing, but the quality of the books depends upon a solid foundation of story writing and the teacher's willingness to cede some of the learning initiative to the students. Once a student has stumbled upon a great idea, it rarely takes more than one or two class periods to watch that student become a teacher to their peers (and sometimes, the teacher), and soon others are doing something new with images, audio, or animation.

My school is situated in a suburban community that is predominantly White and middle class. While adequate funding for the school remains an annual struggle, grants have been secured by our district to purchase two laptop carts with roughly 20 Dell PCs on each cart. Many of my students also have computers in their home, and so basic knowledge of computer applications such as word processing and Internet search engines is fairly universal but never a given. We do not have a computer lab or a technology teacher, and classroom integration of technology has been left up to classroom teachers. In recent years, we have added a media specialist whose primary focus is the library. What this has meant is that some of the faculty never use the carts, some use the computers for Internet research alone, and only a very few of us use the machines for deeper integration into the curriculum. Determined not to let the computers sit idle, I open the cart up all the time. I teach writing to four classes of sixth graders through the course of the day, meaning that anywhere between 75 to 80 students are being exposed to technology on a regular basis. And it turns out that creating and publishing books with the computers opens the doors to some interesting discoveries and learning.

Many teachers have implemented picture book projects with paper to great success, and I would not argue against that approach. I, too, once went that route with my students. Still, I wanted to take it a step further and explore the possibilities of technology with the picture book project. Engagement by learners is certainly one aspect of the answer to why use the computers for composition. The room is rarely quiet during the production of these digital books, but the conversations are almost always on topic, dealing either with story structure or technical assistance. Writers become proud when sharing their books with an audience that is both interested in the story and in awe of the book's creation. I would also argue that the use of a digital platform offers up avenues for expression and communication that the flat page lacks. I am not advocating that the digital book should replace the traditional format; I am only saying that it is different, and that students growing up in an age of interactive media are best served by being composers of this kind of writing as well as readers and participants.

My use of Microsoft's Powerpoint as a software platform is a decidedly mixed bag. There are many conflicting thoughts on whether students should even be taught to use the presentation software. I somewhat agree with Edward Tufte's (2003) argument that slide show software is too often utilized in the classroom for very little creative use beyond formatting an overabundance of information. I turned to Powerpoint for a different use—one in which students are not simply presenting information, but are using the platform for creation of something original while they are also learning some of the deeper layers of the software.

Sharing Digital Books

It is Digital Book Sharing Day at our school one early summer day and the laptops are set up all around the large room, as sixth graders wait for their second-grade audience to be assigned a group in which to begin. After reading and listening to the books, and following hyperlinks to safely vetted Web sites related to the topic of the book, the second graders will move in round robin fashion to another table, and so on, until they have viewed just about every book. I act as a traffic controller, moving groups of readers to groups of writers.

The day before, when my students shared with a class of third graders, the topic of our class post-book-sharing reflection was on how to get the au-

dience more engaged in the books. For some reason, most of the third graders had stood still while the sixth graders used the computer mouse to move
the story along, to click on animation and images, and to guide the computer
to the Internet. Very few questions were being asked by the third graders, even
when prompted by the sixth graders, and my students were clearly frustrated.

"I don't even know if they liked my book," said one of my students. "They
just stared at it and then moved on."

I let a pause fill the room. Some others were nodding their heads in agreement at this statement. "Well," I finally said, "why do you think that was?"
Another moment of silence and a few shrugs. They had assumed their books
were wonderful and engaging and had not considered the possibility that they
would not get feedback. "I think we did too much of the work," said a student. "All they had to do was stand there. We did everything for them."

Yet another one chimed in with a suggestion: "Maybe we need to let them
[younger students] use the mouse. Then, maybe they will ask questions." It is
agreed by the class community to give this approach a try. Today, the strategy
works, for the most part. The second graders seem to relish being in control
of the book and, contrary to the session the day before, they are asking questions about how the sixth graders wrote the story and how they constructed
the story on the computer. The conversations between readers and authors
support the idea that reader involvement in a text, whether paper or digital,
makes for a more enriching experience. In at least three cases that I observed,
the sixth grade writers paused the book to make some quick editing changes
after questions and comments from the young viewers. In one case, two slides
had accidentally been shifted out of sequence, making the story confusing. A
simple drag of the slides put the story back in order, and the reader could
continue. The second graders watched this revision process with fascination,
and although the sixth graders did not know it, they had just given an outsider a glance into the composing process of a writer.

Developing the Picture Book Project

I didn't always use technology as a tool for creating picture books with
my students. In fact, during the first year of teaching, I stumbled upon the
idea of making picture books at the end of the year, when I realized with a
tremor of terror that there were still 4 weeks to the end of the year and I had
no more lessons in my plan book. I had recently come across an article in an
educational journal about the value of publishing picture books for upper elementary students, and it was in this desperate moment that I decided to give
it a try. From the first days when I asked my 12-year-olds to bring in a book
that they considered their favorite, or the first book they remember reading, I
knew I was on to something. Watching my students share a variety of Dr. Seuss

stories (*Hop on Pop* and *Green Eggs and Ham* seemed to be favorites) or some small treasure that made their eyes still glow at the memory, I knew that these would be engaged learners.

Incorporating Technology

For the first few years, the picture book project was another device for developing plot and characters and setting—all things that we had gone over in detail in the year and would now be fleshed out in a publication showcasing their own story and illustrations. By the fourth year, however, I started to envision something grander in scale, and working with first with our math teacher and then with our science teacher, I launched a picture book project that reached across the curriculum. Students would be creating fictional stories based upon a curricular theme (one year it was math, and the second year it was science), using the slide show format of Powerpoint. The shows/books would be shared with an authentic audience of students from the younger grades in our school and with their families via a classroom Web log. For example, one student created a character named Piggy who sees geometric shapes during the course of a typical school day. The character slowly learns how to differentiate one shape from another, based on the number of sides and angles a particular shape might have. Another created a math book based on addition problems that the reader must solve before advancing forward in the story, and the answers were hidden under images that would be lifted with the click of a mouse. I wasn't actually thinking of the ways the computers might push the boundaries of traditional writing and composition. In fact, it was only by watching my students experiment and having them ask me how to do certain things (such as make a character move on the page or hide one thing behind another or add audio to the pictures) that I began to realize that something different was beginning to take place in their minds as writers of digital stories.

The question of how to use my students' interests in the digital world was an issue. I would like to be able to say that my district has provided me with a good foundation of professional development in the area of technology integration, but that is just not the case. Instead, I have had to explore on my own, experiment on a small scale, and borrow ideas from others in the world of teaching through networks of the National Writing Project and Weblogs of others sharing their best practices. The difficult task has been to find a balance between technology integration and the core curriculum that we are required to teach.

Aligning with State Frameworks

This digital book project was not done in a vacuum of accountability. The Commonwealth of Massachusetts (2007) has established curriculum frameworks that center on essential skills the state has determined all students should know upon graduation from high school. Our students are tested regularly on the Massachusetts Comprehensive Assessment System (MCAS), which is a standardized testing program proctored every year from third grade on up in a variety of topics. Teachers are expected to align their classroom curriculum to the Massachusetts Department of Education (2007) Curriculum Frameworks, as MCAS questions are based on the educational concepts found in the frameworks. This digital book project was designed from the outset to align with the state frameworks in the areas of language arts, technology, and science.

For a project like this one, that seeks to create connections between writing and other facets of the curriculum, I knew that collaboration with other teachers would be essential. My team member who teaches science to our sixth graders worked with me to develop a list of all of the major concepts of the science curriculum. I shared this list with my students, who then brainstormed story ideas before focusing on a subject to write about. The art teacher and the media specialist at our school also provided both support and classroom time to work with students on both the art and the construction of picture books from other lens. In examining the wide range of minilessons that form the core of the project—from initial planning and storyboarding, to investigating a science concept, to creating original artwork, to publishing to a real audience—it is clear that our students were touching on a wide number of anchors within the state frameworks.

In English Language Arts (ELA), for example, my students were considering their audience and purpose for their writing, organizing ideas, conducting research, and producing a multimedia project—all of which are central to the ELA frameworks. Science Frameworks were also being met through the contents of the books being produced, drawing from standards that addressed earth and space science, the structure and function of cells, and technology and engineering. There was also some overlap with the Fine Arts Frameworks as students studied picture book art and considered elements and principles of design and artistic connections to interdisciplinary units. Finally, the project fits in nicely with proposed Instructional Technology Frameworks that require students to identify the differences between writing and the design of print and screen media (Massachusetts Department of Education, 2007).

In relation to that last technology standard in our state, one aim of this digital book project is to begin to explore the idea of literacy in its many forms with young writers—from paper to digital platform. *Multiliteracy* is at least one of the terms in the educational field meant to cover this work.

Multiliteracies means being cognitively and socially literate with paper, live, and electronic texts. It also means being strategic, that is, being able to recognize what is required in a given context, examine what is already known, and then, if necessary, modify that knowledge to develop a strategy that suits the context and situation. A multiliterate person must therefore be a problem solver and strategic thinker, that is, an active and informed citizen. (Anstey & Bull, 2006, p. 23.)

The approach of student investigation of technology is also consistent with the concept that students should be innovative in the ways they use computers, which is one of the tenets of the most recent national standards put forth by the International Society for Technology in Education (2007). The group's most recent report entitled *National Educational Standards for Students: The Next Generation*, puts an emphasis on the exploratory process. The report points to such areas as:

Creativity and Innovation

Students demonstrate creative thinking, construct knowledge, and develop innovative products and processes using technology. Students:

- apply existing knowledge to generate new ideas, products, or processes
- create original works as a means of personal or group expression

Communication and Collaboration

Students use digital media and environments to communicate and work collaboratively, including at a distance, to support individual learning and contribute to the learning of others. Students:

- interact, collaborate, and publish with peers, experts or others employing a variety of digital environments and media
- communicate information and ideas effectively to multiple audiences using a variety of media and formats
- contribute to project teams to produce original works or solve problems

The Process of Creating Digital Picture Books

Before my students begin any kind of writing, they reflect on the impact that picture books have had on them as young emerging readers. This understanding of a genre is an important first step for writers moving into that genre. The first phase of creating science picture books, therefore, involves students examining one of the volumes in the Magic School Bus series and reflecting on such topics as layout of illustrations, the character who is narrating the story, and the mix of facts and fiction. What I found is that about half of the students know the Magic School Bus only through the television show and the other half remembers reading the picture books with either their family or in an earlier grade classroom. Most students immediately remember the character of Arnold, for example, who hates going on the field trips and complains all the time about having to go out on another classroom adventure. Others wistfully wonder why they can't have a teacher like Ms. Frizzle (why indeed?) instead of being stuck with me. The point is that the books were engaging to them as readers in a very tangible way. Next, they head to the computers and spend about 30 minutes looking at digital books made in the prior year (in that case, math books), and a classroom discussion ensues about what seemed to work and what did not seem to work for them as readers, and how they would have done things differently if they had been the writer.

It is around this time, too, that students answer a preproject questionnaire that asks them to consider a range of questions—from remembering their favorite picture books as young children to the differences between digital and traditional books. While considering his own book, *The Adventures of Lava Dude* (See Figures 4.1 and 4.2 for excerpts), Brad offered up that, "Digital and traditional books are different because you can make things move and it can have such things as sound, graphics and movement of any kind." The students also have to think about the ways in which audience consideration plays a key role in the writing process. This question of audience is important because the primary audience for the science books are students at our own school, grades one through four. One student, Bill, explained why audience consideration was important to him: "It affects [how you write] because if you were doing it for little kids, you would use less words and more pictures, and you would do the opposite for older kids." They realize that the words they choose, the tone of language, and even the use of pictures to complement the story

Figure 4.1. Lava Dude, Excerpt

Hi kids my name is Lava Dude. Hey do you want to take a journey inside the layers of the earth?

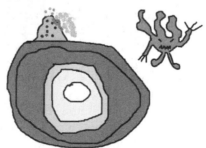

Figure 4.2. Lava Dude, Excerpt

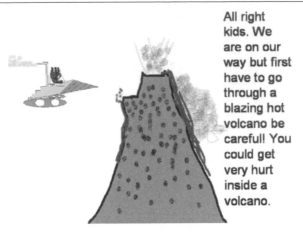

All right kids. We are on our way but first have to go through a blazing hot volcano be careful! You could get very hurt inside a volcano.

are all dependent upon who will be reading their books when everything is complete.

The sequence of activities from that point forward looks something like this:

- **Week One** After some collaborative brainstorming activities, students (working either collaboratively or solo) come up with a scientific concept that is part of the sixth grade curriculum. The writers develop a page-by-page storyboard with sketch drawings and story ideas, and then complete a sequencing chart that maps out the plot of the fictional story. I model the use of storyboards and a sequencing chart by showing a story that I have written. In this initial stage, the students are provided with a rubric assessment sheet that breaks down the expectations in five categories, ranging from spelling and grammar to book presentation and plot structure.
- **Week Two** Students write a rough draft of the fictional science story in Microsoft Word and then proofread. At this time, I provide the class with minilessons on how to use the spell- and grammar-check functions of MS Word as well as using Microsoft Paint to create illustrations. A review of how to use Microsoft Powerpoint may be necessary, which I introduced earlier in the year and students view and discuss examples of the misuse of PowerPoint.
- **Week Three** Students work toward completion of pictures and words. No clip art is allowed. They begin adding multimedia elements such

as audio narration, slide and image transitions, and animated pictures. This deeper level of PowerPoint requires more minilessons and one-on-one instruction. All books are required to have at least two hyperlinks from an end page to Internet sites that further inform the scientific topic that is the center of the book. Again, creating hyperlinks requires more minilessons. Students have access to webcams to create video components to stories as well. Classmates read and critique the developing picture books, providing authentic input for revisions. During the science book project, a highlight was a visit from local picture book author Carol Weis (2006), author of *When the Cows Got Loose*. She talked to students about the process of writing a book for publication, drawing connections between her real-life experiences as a writer and the classroom experience of the students.

- **Week Four** The class invites students from younger grades to tour the classroom in round robin format, reading and/or listening to stories on the computers and asking questions of writers. Writers then reflect on the process and experience, and make any editing changes that have come about from audience reactions.

- **Week Five and beyond** The class publishes the picture books to the Internet (for families and the world), and each student receives a printed copy of his or her book. Students reflect on how different their book is in paper form versus digital form.

Examples of Student Stories

In a story created by Marcus and Bill, for example, a character named Mel the Cell is off on an adventure through the structure of a typical cell. The two boys added audio to capture the voices of the characters, and used animation to help Mel the Cell move through layers of the cell, such as the cytoplasm, and meet such characters as the mitochondria. Sound effects, layers of pictures, movement of characters, and voice narration were all central to the story they created. The links to Internet sites outside of the book allowed the young readers to do an interactive crossword puzzle about cellular structure and then tour the inside of a cell at a Web site. As Marcus and Bill discovered deeper levels of the slide show software, they constantly kept revising their planning. They were more engaged in this project than in any other assignment given to them over the course of the year.

Meanwhile, Penny created a raindrop character who goes through the entire water cycle, explaining such terms as evaporation and condensation while in the course of an adventure, and moving along the pages as the story is being read in the voice of a character as an audio file. Penny adjusted her voice for the characters and viewed the book as a sort of performance art that allowed her even to create a fake author biography page in which she envisioned one billion versions of her book being sold and a fake e-mail address for her fans to write to her.

One other student, Melanie, had friends from class pretend they were the characters of her book. She videotaped interviews with the characters and embedded those interviews into the end pages of her book. As more and more students discovered different tools, more and more of the books began changing through the course of the production. Often it was their memories as readers that led to their discoveries as writers, such as experimenting with how to replicate a pop-up book by using layers on the digital platform.

CHALLENGES OF ASSESSMENT

An analysis by the New Media Consortium and the EduCause learning Initiative entitled *The Horizon Report* (2007) sought to examine some aspects of emerging technologies and literacies in education. One part of the report focused in on the difficulties of assessment of multimedia projects:

> Assessment of new forms of work continues to present a challenge to educators and peer reviewers. Both at the student and at the professional level, assessment is lagging behind creative work. Learning that takes place in interdisciplinary, context-rich environments such as games and simulations is still difficult to evaluate. There is a skills gap between understanding how to use tools for media creation and how to create meaningful content. (p. 6)

My assessment of the digital book project is multitiered, combining reflective writing check-ins, quick student surveys along the way, informal discussions between teacher and student, and a final grade that is based upon the rubric mentioned earlier that I share with all of the students in the first week of the process (Table 4.1). Prior to completing the book, all students are also required to use a basic checklist sheet to ensure that their books have all the requisite parts and have been edited and revised for publication.

When delving into multimedia, however, assessment can be tricky, as this book project is not merely a technology venture. So I try to avoid a direct grading mechanism for the technology itself. This is a conscious decision I have made in order to allow students to find a comfort level with these new skills without the fear of failing. Instead, I weave aspects of those skills—such as color, design and animation—into broader categories.

The quick surveys are presented to students at three different junctures in the project: at the start of the planning process, in the middle of book creation, and then at the end of the project. The final survey sought to gauge impressions of the young writers in terms of what they think they may have

Table 4.1. Scoring Rubric for Digital Book Project

CATEGORY	20	15	10	5
Spelling and Grammar	There are no misspellings or grammatical errors.	There are 3 or fewer misspellings and/or mechanical errors.	There are 4 misspellings and/or gram-matical errors.	There are more than 4 errors in spelling or grammar.
Book Presentation	The book demonstrates excellent use of font, color, graphics, effects, etc., to enhance the presentation.	The book makes good use of font, color, graphics, effects, etc. to enhance to presentation.	The book makes use of font, color, graphics, effects, etc. but occasion-ally these detract from the presen-tation content.	There is some use of font, color, graphics, effects etc. but these often distract from the presen-tation content.
Scientific Concept	The story covers a scientific concept in-depth with details and examples. Subject knowledge is excellent.	The story includes essential knowl-edge about a scientific concept. Subject knowl-edge appears to be good.	The story includes essential information about a scientific concept but there are 1–2 factual errors.	The content in the story is minimal or there are several factual errors. There is very little infor-mation about a scientific concept.
Story Format	The journey story demonstrates a clear and interest-ing beginning, middle, and ending.	The journey story has a beginning, middle, and end, but there are loose ends to the story.	The journey story is somewhat con-fusing to read, but there is evidence of a beginning, middle, and end.	There is no beginning, middle, and end to the journey story.
Cover/Title Page	The book has an interesting title, illustration, dedica-tion, publishing company, and date.	The book is missing one piece of information from the cover and title pages.	The book is missing more than two pieces of information from the cover and title pages.	The book has no cover or title page.

learned from the 6-week project. The following are some of the results from the 64 responses (from the four different classes of sixth graders that I taught in a single year):

- Ninty-seven percent stated they enjoyed working on the book project.
- Fifty-six percent stated that the best part of the project was using tech-nology to create books rather than the traditional methods.
- Only 30 percent stated that they had a better understanding of how books are published.

- Ninty-six percent said that the use of technology made the project more interesting for them.
- Eighty-seven percent said their book would have been very different if they created it in the traditional ways.
- Fifty-eight percent said they are more likely to write and publish their own books now that they know how to do it.
- Seventy-five percent stated they would use technology in creating another book, if given a choice.
- Forty-five percent reported that they consider themselves "advanced" users of PowerPoint (and another 48 percent stated they consider themselves "average").

I find it instructive, and a bit disheartening, that while many of the students were enthusiastic about the use of technology, only a few believed (30 percent) they had a better understanding of the ways in which books are published. That relatively small number gives me pause and forces me to reflect back on whether too much time is spent on the technology and not enough on the writing and elements of publishing a book.

REACTING TO FORMS OF PUBLICATION

Publication of these books takes on a variety of forms, as well. All students were given the chance to bring in a CD-ROM and make copies of their books to bring home for parents and families. A few also brought in portable flash drives. I e-mailed some of the projects home, when CD-ROMs and flash drives presented a problem for families. I also hosted a Weblog for sharing student work with families and linked versions of the books to the site, as well as converted the PowerPoint slides to a PDF version for those who do not own PowerPoint.

Finally, I worked with my school principal to print out paper copies of all the stories so that students, and our school, could have a tangible reminder of the work they created. The paper copies were in full color and staple-bound. For some students, there was a mix of both excitement over publishing something they could hold in their hands and disappointment that much of the technological aspects of their books was lost. The paper holds no sound and shows no video, and pictures can't dance across the page. In a survey of the 20 students who allowed me to use their books for this chapter (I have focused in on 9 of those 20 for this classroom study), every single one of the young writers reported that the paper version was very different from the digital version, and the majority said that they believe the general reader would prefer the digital form over the paper form.

Reflecting on the experience of reading her book in a form different from which it was intended, Michelle, author of *Space Journey* (See Figures 4.3 and 4.4 for excerpts), explained: "I consider my book to be truly digital because some of the best parts (hyperlinks, movement, and so forth) are not part of the paper book and therefore, the paper book isn't really complete at all."

Karen noted that the book she made with her partner that used an original rap song to tell the story of the water cycle was quite different on the flat page because the digital format is "how we made it. We put in the animation and the sounds. They were part of the book and when it is on paper, part of the book is gone." Carrie said the digital book was the "true version" of her story, adding that, "I wrote this book so that you [the reader] can animate the pictures in sequence with the words." And Penny noted that the digital version of her book is geared toward a younger audience and "allows the younger kids to interact with it. Without that [interaction], they [readers] would not be in as much of the 'action' as they were with the digital book."

THINKING AHEAD

As I reflect upon this project in terms of the postmodern picture book, I realize that there are many other possibilities that remain uncharted. One of my students, Murray, who published a book called *Journey into the Cell* (See Figures 4.5 and 4.6 for excerpts), postulated: "I think that books in the future

Figure 4.3. Space Journey, Excerpt

After traveling for many days, Connor reached our galaxy. Our galaxy is called the Milky Way Galaxy and is shaped like a spiral. All of our planets and many stars are in the Milky Way Galaxy.

Figure 4.4. Space Journey, Excerpt

Once inside the galaxy, Connor went to our sun.
The sun is actually a star and is the closest star
to Earth. It gives light, heat, and energy to
everyone on Earth. After searching for the Ecro,
Connor was sweating, but he still hadn't found it.

will have people popping out of the pages and talking, like a miniplay. In the future, you will not even have to read the books—just listen to them."

Even now, there has recently been a resurgence of interest and publication in the Make Your Own Ending novels, in which readers bounce around the text as they make choices in the narrative possibilities. This concept could easily be integrated into a digital book project, using hyperlinks and clues to send readers moving through the text in a very nonlinear manner. Consider

Figure 4.5. Journey into the Cell, Excerpt

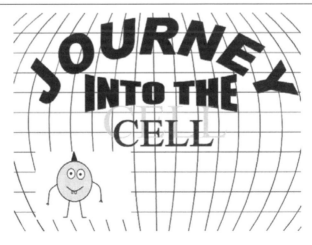

Figure 4.6. Journey into the Cell, Excerpt

the planning that would have to take place by the writer, however, to envision the warren of rooms in which readers might find themselves and the doors that would need to be created to get the reader out. We tinkered with video production with the science books, but only on a small scale. Imagine if every book had a television or computer screen built into the story, and the screen came alive with video related to the story or the topic. And imagine giving readers of these digital books even more authority to move into the story, either by leaving notes for other readers (a sort of digital graffiti) and the writer; or perhaps, allowing the reader to reconstruct the story in another sequence. This would also require great planning and strategy on the part of the writer, never mind the feeling of allowing your own work of art to be manipulated and altered by someone else.

Consider the insightful comments of Dennis Baron (2000):

> The computer has indeed changed the ways some of us do things with words, and the rapid changes in technological development suggest that it will continue to do so in ways we cannot yet foresee. Whether this will result in a massive change in world literacy rates and practices is a question even more difficult to answer. (p.31)

Technology certainly does not hold all the keys to learning and students, like teachers, can often head down a myriad of unfocused paths when confronted with multiple tools and options. I contend, however, that using technology to create digital versions of books can enhance the ways in which students view the compositional process. Further, I contend that this process affords them different kinds of freedom to construct stories that are not confined to the two-dimensional paper page.

REFERENCES

Anstey, M. (2002). It's not all black and white: Postmodern picture books and technology. *Journal of Adolescent and Adult Literacy, 45,* 444–457.

Anstey, M., & Bull, G. (2006). Defining multiliteracies. *Teaching and learning multiliteracies: Changing times, changing literacies.* Pp. 19–55. Delaware: International Reading Association.

Baron, D. (2000). Pencils to pixels: The Stages of literacy technology. (pp. 15–33) Rev. from Hawisher & Selfe (Eds.), *Passions, Pedagogies, and 21st Century Technologies,* Logan, UT: Utah State Univ. Press, and Urbana, IL: National Council of Teachers of English. pp. 15–33. Retrieved July 23, 2007, from http://www.english.uiuc.edu/-people-/faculty/debaron/essays/pencils.htm

Cole, J., & Degen, B. (1986). *Magic school bus at the waterworks.* New York: Scholastic.

Giesel, T. (1960). *Green eggs and ham.* New York: Random House Books.

Giesel, T. (1963). *Hop on pop.* New York: Random House Books.

International Society for Technology in Education. (2007). *National educational standards for students: the next generation.* Retrieved July 23, 2007, from http://www.iste.org/inhouse/nets/cnets/students/pdf/NETS_for_Students_2007.pdf

Massachusetts Department of Education Curriculum Frameworks. (2007). Retrieved July 23, 2007, from http://www.doe.mass.edu/frameworks/

The Horizon report: 2007 edition. New Media Consortium. (2007). Retrieved July 23, 2007, from http://www.nmc.org/20/horizon/2007/report

Tufte, E. (2003, November 9). PowerPoint is evil. *Wired Magazine.* Retrieved July 23, 2007, from http://www.wired.com/wired/archive/11.09/ppt2.html

Weis, C. (2006). *When the cows got loose.* New York: Simon & Schuster.

Wiesner, D. (2001). *The three pigs.* New York: Clarion Books.

Continuing in the Secondary Grades

The four chapters in Part II are based in high school classrooms. Each describes a multimodal project used to enhance students' work within a conventional genre—journalism, poetry, the research paper, and formal public speaking. In Chapter 5, Paul Allison focuses on his use of blogs in a project-based course, New Journalism/Technology, for eighth grade through high school students. For this course students explore topics that they care about and post their compositions to a social networking blog to share with others and respond, creating a virtual writing community of diverse students from across the country.

In Chapter 6, Jeffrey Schwartz examines a collaborative poetry video project, focusing on how composing a multimodal interpretation encourages new ways of thinking and leads to viewing a text as multidimensional. In Chapter 7, Bryan Ripley Crandall describes a research project that concludes with both a 10-page, print text research paper and a multimodal presentation to a panel of students, professionals, and parents. He focuses on how the addition of the new media component has changed both what and how he teaches.

Finally, in Chapter 8, Dawn Reed and Troy Hicks shift the focus to public speaking, teaching it as a composing process that requires brainstorming, researching, drafting and revising, and delivery. Explaining a "This I Believe" project, they show how incorporating podcasting and thereby widening the audience has made students take the entire process more seriously, in particular rhetorical issues of audience and ethics.

CHAPTER 5

Be a Blogger

Social Networking in the Classroom

PAUL ALLISON

Several years ago I decided to see how blogging might fit into my curriculum. Much on the Web has changed since then and we have many more interactive tools available to us now via the Internet, known collectively as Web 2.0, but blogging remains the center of my work with students. Blogging in a school-based social network creates a meaningful, dialogic, motivating environment where students get inspired to measure their own reading, writing, research, and response skills alongside their peers. This environment of self-assessment makes my teacher assessment an afterthought for most students.

My students have personal blogs where their writing posts automatically appear on the main page of the Youth Voices (http://youthvoices.net) site. The software we use allows them to be surrounded by many multimedia resources for their personal inquiries. Students become passionate self-guided learners who seek to improve their skills to keep up with and to impress their peers, some of whom they know quite well because they sit in classes next to them, others of whom they get to know only through Youth Voices.

SNAPSHOTS OF A BLOGGER

To get a picture of how blogging was working in my classroom, I observed one student carefully for a week in late February 2007. Nichole was a junior at the time, and had been a blogger in my New Journalism/Technology classes at a high school in New York City since eighth grade. Nichole and I had learned a lot about blogging by the time I documented her work in publishing her blog "From Love to Social Pressures":

> Is love when your mate shuns you out of their life? Is love when your mate walks past you everyday? Is love when your mate doesn't even acknowledge your existence? Is it love when you haven't kissed your mate in over 3 weeks? Is it love when your mate acts like they only want you for one thing? No, that's not love. Love is when two people show affection for each other and recognize each other's smarts. Not when your partner makes you feel less of yourself and makes you feel invisible.

> Some people believe that for every person born into this funny place, there is a perfect match, or a soul mate. I've often toyed with the idea. Could it be possible that in God's grand design, he was so terribly kind as this? To make somebody so well matched to each of us as to pop into our lives like a battery that fits just right, and never, ever runs out?
> —"Soulmates," Purple Planet Blog (http://purpleplanetblog.blogspot. com)

I used to believe in soul mates, but now I feel that I might not have a perfect match. That there might not be that one person in the world that I am destined to be with. Maybe because I don't get good luck and maybe its on purpose. I believe it has something to do with the fact that I am still very young and I do have my whole life ahead of me. I want to go to college and I want to become a doctor someday. Being distracted isn't the best thing for me to do. That's why I always believe that what happens in high school is ONLY high school and I will get a second chance when I go to college to start my life over. I don't want to make the same mistakes I've made before because it would only lead me down the wrong path again. That's why I feel sometimes my life is pretty screwed up and I cant wait to get that second chance to start fresh.

> Maybe I should be a little more grateful but today I feel as though something huge is missing, like I am nothing but a piddly number in the scheme of life. I do the same thing everyday I see the same people, drive the same route, eat the same food, and deal with the same b. s.
> ———"Ever Feel Unappreciated?" The Life of Mrs. Quad (http:jaxattax .blogspot.com)

I love myself and I live for myself. I care about what other people think of me but to a certain extent. The majority of my life I spend wondering what is missing? Why do I wake up each morning not wanting to get involved with anyone, not wanting to see the world? And that's when I came to the conclusion that I am not a happy teenager. I only have one chance to live young and I am totally destroying that. I'm taking responsibility and eliminating things in my life that shouldn't be there. I can't help it because I was brought up to be nice, and the result of being nice is holding back what I truly feel about things. I swear I wish I wasn't that way, but now I have gotten used to it and bad habits are hard to break. I want to be happy, and I want to smile when I'm doing well, but the fact is that I'm not doing so well. I have so many issues evolving in my life and taking over that it's getting harder and harder each day to take control. It also feels that I am alone in this world because I'm always crying before I go to sleep and thinking of ways to get out. I go around what I know I need to do because I feel it's "too hard". It sounds pitiful, but that's just how I am.

(Posted on Youth Voices (http://youthvoices.net), by Nichole on March 1, 2007)

This was Nichole's 36th blog post and podcast episode since the beginning of the academic year in September. By this time in the year, Nichole had many subscribers and followers or friends who looked forward to her weekly posts and podcasts. Her followers included a group of peers in Salt Lake City, Utah, and Sacramento, California, a solid group of readers in her own school, and new readers in Maine.

Here are day-by-day snapshots of Nichole blogging over one week in late February 2007:

On Monday, Nichole freewrites about a self-chosen question, "What is love?" then crystallizes her freewrite into a focused sentence in which she expresses her feeling that someone else can "make you feel less of yourself." Next Nichole scans several blogs, using Google Blog Search (http://blogsearch .google.com), and reads a post titled, "Soulmates" that had been published a couple of months earlier in the "Purple Planet Blog" (http://purpleplanetblog .blogspot.com)/. Finally, Nichole extends her freewrite, at first by writing in response the Purple Planet blogger, then by writing to herself, developing her inner voice about how things might improve for her in the future.

On Tuesday, Nichole spends several minutes reading over her incomplete post on Google Docs, which is an online collaborative word processing platform, and then she changes the title from: "what is love?" to "From love, to social preassures [sic]." After this, Nichole searches with the word "alone" on Flickr for a Creative Commons image, and soon finds an image of a young girl curled up, almost in fetus position, in front of a window with a shade pulled down completely to block the bright sun that still filters through. Before the end of the period, Nichole saves this image to her desktop, then inserts it into her post, and writes more.

When Nichole arrives in class on Wednesday, she launches her Google Reader to find a blog post in her "love" folder by a woman in Texas, "The life of Mrs. Quad: Ever feel Unappreciated?" (http://jaxattax.blogspot.com), and copies a few lines from that post into her own blooming blog post. As she writes, Nichole reckons back to her own thoughts about how someone else could "make you feel less of yourself and make you feel invisible," and answers tentatively: "I love myself and I live for myself. I care about what other people think of me but to a certain extent." Nichole adapts Mrs. Quad's feeling that "something huge is missing," into questions about "What is missing?", then expresses "the conclusion that I am not a happy teenager," and finally ends the period by writing about why her life leaves her crying at night.

On Thursday, Nichole spends time reading other posts on Youth Voices. She finds an echo to her inquiry in her classmate, Jay's recent post, and comments on his blog: "Hey Jay, Me and you are both worrying about our futures. . . . Just give all that you can and don't worry about what other people are going to say because all of that does not matter." Nichole also responds to two other Youth Voices bloggers, one in Salt Lake City and one in Maine. Finally, Nichole spends some time adjusting the background and the color of her font, and she proofreads, correcting spelling, and adding in all of those apostrophes that she tends to leave out when she freewrites.

On Friday, Nichole copies her writing to her blog on Youth Voices, and records her post using Audacity, a desktop recording software program, then exports it as an MP3 audio file. Nichole uploads the MP3 to her podcast folder on Youth Voices and embeds it into her blog post so that it attaches to the syndication feed for her blog known as RSS (really simple syndication) that allows others to read and listen to her work. Still not finished, Nichole reflects on her work in a community blog, "How am I doing?" where other members of Youth Voices can read it and respond.

Here's what Nichole had to say that last week in February 2007 when this post went up. This is her self-assessment:

> Lately, what makes for a really good blog post is a lot of thought, emotion and a picture. Without any emotions it's almost to a point where it can be dead. The picture adds another kind of taste to it because the reader can actually get a look at how you might feel through a picture. Adding a podcast is also a plus because listeners can hear the tone in your voice, and get a feel of how you feel through how you're talking about the topic. This week I have written about two or three times for my post and I have a picture. And I have a podcast. My post has my opinion and I actually put some work into what I was talking about. I always do that. I just feel that I did it more this week than last. Next week I hope to get a lot more writing done and keep up the good work.

Although the school required me to report a grade for Nichole's work every few weeks, I always de-emphasized the importance of my evaluation. I never grade specific blogs, and instead I keep track of the number of blogs and comments a student produced, giving higher grades for more and better developed blogs and comments. It was the comments from other students to Nichole that mattered the most; these served as the real external assessment.

WHAT DOES A BLOGGING CLASS LOOK LIKE?

Let's change the lens now and take a look at the class where Nichole has been working. By the time Nichole was working on "From Love to Social Pressures," her class had reached an important turning point. I always look forward to this change in dynamics, after which I begin to feel more like a waiter in a busy restaurant than a teacher in a school computer lab. No longer am I working to motivate students to do work for me. Instead, I am working to help each student to accomplish his or her own goals as readers and writers in a school-based social network. No longer am I assessing them; after the shift the students assess themselves, and decide what to do next. This shift, this turning point from teacher-centered to student-centered self-assessment, has come each semester since I put blogging in a social network at the center of my curriculum.

If you were to look into a computer lab like the one where Nichole and her classmates were working, you might see me moving from student to student, troubleshooting computer glitches here and encouraging revision and proofreading over there. Often, you can see me asking students to read aloud what they have written, with me guiding them with this question: "Do you see where you left a word out? You read more than what's on the screen."

Next, you might see me responding to a student across the room who says, "I'm bored! There's nothing to write about, and I've got to get something out or my friends [finger quotes] will be disappointed." Sitting next to this young writer who is feeling the pressure of having a regular readership from across the country is a boy who needs to get back on task. His attention has strayed because yesterday, after listening to a podcast, he couldn't figure out how to make a link to the original MP3 in the response he has begun to write. I show him the simple html code he can use to make a link in his blog post.

Out of the corner of my eye I see that another student who has been relying too much on Wikipedia recently is back on that site again. "It's not that you can't use Wikipedia," I say, "I just want to see you using snippets from other sources too. What blog posts, newspaper or magazine articles, and what podcasts have been collecting in your Google Reader about Will Smith?"

Before this conversation ends, a student across the room blurts out, "When I respond to blogs, do I have to use the sentence starters?" "No," I answer, "but remember the three parts that you have to have. First, quote something that stands out to you from the blog. Second, say why this stands out or make a personal connection to the post from your own experience. At the end make a compliment and be nice." "Do you have to talk so loud?" complains a girl in the corner, "Now I have to re-record my podcast."

What's a Blogging Curriculum?

I'm happy in this busy, sometimes noisy room where students are focused on reading and writing blogs on Youth Voices. With each new class, it takes some time to reach this point. It has something to do with project-based curriculum. Perhaps any teacher who has learned to sponsor projects in the classroom will recognize the turning point that I'm referring to here, where the teacher starts working for the students, instead of the reverse.

Students in my blogging classes develop the learning dispositions that Suzie Boss and Jane Krauss (2007) say "the best projects share." My students exhibit "important learning dispositions, including persistence, risk-taking, confidence, resilience, self-reflection, and cooperation" (p. 65).

In addition, I think that the studiolike atmosphere that I seek comes from a curriculum that asks students to do two things first: find something to be passionate about, and connect with others who share this passion. Students are also asked to evaluate their own progress each day, and to choose from many options what to do with their time.

Finding a Personal Inquiry

I ask my students to find a question or a set of questions that they develop in their own speculative writing, and eventually they do online research about their questions, connecting with others who have published on the Internet, and critically interpreting the welter of information available to them there.

Students grow their blogs over a semester of working with other students and teachers who share their social network, Youth Voices. Together we ratchet up the expectations each week. They begin by posting a barely revised piece of freewriting to their blogs; then they write two times about the same issue over a couple of days, then they add a Creative Commons image and do more writing.

Because they publish their work each week, they see the effort, accomplishment, risk-taking, and level of quality in each others' posts. A student's ability to assess his or her own work grows by the constant exposure to models by students they know and students they don't know. Many times during the semester, I hear students say, "I want to do that too. Can we quote from scientific studies like that? Can we include an image? Or make a video?"

By the time in the semester when I start to feel like a waiter in a busy restaurant, students are working to piece together a blog post that has been revised and proofread a few times over a week or two, that includes at least one Creative Commons image, that takes a stand on an issue, and that includes quotations (snippets) from critically selected online resources such as:

- Wikipedia and other online encyclopedias
- Blogs and podcasts—which can range from online personal diaries to political and professional journalism
- Newspaper articles (from everywhere)
- Creative Commons images (from flickr, for example) and video (from services that haven't been blocked yet)
- Peer-reviewed journals that are now online
- Traditional Web sites that are usually out of date
- Sources from the "hidden Web"—materials that are available through library databases to which we, like most schools, have access

Finding a Niche

Finding a personal inquiry is important, but equally important is the second part of their work in my class. I help students to build an audience, find a niche, develop a network of online friends, and become regular responders on blogs by peers who have similar interests or passions. They do this in Youth Voices. Students and teachers from all over the United States—from Florida to Alaska, from New Jersey to Utah, and from New York to Texas—have joined this site over the past few years, and this network looks like it will continue to grow.

Developing Habits of Mind for a Studio Classroom

Once they become members of a social network like Youth Voices, my students learn how to tag their work with keywords that identify their interests. They allow other students who share their passions to connect, read and respond to particular posts. Then students put each other on their own list of friends to make it easy to follow each others' work in the future.

This social networking technology allows us to ask the essential question: How do you get your work noticed online? Students quickly learn that they need to make both the content and the presentation of their blog posts compelling to a group of peers. They also learn to become good community members by reading and responding to each others' blogs, and eventually by developing ongoing inquiries with each other.

From the first day of a blogging class, I work to create a studio classroom where students can work on passion-based, critical, online research and compelling communication within a school-based social network. It doesn't happen overnight. It takes time to build the trust necessary for students to accept the responsibilities of a studio classroom.

Toward the beginning of the semester, I use minilessons to introduce the multiple skills and ways of thinking that eventually become blogging habits of mind and work. I know these lessons have been successful when students can look at this guide for self-assessment, and not feel overwhelmed because they recognize that they know how to do each of the items listed on the Be a Blogger! matrix (see Figure 5.1). I give this matrix out to my high school students on Mondays, and ask them to choose a place to start. When they complete the work within a particular box, they put an x in that box. Their goal is to have crossed out everything in this matrix every week.

This matrix is an attempt to make clear the multidimensional, multimodal options available to students blogging in a social network. Students are asked to develop a blog post that includes text, images, links, and podcasts. In a one week period, students are asked to work on these modes of expression with four different habits of work: participating (collecting), producing (drafting), perfecting (revising and editing), and publishing.

Any Given Monday

On any given Monday, a student using this matrix might start by Participating with Text by going to Youth Voices or the Personal Learning Space to read posts by other students in their class or community, or on their friends list. In other words, a student might begin his or her week by reading and adding a comment in two blog posts by their peers. To assist students in this process, the teachers in the Youth Voices network give our students "sentence starters" that they can copy and use to guide their comments. Although these can lead to a cookie cutter response at times, teachers using them have found it useful to start with these very structured guides and encourage students to free themselves from them as soon as they seem ready.

Dear [Writer's Name]:
I [past tense verb showing emotion] your message, "[Exact Title]," because . . . [add 2 or 3 sentences]
One sentence you wrote that stands out for me is: "[Quote from message.]" I think this is [adjective] because . . . [add 1 or 2 sentences]
Another sentence that I [past tense verb] was: "[Quote from message]." This stood out for me because . . .

I do/don't [adverb] agree with you that . . . One reason I say this is . . . Another reason I agree/disagree with you is . . .

Thanks for your writing. I look forward to seeing what you write next, because . . . [add 2 or 3 sentences explaining what will bring you back to see more about this person's thoughts.]

Another student might want to begin by Participating with an Image. This student would have a question and a keyword (for example, relationships, Iraq, video games, politics) in mind in order to find an image to jump start his or her writing that week.

Asking students to insert an image into a blog post each week gives us an opportunity to have an ongoing discussion with them about the ethical and legal use of images and other creative content that they find on the Internet. Many a student has said to me, "If they didn't want people to use it, they wouldn't have put it on the Internet!" On the matrix, in our daily lessons, and classroom conversations, I make clear that they may not use images they find through an open Google search, for example, or images they find on a favorite Web site.

However, it's empowering to also introduce students to Creative Commons, a copyright licensing agreement that allows others to freely use material. The model of Creative Commons allows teachers to say, "Even though you can't use anything you find anymore, look at all of the images that Creative Commons has made available for us to use on our blogs! Isn't it exciting to join this movement where we have been given permission by the photographers who took these images to build our blog posts around their work? Makes you feel like part of a cultural movement, almost."

At the same time as I ban the use of Google Images, I provide students with this list of other places where they can find images that they are allowed to use:

- Flickr Creative Commons, which is a collection of photographs that been designated with a Creative Commons sharing license (http://flickr.com/creative_commons/by-nc-nd-2.0)
- Stock.xchng (http://sxc.hu)
- Morgue File (http://morguefile.com)
- Wikimedia Commons (http://commons.wikimedia.org/wiki)
- FlickrCC (http://flickrcc.bluemountains.net)
- Creative Commons Search (http://search.creativecommons.org)

We are constantly updating this list as new services come online. When they publish an image on their blogs, students are asked to cite the image source "at

Figure 5.1. Self-Assessment Matrix: Be a Blogger!

	Participating (Responding)	Producing (Drafting)	Perfecting (Revising & Editing)	Publishing
Text	Read and listen to posts by other students in your class or Community, or on Your Friends list. Add a comment in two of their blogs. Keep focused on the content of that post, not how it is written. Be sure to quote two times from his or her post. Remember to *introduce, insert, and interpret.*	Pose a good question for yourself. Make this the title for a document in Google Docs. *Freewrite* for 10 or 15 minutes. Write a *Focused Sentence,* a perfectly written, opinionated sentence that re-states your entire freewrite. *Freewrite* again this time starting with the *Focused Sentence.* Write 5+ tags for this doc.	Copy your text to Microsoft Word and check grammar (green) and spelling (red). Revise your freewriting: Delete unnecessary words Add more details. Rearrange sentences and paragraphs. Replace slang or confusing words. Look to see that you are *adding to the conversation.*	After you have finished correcting everything in Word, copy back to your Google Docs, then copy the Google Docs file to your blog. Be sure you have: 1. Good Title 2. 5+ tags 3. Set Access to Public, unless told otherwise
Image	Search for Creative Commons images using these sites: * flickr.com/creative commons/by-nc-nd-2.0 * stock.xchng—sxc.hu * morgueFile.com * Wikimedia Commons * flickrCC.bluemountains.net (see more)	Insert a *Creative Commons* image or one of your own. Remember to introduce, insert, and interpret. *Freewrite* for a third time, this time with the image in mind. How does it represent what you are trying to get across in your post?	At the bottom of your post, write: Image Source: 1. "Title," 2. Name or ID of Photographer, 3. link to this photo online	Align your photograph left or right—and give it some horizontal and vertical space—so that the text wraps around. Images should be no larger than 250 pixels wide.

Figure 5.1. (*continued*)

Links	Read blogs, news, and web sites. Subscribe, then find blog posts and news items in your Google Reader subscriptions list. Read and copy snippets or quotations. Also use del.icio.us to collect web sites to use in your blog. Bookmark and tag web pages. Quote from these.	Add two Snippets or quotations from other blogs or news items that you have read—or podcasts you have listened to—about this topic. *Freewrite* a final time with these quotations in mind. Remember to *introduce, insert, and interpret.* How does each quote add to your message in your post?	Make hyperlinks to the *Snippets* or quotations that you have included in your post. If you use the clipboard in Flock the links will be automatically inserted for you.	Use highlighted *Keywords* from the bottom of one of your posts, from your list of *Tags*, or from *Your Profile* to find someone with similar interests or blog posts. Add this person to *Your Friends* list, and *Add a comment* to his or her related blog post.
Podcasts	Use Google Reader to listen to selected podcasts that you have subscribed to. Search Every Zing to find more audio and video about topics of recent interest. In Google Docs write comments about these podcasts with links to the the original source. *Use Podcast Sentence Starters.*	Use Audacity to record. Be sure to introduce yourself with your first name and say the name of your school. Explain what you are about to read. It's okay to say more than what is in your post, but not less. Export it as an MP3, saving it to your folder.	Upload your MP3 to a Podcast folder in your *My Files.* In the description box for your MP3, copy the first sentence from your blog, then type "read more," and make this into a link to your blog post. *See How to set up your podcast files.*	Embed your MP3 file from your online file storage using the *Add* button at the bottom of your post. A small player should appear in your post

the bottom of the post," including a "link to the photo online." This allows the teachers who are monitoring Youth Voices to verify that all images on these sites have Creative Commons permissions attached. When students publish images that are copyrighted, I feel like I've been given yet another opportunity to teach them about the tricky issues of intellectual property rights in the digital age, before I ask them to replace it with a Creative Commons image.

Tapping into the Underground Spring

Although a student could start in many different places on the "Be a Blogger!" grid, most begin at the top of the second column with freewriting about a self-selected question. This is also how I introduce this grid to students: "Let's start in the second column by writing nonstop, anything that comes into your head about anything that is important to you right now." It takes some time each year, with each class to get students to believe that I mean this, that I really do want them to write about something that they care about, not just what their teachers want them to write. Peter Elbow's (1973) description of freewriting in *Writing Without Teachers* is still a good place to begin.

> The idea is simply to write for 10 minutes (later on, perhaps 15 or 20). Don't stop for anything. Go quickly without rushing. Never stop to look back, to cross something out, to wonder how to spell something, to wonder what word or thought to use, or to think about what you are doing. If you can't think of a word or a spelling, just use a squiggle or else write "I can't think what to say, I can't think what to say" as many times as you want; or repeat the last word you wrote over and over again; or anything else. The only requirement is that you never stop. (p. 3)

After freewriting, the next step in the Producing column on the matrix is to write a Focused Sentence, a perfectly written, opinionated sentence that restates your entire freewrite. Then students are asked to freewrite again this time starting with the Focused Sentence.

Students soon get used to shifting their composing gears this way: beginning with open, expansive writing; then writing a careful, precise, power-packed sentence; then going back to expressive, quick writing. This follows Peter Elbow's (1981) "Open-ended Writing Process," which he describes in *Writing With Power* (p. 58):

- Write for 15 or 20 minutes without stopping . . . make sure to let the writing go wherever it wants to go.
- Pause and find the center or focus or main point in what you wrote. Write it down in a sentence.
- Use that focusing sentence for a new burst of nonstop writing. . . .

Elbow might say that once students have finished the prompts for the Text row in the Producing column, they "have used two kinds of consciousness: immersion, where you have your head down and are scurrying along a trail of words in the underbrush; and perspective, where you stand back and look down on things from a height and get a sense of shape and outline" (p. 52). It's important to give the time, and ask students to create substantial personal, committed, passionate pieces of writing each week. I have them collect their freewriting, focused sentences, and more freewriting in the online collaborative word processing platform called Google Documents that they share with me. Over time, each student and I identify the "generative themes" (Freire, 1993) that begin to bubble up in his or her writing.

This type of really free, habitual freewriting is an important first step—an ongoing, underground spring—that allows blogging to become "a practice in catalyzing passion and creativity," not just another school assignment. Once a student begins to write about their insights and discoveries around their area of inquiry, I encourage the writer "by finding niche learning communities that each kid might want to be a part of and build on that" (Brown, 2005, p. 11). Helping students to create and find these niches is what blogging in a school-based social network such as Youth Voices or the Personal Learning Space is all about.

One additional way that students are asked to *re-present* their generative themes (Freire, 1993, p. 109) is by coming up with five tags or key words. I ask students to think of five words to describe their writing so far. "If someone were to search for this piece of writing online, what key words would lead them to your writing?" This is akin to asking students to write a "focused sentence." Asking them to tag their writing with five key words is to ask them to reread and think about what they are writing.

Later, when students add these words to the bottom of their blog posts, they see how key words give them the power to find others who have also published about this theme, which then allows them to respond to these bloggers, and possibly to "friend" them so that following their future posts becomes easier to do. The concept behind friends is that a person in the network connects their blogging site to others, establishing a web of relationships among others in the bigger network.

Midweek Image Looping

Let's jump now to midweek, and zoom back to see the entire class. Whether a student started the Be a Blogger! matrix by commenting on other students' blogs, by finding an image, or by freewriting, in the middle of the week, he or she should have done all of the steps that lead up to Producing (Drafting) with an Image. This activity is similar to ones that I remember from early in my own schooling when my fourth grade teacher would ask us to look at an image and write about it, sometimes to describe it, but more often I remember being encouraged to use the image as a jumping off point. "Write the story that this image brings to mind."

An important difference here is that earlier in the week students were asked to find an image using a key word or tag or some word connected to a theme that they were already writing about. I ask each student to find an image (sometimes one that was taken by the student) to illustrate his or her thinking, then to think further and to write more, with the image in mind.

The image becomes part of the questioning, composing, wondering, inquiry process that helps the student to "loop, as if in an elliptical orbiting voyage" (Elbow, 1981, p. 60), back and forth between what the student already knows and is familiar with to a more speculative, unfamiliar territory.

I want students to go deeper than illustrating their writing with an image. I try to reach back to Freire's (1993) method of developing generative themes with images. Moving beyond my fourth grade teacher and acting like a critical pedagogue, I ask students to use the images that they have found to problematize their writing so far. "Go back to your freewriting now and see what else that image makes you think about your question."

Moving students from merely writing a description of the image to this more thoughtful, inquiry-based writing is one of the challenges of working with images. Instead of just illustrating their texts with images, the students learn to use their images as part of their thinking process. Through example and exhortation, most students begin to recognize the power of using images and text in conjunction, and even sometimes in juxtaposition, with each other. "Don't describe the image. Freewrite about what it makes you think now about what you are writing for this week's blog post. Where can this image take you?"

Rivers of Research Material

Another option on the Be a Blogger! matrix would be for a student to begin his or her week by reading something in their aggregator of syndicated writing and posts, Google Reader. If by Thursday, any particular student hasn't yet put an x through the third box (Links) down in the first column (Participating), I encourage them to go to their Google Reader and find blogs, news articles, and Web sites to read. Of course, before students can choose this option, I have to teach them how to subscribe to these sources.

I have found that students' blog posts are often more compelling when they introduce, insert, and interpret quotations from other sources, especially blogs and news sources that they have found themselves by using Google Blog Search and Google News.

In addition to writing more compelling posts, I want students to understand the differences among blogs, news sources, articles, peer-reviewed journals, videos, and podcasts. Over time, I have found that when students are using these resources in a personally meaningful inquiry they begin to distinguish between the resources that get updated in Google Reader from Web sites, Wikipedia, and other online encyclopedias and information sources.

Since it's easier to use these tools than it is to explain how they work, we have students try them out. Once students have opened an account in Google Reader (http://reader.google.com), we ask them to choose a keyword, something that they might want to research. One example is "Relationships." For the purpose of this demonstration, students use this keyword to find blogs, news sources, podcasts, and articles.

I take students through several steps to set up rivers of information in their Google Readers that will constantly update. Google Reader gives us a place where we can foster in students the habits they need to *select* from these rivers, then *read* (and understand) these sources before using quotations from them in their blog posts. Students learn how to use:

- Google Blog Search (http://blogsearch.google.com) to search the blogosphere to find other bloggers who are writing about their key words.
- Google News (http://news.google.com), looking for their keywords (for example, relationships) in over 4,500 news sources;
- Find Articles (http://findarticles.com) to discover more extended, scholarly articles.
- Everyzing (http://search.everyzing.com) to collect podcast episodes about their inquiries.
- Tweet Scan (http://tweetscan.com) or Summize (http://summize .com) to search for and gather any post on Twitter (http://twitter .com) that uses their keyword.

Students set their Google Readers up so that there is a folder for each of the keywords that they choose to represent their inquiries. Each day, they can come to class, click on that folder, and all the rivers of articles, blogs, news items, podcasts, and Twitter posts that have been collected there based on the settings and interests of the student. This makes the research more integral in their writing and blogging processes. When they sit down at their computers, they pop up their Google Reader and see if there is anything new on topics such as video games, Yankees baseball, mother-daughter relationships, music, or current news.

It is has been a shift for both the students and me to be thinking about information in this way. Instead of saying go find information on a particular topic, I am learning how to ask students to stay with a question for some time and to have a mosaic of Internet resources sent to their Google Reader. What is giving the research purpose is an approach to blogging that asks students to have their own inquiries, their own questions about the world and themselves.

CAN SELF-SPONSORED, PASSION-LED, INQUIRY-BASED BLOGGING BE A CURRICULUM?

As a quick look at the matrix, "Be a Blogger!" might suggest, blogging in my classroom is a multitasked, intricate process of reading, writing, talking, creating media, and doing research. In this era of state tests and mandated, sometimes even scripted curriculum, however, how do I describe this process to an interested but busy colleague, administrator, or parent?

I do not start with the matrix, which can be overwhelming. "One way to understand this curriculum," I say to them, "is to think of it as three different ongoing projects each of which require a student's attention every week."

- Profile: I ask students to add something new to their profiles each week. Profiles are areas on a student's blog that indicates their interests and information about their lives.
- Blog Post: Each week, students are asked to post on their blogs. Each week more thoughtfulness, more quotations, better connections, more effective use of media are required in each of these posts.
- Comments: Students are asked to respond to other students, both within their classes and school and from outside of their schools.

After taking a few questions, I'll continue: "Another way to understand this curriculum is through the media that students are asked to use in their profiles, on their blog posts, and in their comments. I give assignments each week that help students to develop their skills with text, images, audio, and other multimedia.

The Essential Questions for this curriculum are like concentric circles that start with an individual student's passions, and lead out through an online social network into taking social action. Blogging is the tool I use to pose these questions to students:

- What are you passionate about and how do these interests fit with other students' big questions?
- What voices or sources of information do you think are important to include in your search for answers?

- How do you become an effective online networker and get people with shared interests to value your voice online?
- How can you use our social networks as personal learning sites that lead to social action?

Being a blogger is about what young people do when they sit down to work at their computers. It is about creating a space in their lives to safely extend and explore their online voices with a group of peers, both at school, in another part of town, in another state, and around the world. The students in my classes learn about responding to each other's blogs, and how people choose to build together and share their creations and their resources.

By following this curriculum, students move beyond the standards embodied in state exams. They learn to identify the ideas and issues that are of importance to each of them. They learn more about themselves and find other people who share their interests and passions. Being able to have a substantial online presence and to network effectively are necessary skills today for success. Fluency in text, images, and audio are part of this communication. Students use their blogs to connect with their readers, student-to-student.

REFERENCES

Boss, S., & Krauss, J. (2007). *Reinventing project-based learning: Your field guide to real-world projects in the digital age.* Eugene, OR: International Society for Technology in Education.

Brown, J. S. (January 18, 2005). Lecture at San Diego State University. Retrieved on 17 June 2008, http://pict.sdsu.edu/jsb_lecture18jan05.pdf

Elbow, P. (1973). *Writing without teachers.* New York: Oxford University Press.

Elbow, P. (1981). *Writing with power: Techniques for mastering the writing process.* New York: Oxford University Press.

Freire, P. (1993). *Pedagogy of the oppressed.* New York: Continuum Books.

CHAPTER 6

Poetry Fusion

Integrating Video, Verbal, and Audio Texts

JEFFREY SCHWARTZ

I first used a computer to write in 1976 when I was hired as a photo typesetter in Cambridge, Massachusetts. It was as simple as learning computer commands, changing a daisy wheel for every typeface, and detaching a cartridge of rolled photo paper that would be fed through a printer in a dark room. Layout was literally cut and paste. In 1981, I enrolled in a doctoral program at Carnegie Mellon that combined rhetoric, poetry, and technology. On campus, I could write in a computer room (using Emacs & Scribe commands) and pick up the printout a few hours later in another building. In my graduate apartment, I still used an electronic typewriter. The dream at CMU was to link every computer to one giant mainframe so that students and faculty in the near future could communicate with each other and the library. In the summer of 1984 my wife, Betsy Bowen, and I were hired to direct the Apple Cellar at the Bread Loaf School of English. In a mountain campus that had once excluded cars and hair dryers, technology couldn't be kept away. The Apple IIe's we unpacked were part of an early grant from Apple to support word processing and telecommunications. BreadNet, the electronic network of English teachers and students, was invented by Dixie Goswami, Director of the Program in Writing at Bread Loaf. The Apples stayed on the mountain in summer and were loaned during the school year to teachers in rural communities from Maine to South Carolina, New Mexico, and Alaska. Teachers connected via phone lines and very slow modems. My high school students in Pittsburgh conducted an electronic exchange with other student writers in Wilsall, Montana, and on the Pine Ridge Reservation in Sioux Falls, South Dakota

(Schwartz, 1990). In 1989, John Elder, Dixie, Betsy, and I co-wrote *Word Processing in a Community of Writers*, a textbook that was outdated by the time it came out. Since 1988, I've been teaching at Greenwich Academy, which has evolved from several Apples into a model laptop school, where technology is woven seamlessly into the curriculum.

In 30 years, computers have revolutionized reading and writing. Wireless high-speed networks and laptops have made composing and revising easier, faster, and more portable. My students live in a world of mixed media at their fingertips. They multitask between homework, AIM, video chats, iTunes, Facebook, and YouTube. Ask any of them how they spend their time at night. Their computers link them to friends, information, and media in ways that are quicker and more compelling than we can reach them through a textbook. Unlike their parents, who grew up on conventional, linear writing and storytelling, our students' minds work like hyperlinks: one short episode can link endlessly to other episodes that precede it, parallel it, or follow it in time. Inside a text on screen can be detours to articles, music, images, and video. Yes, they must learn to write and read conventional texts. But their understanding of writing and communicating has surpassed that of their parents. To teach reading and writing in a global world, we need to follow our students' lead into a new understanding of media as text.

The project I will describe is an example of where and how media fuse in teaching poetry. For the last 5 years, I've been asking my ninth grade students at Greenwich Academy to interpret poetry in the form of a video. Greenwich Academy is an independent K–12 girls' school in southwestern Connecticut that draws students from as far as Milford in Connecticut and Yonkers in New York. In my three sections of English IX, poetry and media are integrated into a range of reading and writing genres. Students study Shakespeare and Austen, as well as Hitchcock and Kingsolver. They write informally to make meaning, formally in conventional essays, and creatively in prose and poetry. Because Greenwich Academy is a laptop school, students have access every day in class and at home to electronic writing folders, e-mail, multimedia, and the Internet. They are not all previously trained in creating and editing videos on their computers, but they are quick to learn.

The objectives for students of the Poetry Fusion project are to increase their:

- Appreciation of the art, as well as the pleasure, of poetry;
- Understanding of how sound, image, and words are integrated in poems and videos;
- Ability to interpret and analyze poetry;
- Ability to write (alone) and talk (in groups) about poetry;
- Confidence as writers and readers of poetry;

- Knowledge of technology;
- Ability to work and learn collaboratively; and
- Understanding of writing process by seeing videomaking (literally and metaphorically) as a visual way to compose.

The students are able to accomplish these objectives by

- Reading and discussing poems from Billy Collins' (2003) collection, *Poetry 180*, and elsewhere;
- Choosing poems to share with the class and creating audiopodcasts;
- Creating a personal anthology of favorite poems from *Poetry 180*;
- Writing an introduction to their anthologies that articulates taste as well as criteria of quality in poetry;
- Writing and sharing poems;
- Analyzing single poems in essays, both outside class and in timed writing;
- Working collaboratively to choose a poem and create a video (including planning as a group, shooting with digital camera, video editing, and screening of finished projects before a public audience); and
- Writing a self-assessment and a reflection on what they learned.

In the 2006–2007 school year, students used Mac iBooks (laptop computers), with Microsoft Word, iTunes, GarageBand, iWeb, iPhoto, and iMovie. In previous years, before iBooks and iLife (a suite of multimedia software applications), we used a computer lab networked with iMovie.

AUDIOPODCASTS

The video project grows out of a yearlong fusion of poetry and media. Before students pick up a camera, they have been preparing by listening, reading, talking, and seeing. "How do we see?" is an essential question that grounds our acts of observation and interpretation through the year. For the first half of the year, one of my goals is to open up students to poetry for pleasure. We establish a "Poetry Rotation" so that each week one student chooses a poem from Billy Collins' (2003) anthology, *Poetry 180*, to read aloud in class and record on GarageBand. The files are saved to the class Web site as audio podcasts, which students can subscribe to in iTunes. In this informal climate for pleasure reading, students are freer to respond to what they like, what strikes them as cool, and words that elicit feeling and thinking. In relating poems naturally to what they read, they discover that everything connects. Each short discussion of the oral poems is an exploration. Because students are choosing the poems, they are more in charge, and I am more a passenger on this excursion into words. Without my instructing, students are paying attention to sound, image, meaning.

Listening to poems is a different learning experience than conventional reading. Later in the year, students return to the first-semester podcasts and write about what they learned. Adriana writes that "Listening to the poem is different than seeing it because when you listen to it, you are unable to dwell on each word. You only catch what you can. That is why each time you notice something new." According to Julia Grace, "Listening to a poem allows for imagery to come more freely. The poem almost became a movie." Listening takes concentration and effort. Stephanie writes,

> I think listening to a poem is harder than reading it. When I read poems, the words and lines are processed in my head. When I listen to it, I have to make much more of an effort to understand. It is harder to pick up on details when listening to a poem, but it is also more enjoyable. Voice gives a poem life. It is more than just letters on paper.

Students' responses suggest that the podcasts help them to experience the poem as a whole. They don't see the lines or grammar; they can't pause on a word. They have to follow the rhythms and mental images to get to a more holistic sense of the poem. Some close their eyes while listening. One who couldn't get her Internet connection to work asked her father to read her chosen poem. The sounds of poetry enter their homes. Students comment repeatedly on how different it is to focus on hearing versus reading on the page. I tell them sound is a component of all language and writing; the audio podcasts make that real.

MAKING VIDEOS

The video project is a culmination of pleasure reading and analysis that has been developing all year. From the weekly audio podcasts, students are introduced to poetry. Then, during the final weeks of the year, they take a closer look. Concurrent with the video project, students write poems, share poetry aloud, and learn to write an essay that focuses on a close reading of a particular poem, something they do for practice several times before writing a close analysis on a final exam. The timing of the video project is as follows:

- Introduction of the project, including sample videos;
- Assembling individual poetry anthologies;
- Writing about audio podcasts;

- Sharing anthologies, creating groups, choosing one poem;
- Planning the video;
- Shooting the video with digital camera and tripod;
- Editing the video on iMovie (2 to 3 class days and outside class time); and
- Screening the videos: pizza and celebration!

Students are always excited to work on this project. They love working in groups, using cameras, and creating a video. I want them to share the labor equally, even if certain group members are more familiar with shooting or editing. I also want them to think about their poems carefully and pay attention to how film choices, like writing choices, affect meaning. Before shooting the video, they need to prepare by choosing from among a wide selection of poems. Each student creates an individual poetry anthology that includes an introductory two-page statement of poetics followed by at least ten poems from *Poetry 180* and a maximum of five more from other sources. The statements of poetics show the result of our reading for pleasure during first semester. The students genuinely like the poems they select, and they are beginning to articulate theories of poetic language and craft.

In groups of three or four (depending on the size of the class and the number of cameras), students negotiate those poems from their anthologies that would make the best videos. Here, too, they articulate what draws them to certain poems and think about which poems could be reinterpreted with visual imagery, storytelling, and sound. They have already seen sample videos from previous years, so they know the videos must be meaningful. Students are challenged to use their imaginations and take risks rather than to simply illustrate a poem. They are given a checklist to help guide their choices (see Figure 6.1). Even in the planning stage, students begin to consider cinematography (angle, distance, and movement of a camera), location, props, costumes, actors, still versus moving image, and sound. The words of the poem must appear in the video, but there are many possibilities, including voiceover, words that float over images, or words that appear on a black background.

Composing Process

In videomaking, planning is essential. In the long run, it saves time. It also helps students focus, since many are used to home movies, a passive process limited to turning on a camera, taking as much footage as possible, and playing it back with no editing. With some exceptions, poetry videos are restricted to 2 minutes. This is culled from approximately 6 minutes of tape shot during an hour in different locations, in or out of final sequence. Planning grows out of the messiness of talking and brainstorming. Just as with their

Figure 6.1. Poetry Video Checklist

As you work on your video this year, pay attention to your creative choices. How do you compose a video? How is it similar to writing? How do you work as a group? How does this project help you to see? Be prepared to write a reflection on what you have learned about your poem, as well as about the videomaking process.

1. Have you thoroughly *explored* the poem with your group?

_____ Yes _____ No

_____Did you each share your anthology and participate in selecting your poem?

_____Did you discuss your selected poem for meaning and technique?

_____Did you brainstorm together many possibilities for representing the poem in a creative video?

2. Have you *planned* effectively? Before shooting, has your group planned how to show your point?

Consider (where appropriate)

_____ choice of location

_____ script

_____ props

_____ involving other people

_____ sound

_____ camera angle, movement (pan, tilt, zoom), distance

_____ still pictures

3. Did you *shoot* the film effectively and efficiently?

_____ purposeful use of camera angle, distance, movement

_____ use of tripod

_____ time for shooting limited to approximately 6 minutes

4. Have you *edited* effectively?

_____ clear sequence (beginning, middle, and end)

_____ fascinating images

_____ transitions (fade, dissolve, etc.)

_____ special effects if appropriate (color, speed, stills, etc.)

_____ sound (music, narration, dialogue) and silence

_____ total video time edited to 1–2 minutes

_____ credits (video title and list of participants PLUS poet, poem title, and any credits for music, assistance, etc.)

5. Has every member of the group contributed equally?

_____ Yes   _____ No (and explain)

6. Now that you have created your poetry video, how satisfied are you with the outcome? Why?

_____ ecstatic ____ genuinely pleased ____ mildly enthusiastic ____ disappointed essays, I tell students that they need a map or a blueprint to give them a sense of direction, even if the plan changes along the way. The form the plan takes is up to them. Some groups choose to break down their poem line by line with detailed camera directions and shots corresponding to each line. Some make a chart with words in one column and images in another. Some make a simple list that the group could follow. In most cases, I ask them to specify their plans and to consider more options. Many times, the revisions in a plan before shooting are the result of deeper thinking about the poem.

Once shooting begins, the plans inevitably change. Students generally film during class time, so they are limited to available locations, participants, and weather conditions. Their interpretations of the poem grow naturally as they begin to combine words, sounds, and images in the shooting stage.

The actual video-editing process inspires even more choices. Students learn to import from mini DV cassettes to iMovie and then to cut clips down to their essential seconds and place them in sequence on a timeline. As the narrative forms, students have to choose transitions, effects, sound, and how to incorporate the words of the poem. One group realized that Maya Angelou's poem, "Caged Bird" (1983), would be more powerful if read and recorded by many voices rather than one. Another group recognized in the editing process that the still images they had chosen were too sentimental and abrupt. They revised a story of loss, imagining "Lullaby" by Jack Johnson (2006) was more about a family that suffers the death of a father in war, than a love story. The images are subtle and provocative, ending on a still shot of a family that one student edited on Photoshop so that the father is removed. Still another group added what they called *plotlines*, substories branching off the central narrative of Louis Jenkins' (2003) "Football." Embedded into the arc of the football story, which appears in the opening, middle, and end of the video, are four plotlines. Two grow out of Jenkins' suggestion that we live in "a world where anything is possible." Another two show ethical dilemmas that correspond to Jenkins' lines: "One has certain responsibilities,/one has to make choices." The students responded to the poet's humor and associative leaps by incorporating their own stories into his. The videos go beyond illustration to close reading and interpretation of new meanings.

One Group's Interpretive Choices

One of the most successful groups chose Bill Knott's (2008) "Advice from the Experts." This was their third choice after "The Lady of Shalott," a long narrative poem by Tennyson (2005), and "I Finally Managed to Speak to Her" by Hal Sirowitz (2003). According to Amanda, one of the three collaborating group members, "I was originally daunted. We picked a short, humorous poem that exuded a feeling that could not be further from the kind of movie

I wanted to do." Audrey wrote about her first impression of the poem: "There was no reaction, because I had never heard of the poem before. I looked it up in the book, and I read it. Again, there was no reaction. There didn't seem to be any significant meaning." As they proceeded, Molly wrote, "We changed our film dramatically from our initial plan. The plan was initially a very simple, straightforward, almost literal view of the movie." It closely follows Knott's poem:

Advice from the Experts

I lay down in the street and parked
My feet against the gutter's curb while from
The building above a bunch of gawkers perched
Along its ledges urged me don't, don't jump.

The poem is a humorous reaction from the point of view of someone about to jump off a roof. At first the group planned very simple shots of Molly cut between the lines of the poems. They considered a few close-ups, the use of black and white, and "a simple sad piano piece" that Amanda picked. "We were planning on having Molly lie on the road with her feet on the curb. We would film her lifting her foot, as if about to jump, and then flash, 'don't jump.' We planned a simple movie, just like the poem," Audrey wrote.

The film itself is a masterful result of the girls' artistic choices. They were open to adjusting their plan, based on what they were filming and how it looked in the editing stage on iMovie. They worked with a variety of angles and distance, beginning with a long shot of Molly carrying a book. Most of the film alternated between camera work and the words of the poem displayed in white sans serif type on a black background. Knott's short lines, though, were subdivided into single words or phrases that corresponded to the students' interpretation. They chose close-ups and low angles (looking up from Molly's sneakers as she lay on the ground) and long shots and low angles (looking up from one floor below at the two girls, "the bunch of gawkers," waving in front of a fence). They slowed down the narrator who contemplates suicide and sped up the crowd waving and trying to interfere. Because they experimented with angles in shooting, in editing they were able to create a short montage of Molly lying on the road, turning her like clock hands in a circle. Black and white became color. The soundtrack was kept the same, but the section of piano music was changed so that it followed the drama of the story in terms of space, silence, and climax. "The slow music we had chosen required us to slow down certain shots and use slow transition such as cross-dissolves and fade-ins" (Molly). As luck had it, the sun was exactly behind the gawkers and led to some beautiful still shots of their hands in silhouette against an over-bright sun.

The newly discovered images, along with the ones from the plan, became more meaningful as the girls read and reacted to Knott's poem.

> In the process of filming, we decided to move away from a literal interpretation of the poem to include shots of me walking with the book [*The Journals of Sylvia Plath* (1987)] toward a fence. The decision to drop the book was fairly improvisational, but ended up creating a powerful, highly symbolic shot. The book was, unfortunately, broken in the fall, but the way that it naturally fell created an amazingly appropriate shot of Sylvia Plath's face next to her name. (Molly)

The girls were aware of Plath's suicide, which created another layer of their interpretation on whether to jump or not, whether to interfere or to watch, to choose life or death. As with the tone of Knott's poem, part of the video is humorous and part serious. The visual and oral choices create a coherent whole that, like the original poem, is open to interpretation. Plath's book, not a person, ends up falling and breaking. It is a shocking sense of relief that the person didn't jump, and, as a matter of fact, after the group added rolling credits, they included a reverse shot of the book flying up from the ground. The film ends as openly and as ambivalently as Knott's "Advice." "In the end, our movie's deviation from the original plan showed our altered interpretation of the poem itself" (Molly).

Video as Text

Audrey, the collaborator who began the project with "no reaction," agreed that by the end

> the interpretation has changed. Just like in writing, we started out with one idea. Before, there was no reaction, or if there was, it was only about someone listening to another for advice. However, as we developed deeper into the meaning, a new interpretation came out. It wasn't about a person just listening to advice; it was about someone *needing* advice. With this new guidance, this person was slowly able to drop her foolish resolution and begin anew again. This project has not only allowed our group to be creative with a good poem, but it has also helped us delve into the poem in search of a profound meaning to it.

Audrey is aware of her reading process and also how collaboration leads to discovery, further reinforcing a goal throughout the year that meaning is socially constructed. From the first audio podcasts through all of our literary readings, students learn with and from each other about language and thinking.

Clearly, the collaborative experience of filming a poem is itself an act of literary interpretation. The groups that went beyond the literal discovered new layers of meaning. They reinterpreted words in terms of their own reading and also in terms of intentional and unintentional decisions about video images, soundtrack, and use of the poem in the video. All discovered that any choice affected the meaning—everything from sequence to framing, speed, color, angle, transition, sound, light, and so on. The video is a living text that is read, shared, and interpreted both while it is constructed and when it is finished. Like a completed written product, it is also performed or published. At the end of the semester, we celebrated the videos by inviting all of the classes to a public screening of every group video.

Video as Writing

Video is also a text that is composed, much as students' other writing. From observations over time, I believe that there is a positive transference between composing in multimedia and in writing. Students understand the similarities. A group video begins with a germ of an idea that grows through talking and brainstorming. It is structured around an initial plan that expands and contracts during the process. Good writers know that plans are dynamic and that even elements of chance can enhance. Finally, once it is imported into iMovie, the video is manipulated in terms of focus, sequence, transitions, and sound. As with essay or poetry writing, the creators have something important to express that is refined and clarified as they unify the parts and consider an audience.

The concept of revision in conventional writing is incomprehensible to many, if not most, students. In video making, however, students *see* and understand the need for focus, economy, clarity, and engaging an audience. Cutting a clip and choosing transitions and narrative structure are visual and memorable. Style is content. If the connection to writing isn't blaringly apparent, I also ask students to reflect on it in their self-assessment.

ASSESSMENT

Because the video project is so process oriented, it is hard to assess. Over the years, my approach has evolved from not grading the videos at all, to grading the student reflections, to finally grading both reflections and product. The reflections are not hard to grade, given the emphasis throughout the year on response writing that shows a sense of voice, thorough examples, and close reading for discovery and meaning. In addition to their reflections, students self-assess their project on the same rubric I use to give them further feedback. I'm still uncomfortable, though, with my criteria for grading the project and will certainly revise the rubric. In the 2007 assessment rubric (see Figure 6.2), I have tried to focus on process. Next year I might specify the process (for example, incorporating required conferences during planning and editing). I might also try to articulate more what the final product should look like.

Regardless of the wording of the rubrics, they ultimately may not be flexible enough to grade a dynamic, collaborative project that depends on technology. Are amounts of fun or learning quantifiable? Grading must be holistic rather than simply converting rubric scores to percentages. More important than creating a grade, the rubric is a guideline, expressing goals to students.

Sometimes unpredictable and unconventional success can not be measured in a rubric. For example, one video group chose Henry Taylor's (2003) poem, "Elevator Music." Step after step, they ran into unexpected difficulties beyond their control. After all of the preliminary shooting, the first elevator they chose didn't work. They filmed twice, because they thought they had accidentally shot over original footage. Then theirs was the only group that didn't have sufficient memory on their laptops to run iMovie. They borrowed an external hard drive, but in the transfer to the central computer (to combine videos into one DVD), the screen froze, and I inadvertently removed the hard drive before it finished saving. They lost the project, reimported and reedited, but then had unsolvable problems with iTunes copyright restrictions of their soundtrack song (even after I purchased it). The final version was well done, but included compromises that could have been more polished, even though they had put in twice the time expected. With a positive tone, Elizabeth describes her group's process and growing sense of meaning, including how "making this film has really changed my interpretation of the poem." Despite the difficulties and rough final project, the group's adjustment to setbacks and learning could not have been better. The photo of Elizabeth and Anna in Figure 6.3 shows how carefully their group planned a high-angle shot through a glass window, even compensating for the reflective light.

My experience assessing media is that it is an enjoyably messy process. Assessment, like writing itself, is an attempt to express what is too multilayered and complex to be reduced. Having said that, I understand that our students live in a world that demands high stakes testing and grades. This is not a class in test preparation, although students are indirectly reinforcing literacy skills that standardized tests such as the AP and SAT purport to assess. What students learn in a multimedia classroom in ninth grade unquestionably enriches their literacy as readers and writers. In particular, the video project meets all of the English Language Arts Standards developed by NCTE and IRA

Figure 6.2. Poetry Video Assessment

Your Name: _____

Circle a number between 1 and 4, where
4= Strongly Agree, 3 = Agree, 2 = Disagree, and 1 = Strongly Disagree.

Criteria	Student Assessment				Teacher Assessment			
The group completed a **plan** (attached) before shooting the film.	1	2	3	4	1	2	3	4
The film is **creative** and **original**.	1	2	3	4	1	2	3	4
The **interpretation** of the poem goes beyond the literal to a thoughtful, fresh reading.	1	2	3	4	1	2	3	4
The group made **camera choices** (angle, distance, movement) that contribute very effectively to the video.	1	2	3	4	1	2	3	4
The **music** complements and doesn't compete with the images and words of the poem.	1	2	3	4	1	2	3	4
The video is **edited** to two minutes—or to its most concise form so that every frame and transition is absolutely necessary.	1	2	3	4	1	2	3	4
The group truly **collaborated**; each person shared equally in the whole process.	1	2	3	4	1	2	3	4
Group members **learned more about the poem** by interpreting it in a video form.**	1	2	3	4	1	2	3	4
Group members **learned more about video composition** and how it resembles writing process.**	1	2	3	4	1	2	3	4
The project was **fun**.	1	2	3	4	1	2	3	4
Comments and Grade								

** In your video response, write more about your process and what you learned.

Figure 6.3. Anna and Elizabeth Compose a High-Angle Shot Through a Glass Wall to the Floor Below

(1996) on process, strategies, diversity of language, and technology—from Standards 1 "Students read a wide range of print and nonprint texts"—to 12 "students use spoken, written, and visual language to accomplish their own purposes" (p. 25). These standards, which provide the theoretical foundation for my department, also inform my practice as does the NCTE (2005) guideline on Multimodal Literacies. It advocates that "The use of different modes of expression in student work should be integrated into the overall literacy goals of the curriculum."

25 YEARS WITH TECHNOLOGY

The poetry video project I've described does not replace conventional writing tasks in my classroom. Especially because Greenwich Academy is a highly competitive independent school, conventional literary analyses still have prime importance. Underpinning the goals of the course, though, is a philosophy of writing that makes room for multiple genres and purposes. In that regard, my classroom has stayed the same for the last 25 years. Writing still focuses on principles of process, rhetoric, and assessment, particularly self-assessment in the form of an ongoing portfolio and frequent student reflection on and grading of their own essays. Even technology has been consistent in my classroom, from initial attempts to incorporate telecommunications and to require word processing through today's hyperlinked, multimedia universe available instantly on a wireless network that reaches every inch of school property.

Besides speed and availability, what has changed most is our notion of *text*. In addition to linear, single-authored, printed narrative texts, my classes also read and compose texts that are nonlinear, collaborative, and layered with sound, visual images, and writing. Previously, I had happily taught poetry solely on the page. Students learned a lot, but they didn't learn in the same ways as they do making audio podcasts and videos. At the end of her three-page video response on how meaning evolved in her group video, Alexa wrote:

> Making the poem into a movie helped me discover so many nuances about the poem. No matter how many times I read it [Gary Soto's (2003) "Saturday at the Canal"], it seemed like a story about teen rebellion, about a "teenage wasteland." But when we started putting images into it, it became so much more. It became restless, unsatisfactory, dirty. It was the editing that made all the difference. I had never thought about how important that was until working on this movie.

In fusing media, students are challenged to think in new ways. Reading and writing video texts creates metaphors for composing in writing. One transfers to the other: What could be clearer than cutting the extra seconds out of a good shot? Get to the point. Use all of your creative and analytical resources to express your meaning to your audience. Pay attention to the language. Be aware of how you work and what you say, including the creative surprises and unintended meaning that you might not even notice until after you're finished. Respect and listen to your collaborators. You will learn from them. Be proud of what you have created. All of your choices determine the quality and the art of the final product. But the learning, the learning together is key.

REFERENCES

Angelou, M. (1983). *Shaker, why don't yon sing*. New York: Randon House.

Collins, B. (Ed.). (2003). *Poetry 180: A turning back to poetry*. New York: Random House.

Elder, J., Goswami, D., Bowen, B., & Schwartz, J. (1989). *Word processing in a community of writers*. New York: Garland.

Jenkins, L. (2003). Football. In B. Collins (Ed.), *Poetry 180: A turning back to poetry*. New York: Random House.

Johnson, J. (2006). Lullaby. In *Sing-a-longs and lullabies for the film Curious George* (p. 140). Los Angeles: Brushfire Records.

Knott, B. (2000). Advice from the experts. *Laugh at the end of the world: Collected comic poems, 1969–1999* (p. 103). Rochester, NY: BOA Editions.

National Council of Teachers of English. (2005). Multimodal literacies. NCTE Guideline. Retrieved August 25, 2008, from http://www.ncte.org/edpolicy/multimodal/resources/123213.htm

National Council of Teachers of English and International Reading Association. (1996). *Standards for the English Language Arts*. Urbana, IL, and Newark, DE: Authors.

Plath, S. (1987). The Journals of Sylvia Plath. (F. McCullough, Ed.) New York: Ballantine Books.

Schwartz, J. (1990). Using an electronic network to play the scales of discourse. *English Journal, 79*(3), 16–24.

Sirowitz, H. (2003). I finally managed to speak to her. In B. Collins (Ed.), *Poetry 180: A turning back to poetry* (p. 108). New York: Random House.

Soto, G. (2003). Saturday at the Canal. In B. Collins (Ed.), *Poetry 180: A turning back to poetry* (p. 229). New York: Random House.

Taylor, H. (2003). Elevator Music. In B. Collins (Ed.), *Poetry 180: A turning back to poetry* (p. 207). New York: Random House.

Tennyson, A. (2005). "The Lady of Shalott" in M. Ferguson, M. J. Salter, and J. Stallworthy (Eds.), *The Norton anthology of poetry*, (Shorter 5th ed.) (pp. 621–625). New York: W. W. Norton (Original work published 1970).

CHAPTER 7

Senior Boards

Multimedia Presentations from Yearlong Research and Community-Based Culminating Projects

BRYAN RIPLEY CRANDALL

On the mornings reserved for senior culminating projects I'm a nervous wreck. I arrive at school earlier than usual in order to double-check the technology and to make sure everything is where it should be. Students have scheduled multimedia presentations in two rooms, and I pace between them like a madman trying to empty the ocean with a fork. I am a facilitator and a host for my students who will showcase their yearlong research and culminating projects to an invited panel of four guests: three adults and one student. I place scoring rubrics at each table; 12 students present every day: 6 performances per room. My students are ready. They will be fine. Seniors have already spent 4 years preparing for state-assessed writing portfolios and on-demand writing prompts. Most have also applied for their post-high school lives. Yet, at the Brown School, seniors are required to participate in an additional presentation of research and community involvement. These projects assist their state-assessed writing in several, real-world ways.

I place refreshments in one of the rooms, and the first senior arrives. He has spent the year researching water issues in Zambia. From his practice sessions in my English class, notes from a sociology teacher, and lessons from an environmental science course, he's written a paper on Zambia's ecological problems. He's referenced Maslow's hierarchy of needs and researched the watersheds of Zambia. He spent 6 weeks last year reading Alan Paton's (1948) *Cry the Beloved Country*. With BreadNet computer software made available by the Bread Loaf School of English, he was able to become a correspondent with students in Nairobi, Africa. His community network is global because of current technology. He worked closely with a mentor at his church, too, and held a pancake supper to raise money for water wells. At the supper, he handed out bottles of water and taught others about Zambia's current conditions. He instructed participants to keep the water bottle he provided and to fill it with spare change once it became empty. Because it was near Lent, he recommended giving up a habit in order to support those who are less privileged.

"Are you ready?" I ask him.

"I'm ready if the technology is ready," he admits.

The student clicks the computer and a projector throws his words onto a large screen: "Imagine waking up everyday knowing it will not be easy to provide enough water for your family to drink, knowing the fields are dry outside, and feeling as though there is no one there to help you." He clicks the mouse and produces a Tibetan proverb, "Words are mere bubbles of water; deeds are drops of gold."

I ask him, "Did you remember a copy of your research paper?" He pulls the work out of his bag. It's entitled, "Splashing Through Still Waters: The Crippling of Zambia as a result of AIDS and Hydrologic Poverty." I tease him that his use of Wikipedia is a good place to start a research paper, but once he enters college in the fall, he should begin looking at more primary sources. He's written an excellent paper, and I'm kidding. He's met the criteria for the research requirement at the Brown, and now he's about to present his work to a panel using audio, video, and a well-rehearsed PowerPoint presentation.

There were 53 projects presented at the J. Graham Brown School last year, all of them assessed for partial credit toward graduation. With each project, students learned research, organization, and presentation skills. In addition, much of the writing that occurred during this process was entered into the celebrated, state-assessed Kentucky writing portfolios (Hillocks, 2002). In an age of digital literacy, presentations from student-research projects are an excellent preparation for the future. The technology available to students allows them faster acquisition of resource materials and improves the way they are able to present what they know. Over the last decade, these culminating projects and research presentations have become more multimedia, however, and as an English teacher, I've had to adapt with new technology to keep up. I feel obligated to provide students the best technological resources I can because I recognize an online, digital life is what my students know and where they'll be in the future. Digital literacy is a growing expectation of higher education, employers, parents, and students. I adhere to local and state regulations as well, trying to incorporate as much technology as I can. My students use the Internet for research and the Bread Loaf School of English's BreadNet software to communicate with writing partners across seas. They are familiar with word processing tools and software because they have been a part of their world since they began school. More and more, students are becoming more comfortable with video and audio editing software, too. As super communicators (Associated Press, 2008) and digital natives (Prensky, 2001), they are used to technological environments.

HISTORY OF THE SENIOR PROJECT PROCESS

In 1997 I began teaching English at the J. Graham Brown School in Louisville, Kentucky, a K–12 public school designed with a mission for diversity, self-directed learning, and the promotion of individuality. The school holds approximately 600 students—usually one boy and one girl from each of the city's zip codes—and I'm responsible for the junior and senior classes. Before I arrived, several leaders at the school were active with the Coalition of Essential Schools (CES) and were introduced to senior exhibitions as a graduation requirement. Seniors were still assessed with on-demand writing prompts and a writing portfolio as part of their state assessment, but they also were provided with a new requirement: to present research and a culminating project during Senior Boards. Another CES teacher, Peggy Silva, (Silva & Mackin, 2002), describes the culminating work as

> an active project in which students choose a topic of interest, something that they really want to learn more about. They read about it, they research it, they interview people, and they choose an expert in the field and have conversations. Students choose an essential question, or an inquiry topic, and engage in a process in which all learners work to become an expert. Students have to demonstrate application, to show that they can use this knowledge in a new context. (p. 101).

At the Brown School, the senior culminating project process guides the senior year, and as technology changes, so does the design of what I teach in my classroom. From August to May, students are in one phase or another toward their final goal. Recent technological advancements have changed what I expect my students to do in my English class.

Senior English at the Brown School is divided into four major areas: 1. state-assessed writing portfolios, 2. a senior research paper, 3. a year-long project, and 4. the presentation of both research and the culminating project. All writing produced during this process is viewed as an important factor to a student's senior year success. The audiences for the presentations are authentic (that is, genuinely interested in the substance of the presentation), and therefore the students' writing transcends the "teacher as assessor" model. More often than not, written work for their senior projects are included in Kentucky's assessed writing portfolios. This writing is more credible, purposeful, and useful than writing done solely for testing purposes.

NEW WRITING EXPECTATIONS

In 2006–2007, the State of Kentucky revisited its writing program and switched a portfolio-scoring rubric from a *holistic* measurement to an *analytical* one (see Kentucky Department of Education, 2007). Observations made by business sectors in Kentucky noticed high school students needed more workplace, practical writing, while academic institutions saw a need for preparing students better with analytical writing. The result was an analytical/technical writing requirement for all high school writing portfolios in Kentucky.

Required Portfolio Entries

The 12th grade writing portfolio assessment has four entries instead of the previous five. The first is a literacy reflection, where students address themselves as writers through the lens of reading and writing. This writing is an opportunity for students to think deeply about their accomplishments as readers and writers. The second piece is a personal narrative, memoir, essay, short story, script, or poem. Here, students choose their best literary piece to enter as a demonstration of their personal/literary talents. The third and fourth pieces are entitled transactive writing: writing with real-world purposes to real world audiences. One of the two transactive pieces MUST be analytical or technical in focus. As the *Kentucky Writing Handbook* (2006) notes,

> Transactive writing, which is written from the perspective of an informed writer to a less-informed reader, is functional writing intended to present information. Transactive writing is writing for a variety of realistic purposes that is intended to "get things accomplished" or to help the audience understand something better. Much of the writing completed in academic contexts and in the workplace is transactive writing. In fact, academic writing and technical writing are examples of transactive writing that can be potentially publishable and portfolio-appropriate.
> In order to present authentic purposes to real-world critical readers, students may choose from a variety of forms such as: a letter for the local newspaper, an editorial published in the school newspaper, an article for a class or team magazine, or a speech or proposal for the school based council. (p. 87)

Finally, at least one piece entered in the writing portfolio must originate from a content area other than English. This requirement mandates English departments to work closely with all colleagues in other content areas so cross-disciplinary writing is produced. Writing across the curriculum is a state mandate.

Senior Research Papers as Transactive Writing

Brown's senior research paper qualifies as a transactive piece of writing because it requires students to analyze available resources and to demonstrate new learning. The goal of this assigned paper is to gain skills that might serve as an introduction to the academic writing they may encounter if they choose to pursue a college education. Students at the Brown are not tracked. Every classroom encourages students with learning disabilities, students with average abilities, and students with exceptional abilities to accomplish their personal best. Diversity is the school's mission, and holding high standards for all students is a cultural norm. Every individual who graduates from the Brown School writes a research paper and is held accountable to the goals set forth from the senior project experience. Flexibility exists within these goals, however, to accommodate the needs of individual students.

The senior class begins research in August and continues accruing information throughout the first, and the beginning of second, semester. Within the entire process, students are given advice on how to best use the Internet, school library, and local library to gain the best sources for their topic. The first draft of the research paper is submitted at the end of January. Students are offered feedback within workshops and use an adapted protocol for looking at student work (Blythe, Allen, & Schieffelin-Powell, 2007). Seniors also have access to an online community through Jefferson County Public Schools and are able to post their work for one another. This online community allows teachers to post assignments and keep an eye on student progress. In addition, weekly conferences between the teacher and students occur. The second draft of the paper is collected in March. In total, two drafts are required, but students may submit additional drafts if necessary. The goal of the research paper is to build academic knowledge for the yearlong project that culminates with the Senior Boards. The process of research and planning is more important than the product of a paper and a presentation.

Many students submit their papers as part of the state portfolio assessment in the analytical/transactive category. Research is mentored by subject area teachers and relies heavily on them for guidance as to content. For example, a student may choose to research global warming and need the guidance of teachers in the science department. Research skills, however, are taught in English class where the paper is guided into completion.

Brown School seniors are given a checklist during the first week of their senior year that frames the research process entirely. When they are able to answer yes to each of 16 questions, they have a successful research paper. This checklist is revisited throughout the year and is a guide for students as they work their way through the process:

1. Do I have a title page with my name, Senior English, and the date on it?
2. Do I have a preface?
3. Do I have at least ten pages beginning with the introduction page?
4. Do I have a strong essential question that can be answered in an original, thought provoking way?
5. Do I have a clever introduction with a strong thesis statement?
6. 1s my paper proofread for grammatical/spelling errors?
7. Do I organize my paragraphs?
8. Do I cite at least seven sources within my text?
9. Do I cite them correctly using MLA referencing?
10. Do I have a conclusion?
11. Do I have a bibliography that is in MLA style?
12. Do I have at least five books as resources (excluding encyclopedias, dictionaries, etc.)?
13. Do I have at least two Internet cites with the web address, author of the cite, and title of the cite, if available?
14. Does the paper show a semester's worth of research?
15. De I give reference to the proper authorities in my paper and avoid plagiarism?
16. Is the paper interesting, engaging and educational to read?

Senior Research Prefaces as Personal Narrative

Unique to this yearlong process is the assignment of a preface to the research paper (#2 on the Checklist). The preface is a personal narrative on why a student takes an interest in his or her subject. Here, students write the story behind the work. Often, students use their preface as a personal/literary entry for the state-assessed writing portfolio. The genuine interest students have for their chosen subject makes for better writing, and the prefaces are usually quite strong. Students also tap into this narration when they present their multimedia presentation at the Senior Boards.

Danh, a Vietnamese immigrant and 2007 Brown graduate, spent his senior year researching the history of American-Vietnamese immigration. For Danh's senior project he volunteered with a youth group at his church and led several activities. He researched Vietnamese political refugees and offered the following as part of his personal connection:

Ever since I was little, I have been known as the quiet boy who was unable to express his feelings to anyone. Rather, I'd keep my thoughts to myself and rarely ever did I voice my opinion. After I started to attend the Vietnamese Eucharistic Youth Society, however, I realized it was okay to step outside of my sheltered bubble my parents had created for me. I realized it was okay for me to let things out every once in a while and I did not have to keep everything in. Realizing this, I stumbled onto my senior project idea.

As a senior at the J. Graham Brown School, I am required to have a yearlong culminating project as well as a paper on a topic related to what I am doing. Personally, my project is working with the children in my youth group, where I help out with activities, bible studies, and events such as field trips, or the annual Christmas play. The work takes place every Sunday before Church services. In my research, I'm exploring the life of Vietnamese immigrants who came to America, addressing why they moved here, and learning what they did once they arrived. Consequently, my paper explains a little bit about my project as well.

Danh wrote from personal experiences to guide him to this subject. He is a first generation Vietnamese student. Given the freedom to pursue his topic of interest (as opposed to a specified assignment), the writing became more meaningful. He continues:

I am Vietnamese. My parents come from Vietnam and I was born there in a little suburb in the south area (I can't recall exactly where). A little while after I was born, my parents decided to have me baptized and thus I became a Catholic. A year after I was born, though, they also decided they would move to America in order to find a better life for my siblings and me. This is why I don't remember much about my home country.

An extended narration of Danh's essay fulfilled the student's literary/personal piece expected for state accountability, but also served as a background for his entire research paper and culminating project. During his end-of-the-year presentation, Danh was also able to navigate between photographs from his work in the Vietnamese community, his personal story of why this work was important to him, and his research on political refugees. Using PowerPoint, he organized the topic through an introduction, his personal narrative, the research conducted on political refugees, and his implemented project in the Vietnamese neighborhood. The personal connection allowed him to tell his story behind the research while also becoming an option for state assessment. Seniors often use variations of these research prefaces for college applications, because they turn into a strong declaration of the self, as well.

Writing for the Real World

Writing for the culminating projects isn't just analytical and research oriented. Early in the academic year, students are taught the skills for writing business letters that make things happen. Kentucky's writing portfolios call for at least one entry in the transactive category to be analytical *and/or* technical. Students may choose to submit a proposal, business letter, or laboratory report to model the writing that occurs in professional fields. Students do not have to submit research papers if they choose not to. As a result of this, a few weeks are spent early in the senior year on the art of writing letters to get something done. Each student gains skills with how to write a proposal, and every senior is required to have her or his project approved by the School Based Decision Making (SBDM) council (another real-world audience). Some students network their plans via business letters—again, real-world writing— to seek assistance with their senior projects. One senior from last year's class, for example, kept a strong business tie with the Victory Junction Gang Camp of North Carolina and networked with them as she pursued an interest in equine therapy.

ASSESSMENT

During second semester of Senior English, 25 percent of a student's total grade derives from the presentations at Senior Boards; 25 percent from the senior research paper; 25 percent from the State Assessed writing portfolio; and 25 percent from the class work, participation, and homework that is carried out to support these processes. Class work is often carried out through discussions that acknowledge student online postings and in class concerns. It is difficult to keep up with all the online activity the students are involved with. The online community, then, becomes a discussion forum for the students to generate ideas before they are brought to the teacher's attention.

The new Kentucky Writing Scoring Rubric looks at student writing using three domains: content, structure, and conventions. Within the three domains, subcategories are provided to assess a piece of writing. In the content domain students are responsible for purpose and audience, idea development and support. In the structure domain students are scored for their organization, unity and coherence, and sentences (structure and length). Finally, students are given a score in the conventions domain: language choice, grammar and usage, word choice, and correctness in spelling, punctuation, capitalization, abbreviation, and documentation. Elaborate training is provided for all Kentucky teachers wanting to score student writing; each piece is given two readings to assure accuracy. If two assessors score a written piece differently, a third reading is required.

Most writing in Kentucky schools is held to the Kentucky Writing Scoring Rubric, including the senior research paper at the Brown School. The research paper that responds to the 16 questions of the checklist discussed earlier is likely to score well with the new state rubric. In particular, research papers are written with a specific purpose for a direct audience. Much attention is paid to idea development through supported research (hence, it demonstrates analysis). Students are deliberate on how to best organize this writing, and lessons are provided in their English class to accomplish this. Workshops and peer readings also help students pay close attention to conventions.

Beyond the Kentucky Writing Scoring Rubric that guides student writing, Brown School seniors also become familiar with the Senior Boards Evaluation Sheet. The categories on this evaluation sheet become the rubric that students use to guide their senior research and projects. Like the Kentucky Writing Handbook (Kentucky Department of Education, 2006) that guides state writing portfolios, the Senior Board Evaluation Sheet provides a framework for research, culminating projects and presentations.

The culminating projects that grow out of the research papers showcase the individual student's talents, intelligence, leadership, and ability to contribute toward a better world. The work can't be accomplished overnight; instead, it demonstrates the labor needed to investigate, plan, design, and implement a project. Culminating projects take on many forms, and each is designed to match the interest of the student. In year's past, projects have included the following:

- Art projects. Throughout the school and local community, students have donated pieces of art created out of their research.
- Teaching. Several students choose to teach small units within the Brown, but also in the community: churches, after school programs, parent groups, volunteer organizations, hospitals, and so forth.
- Community festivals. Some students provide evenings for poetic entertainment, song, comedy, and art. Others create drama programs. A few more have designed Earth Day programs, while many implement benefit shows with their bands.
- Volunteering. Several students give their free time to assist others in need. They work with refugees, at local charities, or for national programs. They assist with charity walks, mailings, and dinners.

Each culminating project is designed from the research conducted by students and provides an opportunity for Brown School seniors to take on leadership roles.

For the Senior Boards, seniors prepare a half-hour to an hour presentation on their yearlong work using PowerPoint or Keynote to outline their efforts. They present a title slide, information on why their subject is of personal interest, key findings from their research, and a timeline of how their culminating project occurred. In these presentations, students upload video clips of their work, photographs of their accomplishments, and hyperlinks to some of their resources. They use a partner to help them click the slides as they present.

One student, for example, spent his senior year researching the history of Improvisation and used technology to help the panel learn about the yearlong effort. His first slide was entitled "Life is Improv," and from here, he designed slides to discuss definitions of theatrical improvisation and included an audio clip of William Shakespeare's "All the World's a Stage." When the audio finished, he discussed his personal connection to the subject, and then went through several of his key findings. He walked members through a timeline of his year, discussed important dates, and shared the knowledge he learned from his research. He also played video of several of his Improv shows to demonstrate how his new learning influenced the performance group he created. He was able to create course material for a humanities teacher at our school, as well. At the end of the presentation, he reflected on the process in its entirety and offered suggestions for others who might like to follow in his footsteps.

A second student spent her senior year looking at AIDS in the African American community. Working with local agencies, she created a presentation from her research that included several photographs taken during workshops she conducted throughout the city. She created an audio slide show of a student group she was able to organize for a local AIDS Walk. Handing out her finished research paper to accompany the presentation, she succeeded in demonstrating to the panel that she was ready for the next phase of her life.

Senior Boards are assessed using the following Senior Boards Evaluation Sheet as a rubric. Technology use was added to the rubric after 2002 when panel members made specific requests that students should use available technologies to make their presentations more mature. As a teacher, I now expect students to use presentation software and hyperlinks when they present. I also encourage the use of video and audio. In each category, 10 points may be rewarded for a grand total of 100 points:

1. Purpose/goal for project
2. Personal connection/motivation for project
3. Research behind project

4. Evidence of yearlong effort (September–April)
5. Contribution to community
6. Student growth/reflection on project and research
7. Feedback from mentors, audiences, and/or teachers
8. Visual aids/technology use
9. Speech/articulation/clarity
10. Overall presentation

Students have the right to redo their presentations if their total does not equal a passing grade. In these cases, members of the panel discuss with the student what they saw from the presentation and where further work is needed. Students do not usually fail the Senior Boards because the yearlong process and the practice presentations in senior English are designed as check points to offer guidance and support. Students usually enter the boards knowing they have done a great job.

CURRICULAR ADAPTATIONS AS A RESULT OF TECHNOLOGY

When I first began teaching at the Brown School in 1997 it was common for students to turn in handwritten state writing portfolios and senior research papers. Students did not use computers for any of their end-of-the-year presentations; instead, they utilized storyboards, photographs, and booklets to demonstrate their work. I didn't have a computer, myself, until 1996. Before that I wrote with a typewriter and then moved to a word processor. The Internet was not available as a tool in my teacher preparation. It was just barely introduced to the MAT program I attended the year after I graduated. My classroom teaching experience with technology has evolved with the recommendations of the policymakers in Washington (U.S. Department of Education, 1996, 2000, 2004). Changes on how I teach are influenced by the education technology policies in the United States and the professional development offered to me through my district and programs like the Bread Loaf School of English. Using software like Bread Net helps me connect my students with others around the world. It also helps me stay in close contact with teaching professionals in other countries who offer new perspectives on my career and feedback on my ideas. As an online community, Bread Net operates with e-mail, discussion forums, and newsletters. Those who teach in my school and district aren't my only colleagues. They are also teachers around the globe who help me keep up with newer, better technologies when they are introduced. In some ways what was once revolutionary is now, ho-hum, normal: podcasts, QuickTime, chat rooms, blogging, and so forth. I'm given a lot of power knowing that as a classroom teacher, I can bring my questions to the Internet and resolve them quickly.

Still, my students are more technologically savvy than I. They grew up immersed in technology. All students now word process their writing portfolios and use multimedia techniques to present their work at the Senior Boards (teaching me new tools every year). Guests want to see technology during presentations, and coming from other professions—many that aren't in educational careers—they feel the more modern the presentations, the more mature and prepared the students will be for their future. As a result, I vow to learn as much as I can each year so I'll better prepare my students for the changing world they'll inherit.

The availability of e-mail for all students has also made it easier to share multiple drafts of their work and has made writing workshops a little more practical. Students can send one another their drafts. The Internet allows information to be more accessible to my students at a faster rate; therefore, I now spend more time discussing good online sources over good library sources than I did in the past. I find myself facilitating how to access information instead of pouring out knowledge as if I am some sort of faucet of facts. The volumes of information students sift through on a daily basis has multiplied, yet so has the necessity for teaching skills to recognize credible sources. For example, in senior English class, a lot more discussion occurs around what constitutes expertise in any given field. These discussions, complemented by Gerald Graff and Cathy Birkenstein's (2006) text, *They Say, I Say: The Moves that Matter in Academic Writing*, have been very useful.

It has also become a ritual to work collaboratively with the school librarian on best practices for Internet/library research because she has the most up-to-date training on these issues. Our librarian trains students by using Purdue University's online OWL, (http://owl.english.purdue.edu/) as a quick overview and leads a discussion about the library copies of the MLA handbook available to students. In addition, Jefferson County Public Schools allow students access to community software and Internet programs where additional resources are available. Here, students and teachers can correspond in chat rooms, use e-mail, and access assignments. Materials can be posted so students have access at home.

Thursdays at the school are now deemed "re-thearch-days" where seniors can work on the research and project process in the English classroom, the library, or at a computer lab. My role as the English teacher on Thursdays is to conference, guide, mentor, and support the work students are doing. On these days, the students are very self-directed.

Several students now make I-movies, use Final Cut Pro, design Web sites, and/or post flash animation as ways of displaying their senior work. Such advances, however, do not necessarily derive from our school's resources (although the technology teacher does amazing work with the staff to keep us up-to-date). Instead, much of the knowledge for these programs is brought to school from home. Students today have grown up in a world where technology has always been available to them, and they therefore know much more about navigating through a technological world than most teachers do. I've become a student of what they know. In fact, I've reserved a part of my professional development each year to include learning more from my students about their technological world.

Another change I've made to assist the senior-year process at the Brown is to create a 6-week unit on presentation skills. Students arrive technological savvy, but it doesn't mean they've had experience with how to present in front of others. Instead, I've come to learn that a lot of practice and rehearsal still needs to go into such presentations. During the 6-week unit, students and I look at persuasive techniques, rhetorical strategies, as well as ways to use modern technology as a means of becoming more effective presenters and speakers. Students begin to realize how one picture/semiotic can represent a thousand things to any audience. This results in carefully planned photographs and graphics to best capture their research and project experience. Students learn that a single image in a PowerPoint slide can be a great way to allow panels to discuss what they see and know—a great icebreaker and presentation opener. Those who utilize audio clips or movies as a part of their presentations recognize, as well, that careful effort is needed for adhering to time frames and purpose.

These conversations arise from a series of minilessons on public speaking. From mid-March to mid-April, students are assessed on practice presentations to get ready for the bigger one in May. The first round is a traditional how-to speech. The second round is an argument speech and the third round is an informative speech from the research paper they submit. Practice presentations are timed so students can understand how to pace themselves. For practice presentations, students help me create rubrics via the Rubistar Web site for Teachers: http://rubistar.4teachers.org/index.php and new criteria for presenting are given to them. They may have to use a prop one week. Then they move to a PowerPoint. From here, I ask for hyperlinks in their presentations. Each step of the way, students become more comfortable before an audience and receive further training on using technology within their presentations—especially with learning how to pace their efforts. We discuss what we're learning as each student presents his or her work. My classroom becomes a conference hall with a computer-ready television, projectors, and student-led forums. From 8 a.m. until 11 a.m., seniors teach each other while gaining practice through slides, DVDs, props, and the use of a computer-clicking peer—the student they choose to help them with their presentation (an issue that also has a learning curve).

With the technology changing as rapidly as it has in the lives of my students, I've learned to trade the traditional English classroom for a more progressive environment. I still facilitate literature circles and offer lessons on literary analysis. I continue to help prepare students for the SAT and ACT through minilessons on grammar and sentence structure. Yet, I find my classes becoming less book-text focused and more student-centered and multitextual with Web sites, articles, interviews, movies, YouTube clips, and podcasts. I recognize that reading, writing, and presentation skills will carry them further than any type of multiple choice test I might design around a particular textbook. My instruction has become more skill oriented. I seek to learn what they know as much as they seek what I know. I'm aware of what I want students to be able to do by the time they leave my classroom, and I've become more proficient at scaffolding the ways of getting them there.

Although overwhelming to me at times, I've grown comfortable with allowing technological digression in my classroom. More often than not, such meandering is useful to the goals I have for the class. This became especially true through my discovery of podcasts. Once students explained to me what they were, I found several essays and articles in audio-form online that were useful in helping my students research and become better writers. One senior, in particular, enjoyed a downloaded version of Emerson's essay on individuality and used it as a primary text for her senior research. Her inquiry was, "How do individuals 'really' make a difference in their world?" and a part of her research came from listening to her IPod.

As each class graduates from the Brown School, they leave the legacy of their projects and research behind. Research papers are filed, and copies of their presentations are saved on the school's server where other teachers and students can access them. In addition, several culminating projects result in school murals or created art spaces that leave their mark in time. Seniors often mentor students in the junior class on how they accomplished their senior year work, and more often than not, they hand the baton over so that their projects can be continued and further research can be added. Stories of success from the previous year become the norm for the next generation of seniors. In this age of digital literacy, research and the Brown's culminating projects continue to grow more engaging and mature. The technology available allows for fast acquisition of resource material and improves the ways students can present material in a mature, real-world way.

CONCLUSIONS

Technology is a tool that enhances my profession as a reading, writing, and thinking high school teacher. Technology is expensive, though, and it causes a strain on an already frantic week of teaching, grading, planning, and learning. When students first began using online communities to share their thinking, e-mails and discussions, it became extremely difficult to keep up with all their online postings. The majority of my time needed to be spent reading the writing prepared for their senior writing portfolios and research papers, so I found assessing our online communities to be difficult. I had to begin training students to be better critical friends with each other before I gave them a writing grade.

With this said, the culminating project and research expectation allows me a yearlong structure to accomplish goals that are important to me as a writing teacher: idea development, audience awareness, voice, purpose, sentence structure, organization, and so forth. Student writing expectations and presentations are the vehicles that help students build skills. The students who graduate from the Brown School are ready for the future of America and what that might bring.

Technological advancements, however, come faster than a school can afford. With this economic concern, I also acknowledge that not all homes of the students I teach are online and ready to grow with the nation. Some students rely heavily on computers at school—computers that are in demand by many students from several grade levels every hour of the day. All educators want the best for their students, but the best isn't always available to all students all the time. In fact, as Jonathon Kozol (2005) has shown us, the inequities within American schools are shameful, and the digital divide (U.S. Department of Commerce, 2007) needs to be further addressed. Keeping technological standards high is tricky when not all individuals have fair access to it.

Recognizing that the digital pencil (Lei, Conway & Zhao, 2008) is now ubiquitous in America's classrooms, I've become more adaptive to this technological ecosystem (Zhao, Lei, & Frank, 2007). With this noted, I am able to conclude with a few insights about being a high school English educator in an ever-changing, technological world:

- It takes a teacher to teach how technology can be used as a resource to his or her students—even in the English classroom. Computers can't do the work of teachers. Teachers need to coach students with how to best use technology as a resource.
- A good teacher teaches skills. If the skills required for readers and writers are changing, so should the practice of teachers. Literacy has become more digital so digital literacy should be addressed by English departments and faculties.
- At any given time, the work created by students and teachers can disappear into the land of faulty hard drives, lost e-mails, and sabotage.

There's nothing more frustrating than knowing that one's work and preparation can disappear without warning. Teaching students to have backup plans is important.

- Marrying the expectations of individual schools, districts, states, and nations with common technological goals is difficult work, but it is work that needs to be done. Relax and enjoy the process.
- The culminating project, research paper and Senior Boards provide an excellent foundation for preparing students for a post-graduation life, because they offer skills in research and presentation, assist the state-mandated Kentucky writing portfolio, and foster the use of technology.

Advances in technology allow for much more material to be available to teachers and students a lot faster than it used to be. The pace is rigorous, exhausting, and revolutionary. Skills necessary for success in an English classroom are changing every day, and I wonder what skills I'll set aside to make room for new technological skills yet to arrive. As technological advancements are made, expectations become greater for classrooms and schools. The Brown's unique program is one example of how technology is utilized in a modern high school English classroom as it coexists with writing expectations in the State of Kentucky. The multimedia presentations at the end of the year provide an excellent audience for showcasing new talents and gaining necessary skills.

REFERENCES

Associated Press. (2008). Technology demands ed. changes. In *Teacher Magazine*, Published and Retrieved February 10, 2008, from http://www.teachermagazine .org

Blythe, T., Allen, D., & Schieffelin-Powell, B. (2007). *Looking together at student work: A companion guide to assessing student learning* (2nd ed.). New York: Teachers College Press.

Graff, G., & Birkenstein, C. (2006). *They say, I say: The moves that matter in academic writing*. New York: Norton.

Hillocks, G. (2002). *The testing trap: How state writing assessments control learning*. New York: Teachers College Press.

Kentucky Department of Education. (2007). Writing. Retrieved June 6, 2007, from http://education.ky.gov/KDE/Instructional+Resources/High+School/ English+Language+Arts/Writing/

Kentucky Department of Education. (2006). *Kentucky writing handbook: Helping students develop as proficient writers and learners*. Kentucky Department of Education. Frankfort, KY.

Kozol, J. (2005). *The shame of the nation: The restoration of apartheid schooling in America*. New York: Three Rivers Press.

Lei, J., Conway, P. F., & Zhao, Y. (2008). *The Digital pencil; One-to-one computing for children.* New York: Erlbaum.

Paton, A. (1948). *Cry the beloved country.* New York: Collier Books, MacMillan Publishing.

Prensky, M. (2001). Digital natives, digital immigrants. *On the horizon,* NCB University Press, *9*(5). Retrieved February 6, 2008, from : http://www.marcprensky.com

Silva, P., & Mackin, R. A. (2002). *Standards of mind and heart: Creating the good high school.* New York: Teachers College Press.

U.S. Department of Commerce. (2007). *Falling through the net, defining the digital divide.* Retrieved March 3, 2008, from http://www.ntia.doc.gov/ntiahome/fttn99/contents.html

U.S. Department of Education. (1996). *Getting America's students ready for the 21st Century: Meeting the technology literacy challenge.* Washington, DC. Author.

U.S. Department of Education. (2000). *E-learning: Putting a world-class education at the fingertips of all children.* Washington, DC. Author.

U.S. Department of Education. (2004). *Toward a new golden age in American education: How the internet, the law and today's students are revolutionizing expectations.* The National Educational Technology Plan. Washington, DC. Retrieved April 2, 2008, from http://www.ed.gov/about/offices/list/os/technology/plan/2004/plan.pdf

Zhao, Y., Lei, J., & Frank, K. A. (2007). The social life of technology: An ecological analysis of technology diffusion in schools. *Pedagogies: An International Journal, 1*(2), 135–149.

CHAPTER 8

From the Front of the Classroom to the Ears of the World

Multimodal Composing in Speech Class

DAWN REED
TROY HICKS

Four weeks into class, after reading about "You" as the person of the year from *Time* magazine (Grossman, 2006), and discussing how YouTube was changing the way people share their lives online, my students were not buying it. In Time, Grossman asked, "who actually sits down after a long day at work and says, 'I'm not going to watch "Lost" tonight. I'm going to turn on my computer and make a movie starring my pet iguana?'" (p. 40)

In reply, one student quipped, "Why would anyone want to do this? Why would you create a video for YouTube when "Lost" is on TV?" Another student wondered aloud: "This is unnecessary, why would we podcast, when we should be presenting in front of class? I need practice talking in front of people because I get nervous."

Clearly, this was not going as I had expected. Yet, 3 weeks later, when the first student-produced podcast went public, their sentiments began to change:

"Mrs. Reed, you will never believe who responded to my podcast."

"I understand my speech differently now that people are commenting on the blog," he sighed. "I suppose that everyone in class heard it one way, but now I see how it could be understood in a different way."

In the spring of 2007, we—Dawn, a high school English teacher, and Troy, a teacher educator—explored how students might use blogging and podcasting to create, revise, share, and respond to speeches. We worked to discover how the writing and speaking process as well as evaluation of students' work would change when students composed multimodal texts. Because podcasting extends their audience and allows students to move their speech beyond the initial and temporal experience of delivering a talk only once within the classroom, we felt that this project would provide students an opportunity to learn technology skills for authentic literacy. What we discovered along the way showed us that students valued this experience and that podcasting provides opportunities to rethink the writing and speaking process as a unique situation for multimodal composing.

CONTEXT FOR THE PODCASTING PROJECT

In the chapter that follows, Dawn, speaking in the first person singular, describes her experience in using podcasting in her speech class. At the end of the chapter, both of us discuss the implications of our project.

Charlotte High School, located in the middle of Michigan in the rural/suburban city of Charlotte, serves about 1,000 students in grades 9 through 12 (Great Schools, 2008). Classes are set up on a 4 × 4 block schedule with 18-week fall and spring semester courses, each with two 9-week marking periods. Speech is a 9-week English elective offered in grades 9 through 12 to students who have completed the prerequisite English Nine. In 2007, students could take Speech to fulfill a half credit elective of English needed for graduation. In early class discussions, several students indicated that they had enrolled in the course to fulfill the requirement, although many also took the class with the desire to become better speakers. My Speech class included 18 students, 8 men and 10 women. The majority of the students were high school juniors or seniors, but the class also included one freshman, one sophomore, and one foreign exchange student from Germany. While Speech class has been in the Charlotte High School curriculum for years, this was my first year teaching a speech class.

In the course, students practice oral communication to prepare for a future career or to feel more at ease with public speaking. Goals include communicating accurately for meaning, analyzing skills used in communicating, and using the English language effectively. In addition to these goals, I wanted students to communicate in front of our class audience, in small groups, and, through multimedia, to a larger audience. Through the use of multimedia, students would analyze the role of audience and purposeful language use for speakers that they listened to and for their own podcast speech, since anyone could access their speech.

STATE REQUIREMENTS, MULTIMODAL RELEVANCY, AND A NATIONAL INVITATION

During the time I was preparing to teach this course, the Michigan Department of Education (2006c) released new requirements for high school students, including the requirement that students engage in a meaningful online experience at some point in their high school career. I was curious about the manner in which public speaking is changing through the use of technology, and now the state content and technology standards required students to create multimedia compositions such as digital stories, to research and evaluate nonprint media, and to develop other online writing (Michigan Department of Education, 2006a, 2006b). Like many other states, Michigan's standards were produced and disseminated to schools, yet rarely assessed formally. Moreover, multimedia composing remains a new and often ignored component of a school curriculum that must bow to the demands of standardized testing.

With this context, and given my interest in multimedia composition, I wanted to integrate my own interests and the state high school content expectations into this Speech class. Therefore, in addition to traditional experiences of speaking in front of the class, the students would explore communication in a digital world, specifically though podcasting. Approaching Speech class in this manner, Troy and I believed, would provide opportunities for my students to have a larger audience and extend their voices beyond the one time speech at the podium, essentially eliminating the constraints of time, place, and the walls of the classroom. Podcasting would allow them to focus on their voices in the delivery of a speech, as well as revise it to their satisfaction. Furthermore, since students often limit their comments to one another's work with simple replies such as "good speech," and others—teachers, parents, community members, and students from other classes or schools—could not be a part of our speech class, podcasting would allow for feedback from those who may offer a different perception of the ideas presented. Finally, as noted above, the digital literacies required to create and publish a podcast aligned with our vision of an online experience.

For this speech podcasting project we followed the "This I Believe" format based on National Public Radio's (NPR, 2007a) series of the same name because it offered a rich model for public speaking, including diverse options of speakers and speech topics (NPR, 2007b). We listened to NPR's "This I Believe" podcasts, and I invited students to craft their own essays about their beliefs. By doing this, my students engaged in an assignment with a national invitation so that they could connect their ideas to those of other famous people—such as Tony Hawk (2007), Bill Gates, and Colin Powell—as well as everyday citizens. Throughout the project, students knew that they would have the option of posting their final version of their "This I Believe" essays on the class blog. (Visit http://reedd504.edublogs.org/ to read the blog posts and listen to the podcasts.)

The personal nature of the essay—along with creating it in a manner that would eventually be spoken, not just written—influenced the composing process for several students. They began to make sure their speech sounded right based on their reading and revisions, and they began to see themselves as having a speaking personality. For instance, one student wrote her piece with fragments and slang terms because she wanted to emphasize these points in her essay, a rhetorical move that she likely would not have made if turning in a traditional paper or, we contend, giving a speech for the class. By exploring their beliefs, writing, listening, revising, offering feedback, rerecording, and posting their work online, students engaged in a multimodal composing process that influenced the entire process, from initial writing, to response, revision, and recording; to the final posting and feedback. We explore these processes in the sections below, while Figure 8.1 summarizes key moments from each part of the process.

Figure 8.1. Key Moments in the Podcast Composing Process

Initial Writing, Recording, and Revising	Peer Response and Collaboration	Posting and Feedback
• Spending more time on drafting initial speech	• Getting support for revision from writing group	• Overcoming interface and file saving problems with the blog
• Hearing one's voice through digital recording; identifying and fixing mistakes	• Taking speeches more seriously because of the nature of the task	• Imagining their new roles as content producers
• Improving confidence because of ability to pause and rerecord	• Modeling of editing process in Audacity (creation of podcast introduction)	• Understanding their peers in different ways based on their statements of personal belief
• Monitoring tone of voice in speech	• Overcoming recording and installation problems with Audacity	• Receiving feedback from their school, community, and others
• Working through entire speech without audience distractions	• Expressing interest in working collaboratively	• Reading comments on podcast selectively and choosing whether or not to respond
	• Understanding citation and copyright	

INITIAL WRITING, RECORDING, AND REVISING

People don't know what you look like when you podcast, so you could be anybody. And you could be yourself, and not have to be scared to speak out.
—Sally, a student in the podcasting project

A "This I Believe" speech was different from the traditional informative speech found in speech class, because we would record the speeches and podcast them, thus requiring an extensive amount of writing. Unlike the outline plans we studied at the beginning of the course, students were expected to fully draft and revise their "This I Believe" speeches. While I participated in the composing process with my students and received feedback from my students and my peers I discovered that just as the "This I Believe" curriculum suggests, this is a hard paper to write. Coming up with a topic was the first challenge. One student, Danielle, reflected on this part of the composing processes:

> When we started writing our papers, about what we believed, I had no idea what I was passionate enough, to write about. After listening to a lot of different "This I Believe" speeches on NPR, I realized that it didn't have to be something that would change the world. It could be something simple, but something that anyone would be interested in reading.

Danielle's reflection suggests a learning opportunity in which writing instruction engaged not only "higher-order thinking skills for *all* students but skills that provide students opportunities to use their writing in personally and politically empowering ways" (Dornan, Rosen, & Wilson, 2003, p. 14).

Along with the fact that the "This I Believe" format inspired them to write about statements of personal conviction (and that may have led to some increase in the amount of time they were willing to spend drafting their speech), we contend that students knew that a podcast was a fundamentally different speech act than standing in front of the class. As Jackie explained:

> At first, I didn't really understand speech and technology together because Ms. Reed kept trying to explain it to me and I still wasn't really getting it. But, after doing the "This I Believe" speeches, um, I really did like it because it helped me dig deep and actually look at what I actually believed in and helped me get it down and let myself share it with everyone else.

Thus as students engaged in initial writing and recording, they found a number of elements in the composing process that helped them refine their work along the way, honed on the ability to record their voice, play it back, and re-record if necessary.

For instance, having discussed the concept of *voice* while analyzing sample speeches from the "This I Believe" Web site, students were constantly monitoring their own tone and word choice; the role of emotion and intonation became central to the conversation about composition and delivery. Although students were disappointed that they would only hear the speaker of these essays and not see them, students began to respond with deeper appreciation about the role of voice in speaking. One student, Justin, put it this way:

> I learned how to portray a speech personality. What I mean by a speech or speaking personality is what a person can judge about you based on how you sound, my personality has to be best portrayed through sound because podcasting doesn't include video. It's hard to display yourself in your voice because you're not used to it. It's also important, because like I said earlier, you can't have any visual gestures.

When Justin began the course, his voice was fair in speechmaking, yet just like the majority of students in the class by their own admission, he had not fully embraced the role of voice in public speaking. Throughout the class and in all their non-podcast speeches, several students spoke in a monotone and paid little attention to word choice. Here Justin's response shows how he, like others, learned about inflection and tone by listening again and again to his own recording.

Students also reported that they could see the amplitude of their voice reflected in the Audacity sound editor, so they could know when they were modulating their voice and tone, or not. In an interview, one student described how Audacity literally helped her *see* the way her voice popped with Ps and Bs, based on the peaks and valleys in the audio track. By hearing their own voices through digital recording, they were able to identify and fix mistakes in pronunciation or inflection.

This strikes us as significant for another reason. Because they were able to rerecord and work without the distraction of a physically present audience, many students reported that they felt more confident. Danielle, described her new confidence in this manner:

> I think for me, too, it was a confidence booster, 'cause when I listen to myself speak I'm like, "Oh, I'm really not that bad at speaking in front of people or, like, making a speech." And, when I just go up in front of the class and make one right away, then I'm like "Oh, that probably sounded really bad."

She went on to say:

> It was kind of easier to podcast because I knew if I messed up my recording, like something that I said, I could go back and fix it rather than stand up in front of the class and look dumb because I just messed up everything I was trying to say.

The ability to hear one's self in private was certainly part of students' feeling of comfort. Furthermore, through our observations and students' reports in their writing and interviews, the time and effort spent writing their speech for the "This I Believe" podcast was substantially more than what they did for any other speech. For all students, the time they reported spending on drafting their initial speeches was at least as much as other speeches; for most, they spent much more time. One student described the hours and days that she spent preparing, recording, and rerecording. The writing process guided their work from initial drafting through final revisions and contributed to the success of the project. In addition, the students probably sensed my excitement about the project, and that could have influenced their motivation. Yet, we also believe that students were willing to invest more personally in this work due to the nature of the topic and the fact that it would be posted online as a podcast.

In another example, Jonathan, a student who seemed less engaged or interested in the project, clearly tackled major issues of revision, as he noted in his reflection on the project:

> The most important thing I learned was how to put my true thoughts and point of views into writing and process complete thoughts. This I believe essays helped with shaping and creating my speech in there speeches I noticed the emotion and realism in there [sic] voice which showed that they had a genuine belief in what they were saying. After listening to there speech I decided to go out on a limb and try to match there creativeness. Once I had all my thought down on paper It took so long before I had changed everything to the way I seen fit. Hearing my voice in Audacity was a wake up call I found myself rewording many parts of my essay because I didn't feel it sounded right coming out of my mouth.

Jonathan taps into major aspects of this experience. When listening to other "This I Believe" podcasts, he could hear the speaker offering emotion and realism, which is important to a speaking voice. He also notes that the topic had to be something he felt strongly about and believes in. Moreover, Jonathan was following speech models or mentor texts and challenged himself to be creative. Revision seems to have found a new meaning for Jonathan in this process. He changed the material and then found, when he thought the work was ready, that more revision was needed.

While Jonathan shows ideal understanding of the goals of the assignment, particularly through his awareness of the revision experience, we also found the role of audience influencing students' work. This first came to our attention when considering citations. Unlike research papers from other courses, students were able to find real purpose in using citations. Students were clearly concerned about getting citations right; because they were publishing for an audience beyond the classroom, they knew the importance of correct citations. Moreover, discussions around copyright, fair use, and Creative Commons influenced their perceptions about what is, and what is not, appropriate to share on the Internet. For instance, students created end credits for all the podcasts. While they cited National Public Radio and the Podsafe Music Network, they also added citations of other sources as applicable to their "This I Believe" essays, even though they were not required to include additional sources.

PEER RESPONSE AND COLLABORATION

Teachers and researchers in composition have touted the benefits of classroom community for decades. Classroom community was essential for this project. In order to teach students how to respond to one another, I first established a community in my classroom with introductory activities. Students collaborated on speeches from the beginning of the course. In addition, I modeled and discussed how to respond to speeches; early on, students responded to one another's speeches via letter and through group debriefing sessions about each student's speech. Second, when writing their "This I Believe" informative speeches, students formed writing groups to work with one another on their writing (eventually, they would also act as the introductory and closing narrators in their partners' podcasts). At times, in speech classes the rough draft of a student's speech is also its world premiere. With this project there was time for response and revision, time to write and rewrite, time to review content and delivery.

Moreover, the project challenged students to be metacognitive about their work. As Jackie explained, she was able to hear herself say *like*, and listening to herself made it easier to find and fix those kinds of mistakes. Because listening forces you to *hear* (and Audacity helps you *see* in sound and images of the sound) your mistakes, this multimodal composing process differed from peer response, where students reported that sometimes they just tried to be nice rather than give substantive feedback. Self-evaluation, in this case, came through one's headsets, in one's own voice, and made the urge to revise more real.

Additionally, Clara, a student who feared the project because she was concerned she wouldn't be able to work with the technology, came up with the idea that the class should create an introductory clip to our podcasts that included each one of our beliefs, similar to the introduction from NPR. These clips overlay a number of speakers, each stating, "I believe in . . ." creating a multilayered soundscape, accompanied by piano, which introduces the program. To begin with, students recorded a short line stating their belief for this collaborative introduction. One student recorded her line and then, after revising her piece, returned with what she deemed a better line. Other students helped one another compose and revise their belief lines. When all of the lines were recorded, I then overlapped them. Next I took the draft of this text to class and asked students for ideas on revision based on how students wanted the piece to sound. As a class we had conversations about why we make specific choices in writing, why a piece of audio should sound a certain way, what the length of the clip should be, where the sound level may need tweaking, and how an audience might perceive the clip. When the clip was finally together, I played it again and the class agreed that they liked the result. While I took the lead on that part of the project, like a good minilesson in writing, the steps that the class took together modeled revision strategies for the audio editing each student would be doing in their individual clips. Consequently, as collaborators and a community of writers, the entire podcasting experience was propelled forward, allowing students to do something with their writing as they excitedly posted podcasts and anticipated hearing each other's work.

POSTING AND FEEDBACK

Time was not on our side when students posted final podcasts and began generating responses for one another. This was only a 9-week course, and students had completed a variety of nonpodcast speeches in addition to this podcast. Still, there were many elements of this final stage of the process that yielded positive comments from the students. They felt that they were able to overcome interface problems on the blog and problems with saving podcast files. They began to imagine themselves as content producers and by hearing the podcasts of their peers, understood these classmates in different ways as well. Finally, they saw how others in their school, community, and the broader audiences on the Internet responded to their work and how they could choose (or choose not) to respond to those comments. Students received comments from a wide audience, including staff members and students from our high school in Charlotte, students from the Youth Voices Project (2007) in New

York City and Utah, Michigan State University faculty and students, Red Cedar Writing Project Teacher Consultants and their classes, as well as our family members and friends. The students had also decided that they should put fliers in the hallways advertising the blog, with the URL to the site printed like a phone number on an ad, ready to be ripped off. Rick noted in a written reflection on the project that "within the first day we had many people pulling off the little slips of paper hanging from the flyers containing the address of our site."

Students were excited about having this larger audience. And while there are not many posted comments from students at the school, I anecdotally knew that these students too were reading the blog. One day, for instance, I overheard a student ask, "What's that [flier] about? I am not in Speech class." Another student responded, "Oh yeah, they have a Web site, you can hear their speeches." Yet another time I heard one of my students say to a friend, "That's for my Speech class. We're online, you should check it out."

These positive implications for students, and their willingness to share information about their Speech class, come in the context of a high school where, like other high schools, it is not always considered cool for students to promote class work in this way. Over spring break, students were voluntarily writing comments on the blog, representing what Richardson (2006) suggests as a big shift in education where there are "many, many teachers, and 24/7 learning" as students "no longer just consume the content" but are able to connect to others and to more content through the use of technology (p. 128).

Despite the many technical problems we experienced setting up my first, then second blog, getting Audacity installed and operating on the school computers, and finding a space to save the podcasts online, students were able to imagine their new roles as content producers. This was an important change in attitude, as Danielle notes:

> I never thought that it would be me doing it [podcasting]. Like, I have always gone online and listened to other people, but I'm like, "I would never do that. I would never put myself online and, like, let other people hear me." But, it really wasn't that big of a deal and it was kind of fun to be able to do that.

Perhaps because it was the end of the marking period and the students had already done a lot of work on the project, and because getting feedback from a virtual, anonymous audience was a new experience, some students indicated in their interview that they would read comments on their podcast selectively and choose whether to respond or not based on how interesting the comment was or on their knowledge of the comment's author. As we invite students to become global citizens, we think that teaching them how to respond in a timely manner must be a component of any read/write Web project and will be more aware of that in our own teaching. Yet, despite our difficulties with this stage of the process, we believe that the comment-and-response had some value to the students. Clara describes her new confidence in her own work, and her pride in her comment:

> My finished product was, to my surprise, pretty good. I was actually amazed at the finished product. I really didn't like the thing at first, but now I feel more confident about it. I wouldn't mind doing it again. I think I might try and visit the blog and check my comments and everything, its pretty interesting.

IMPLICATIONS FOR INSTRUCTION, CURRICULUM, AND ASSESSMENT

Any implications that we draw from our experience of this course need to be seen in relation to the context of Dawn's school. In particular, we need to consider several aspects of this context: the school's curriculum, available instructional support, and the school's technology infrastructure.

School Context

We begin with the relationship of Dawn's class to her school's curriculum. Dawn's class was an elective. For this reason, she was not directly encumbered by the content expectations faced in other courses. The importance of this fact cannot be underestimated in the overall scheme of how and why she was able to invest so much time in a technology-rich project. To fit the technology project into the course, other assignments were shortened. Looking ahead, in future courses Dawn's students may give one fewer speech in front of their peers. Based on our observations, student comments about their learning, and assessment of their work, we feel these adjustments were more than worth it. Not only did students continue to be involved in the blog immediately following the course; more than a year later Dawn still received e-mails from students about the blog. Further, the interest in the course has increased, as has enrollment.

A second crucial element of Dawn's school context is that she had available considerable instructional support. Dawn, a strong teacher to begin with, could draw on the support of a National Writing Project site. In addition, she could rely on the support of Troy, the professional development coordinator of Red Cedar Writing Project. We realize that not all teachers have access to NWP professional development or to the direct support of a classroom technology coach.

A third element is the school's technology infrastructure, a challenge faced by all teachers who bring technology into their curriculum. Among the problems that we worked through, typically by Dawn e-mailing Troy, with many options discussed and debated, included:

- Setting up a blog that was not filtered by the schools system with easy podcast integration (we eventually chose Edublogs.org);
- Arranging permission and assistance from the school's IT department to download and install Audacity in a timely manner and then get it working with the headsets and LAME MP3 encoder;
- Location to upload and store the podcasts, originally meant to be saved on the school server, then in a separate online space, neither of which were available. Finally, they were able to be saved in Edublogs;
- Obtaining access to the computer lab with Audacity installed on a consistent basis.

We mention these components of our project because they directly affected the multimodal composing process that students engaged in. We agree with DeVoss, Cushman, & Grabill (2005), in that "although these structural aspects of teaching new media might easily be dismissed as mere inconvenience when they break down or rupture entirely, they are, in fact, deeply embedded in the acts of digital-media composing" (p. 16). In order to have our students compose in this manner, we have realized that teachers need to take an advocacy role in promoting technology as a part of their curriculum and their own professional development in order to obtain access to certain technologies and Web sites in what has often become a locked down, filtered out school environment.

Standards and Assessment

As we set this stage for a discussion on assessment, it becomes increasingly clear that the old adage, "what gets measured, gets treasured," will become increasingly complicated in coming years. For us in Michigan, the misalignment of the state's new high school content expectations and the Michigan Merit Exam are acute. Praised widely as a new model for education around the country (Steptoe, 2006), our new high school graduation requirements for all students adhere to a college-prep type of curriculum and require students to take the ACT as a part of the merit exam. On the one hand, these new standards are encouraging teachers to use technology. All students are required to have an online experience (which Dawn's use of blogging and podcasting fulfills without their having to take an online course, a debate to be saved for another time), and the new content expectations mention *multi*, *electronic*, or *digital* 22 times in 11 pages.

On the other hand, much of what we see in the enactment of this curriculum (as a result of the tests) does not engender the kind of changed mindset that a new literacies perspective requires: one that is characterized by openness, collaboration, collective intelligence, distributed authority, and social relations (Lankshear & Knobel, 2006). In contrast to an industrial view of education in which objectives can be clearly met through a one time assessment of writing that requires both the timed writing of a persuasive essay and multiple-choice sections on grammar, a view that embraces multimodal composing is recursive, networked, and collaborative. In short, the test still tests reading, 'riting, and 'rithmetic (as well as science, math, and social studies). In no way does it reflect the types of multimodal composing processes that the Michigan content standards suggest or that, in our experience, podcasting requires.

This is not to say that Dawn's course as a whole, or this project in particular, did not meet the statewide standards. The course and project met at least these writing and technology standards:

- Creating and sustaining an argument
- Adding details and examples
- Revising one's own and others' writing
- Having critical media awareness
- Having the ability to analyze electronic sources (with the corollary of remixing and producing new digital media in ethical and responsible ways)

The problem is that this project occurred in isolation, in a high school that is hamstrung by concerns about Adequate Yearly Progress, and in a state that struggles to produce enough jobs for its college graduates.

Engaging Digital Literacies

Acknowledging and drawing from what students know and are familiar with, teachers also can engage the cultural resources of students. Anne Haas Dyson (2003) suggests tapping into student's cultural landscapes—their cultural and environmental background, as well as texts from their everyday lives—to make formal education accessible for various students. This way, students may "more deliberately maneuver on an expanding landscape" as they are also engaging in "recontextualizing—borrowing and revoicing—this material in school contexts" to "expand their knowledge about symbolic systems, social practices, and the ideologically complex world" (Dyson, 2003, p. 15). Dyson asserts that drawing on students' home literacies will help them engage with school literacies. While Dyson's work does not directly comment on shifts in learning resulting from digital literacies, the general concept of literacy development through engagement with home and school literacies aligns with Prensky's (2001) concept of today's children being digital natives and, by extension, that we as teachers should engage in these literacies with them at school.

During her group interview, when asked what they would take away as students in this project, Sally immediately replied, "That anybody can do it." In reflecting on the project, Danielle, a senior, noted:

> I think that the creation of our Web site, with all of our speeches on it, is a very cool thing. I have never done anything even close to this in any other class. I hope that our Web site can still be used over the next year, not just by us, but people all over America. I believe that other classes should start incorporating technology into their curriculum, because in today's world, everything is developed around technology and computers. The whole experience of blogging and podcasting was different, but fun thing to do. I hope that a lot of other students will get to experience this in the future.

Rick, another senior, expressed a similar view, stating "in no other classes have I ever used technology in this way. This project taught me a lot, and was fun and exciting at the same time, something that seems to occur less often in today's schools." Like Danielle, Rick also expressed the desire to influence education, when he wrote, "this entire project has really changed the way I view technology in today's world. This has really woken me up to the fact that technology is affecting the way we live our lives."

Gauging Audience Reactions

As Dawn gauged from student response in class, comments on the blog, and talk around the school, people were excited about the great work students were involved in through the podcasting project. Students were interested in comments they received about their speeches. Erica wrote that "I'm really happy with how it turned out, I'm actually excited to see the comments I might receive." Sally sent Dawn an e-mail in which she said, "IM so excited i didnt [*sic*] think people would actually read my speech." Unlike a speech that evaporated once delivered from the podium, the podcasts kept garnering comments days and weeks after their original posting.

Our audience members even seemed excited about the project. A colleague at the school, Christine Halsey, told Dawn that she had chills just listening to the collaboratively authored introduction (personal communication, April 2007). A National Writing Project colleague, Leah Zuidema, from Iowa wrote Dawn to say "Your students' voices come through so strong—it's like they compel a response" (personal communication, April 12, 2007). Our student tech aide, Donovan Latimore, a high school senior who helped install Audacity on school computers for us, sent Dawn an e-mail stating, "I'd love to see this grow, and after hearing some, I think that you have struck gold on making assignments far more exciting to complete." One parent comment offered valuable insight to the importance of the project, when a kid's dad wrote:

> These are all powerful essays. I think it's especially wonderful for the kids to be able to podcast them as well. It's likely going to be a major communications tool for their generation. But tools are worthless without careful thought, self-examination, and passion. I found elements of each of these in all of the essays. Very impressive, and congratulations to all of you. Best of luck as you pursue your dreams.

Reflecting on the Project

In class, when we began our discussion about speech in a technological world, James, a fan of the TV show "Lost," seemed nearly offended that *Time* magazine would praise someone for creating a multimedia composition instead of watching "Lost." In this light, his final reflection on the podcasting project was insightful. He wrote:

> Doing this pod casting project had changed my outlook on public speaking. I used to think that public speaking was really just for the public around me. But this pod casting project has shown me that when your audience it [sic] limited that you will need to get a bigger one. The TV and radio are really good ways of telling your speech to the masses. But what better than to give your speech on the World Wide Web.

For us as educators, then, the largest implication of this entire project is the value that students found in producing content for a larger and authentic audience. In so doing, they joined a conversation as members of a global society, moving their voices from the front of the classroom to the ears of the world.

REFERENCES

DeVoss, D. N., Cushman, E., & Grabill, J. T. (2005). Infrastructure and composing: The *when* of new-media writing. *College Composition and Communication*, *57*(1), 14–44.

Dornan, R. W., Rosen, L. M., & Wilson, M. (2003). *Within and beyond the writing process in the secondary English classroom.* New York: Pearson Education Group.

Dyson, A. H. (2003). *The brothers and sisters learn to write.* New York: Teachers College Press.

Great Schools. (2008). *Charlotte Senior High School.* Retrieved August, 2008, from http://www.greatschools.net/modperl/browse_school/mi/783)

Grossman, L. (2006, December 25). Person of the year. *Time,* pp. 40–41.

Hawk, Tony. (2007). Do what you love. *National Public Radio This I Believe.* Retrieved April 23, 2007, from http://www.npr.org/templates/story/story.php?storyId=5568583>

Lankshear, C., & Knobel, M. (2006). *New literacies: Everyday practices and classroom learning* (2nd ed.). Maidenhead; NY: Open University Press.

Michigan Department of Education. (2006a). *Grade level content expectations: Technology.* Retrieved September 10, 2006, from http://www.michigan.gov/mde/0,1607,7-140-28753_33232_37328—,00.html

Michigan Department of Education. (2006b). *Michigan Merit Curriculum—English Language Arts.* Retrieved June 21, 2006, from http://www.michigan.gov/mde/0,1607,7-140-38924_41644_42674—,00.html

Michigan Department of Education. (2006c). *Michigan Merit Curriculum—Online Learning.* Retrieved June 21, 2006, from http://www.michigan.gov/mde/0,1607,7-140-38924_41644_42825—,00.html

National Public Radio. (2007a). *This I Believe.* Retrieved April 3, 2007, from http://www.npr.org/templates/story/story.php?storyId=4538138

National Public Radio.(2007b). *This I Believe* Curriculum. Retrieved April 21, 2007, from http://thisibelieve.org/educationoutreach.html

Prensky, M. (2001, October 5). *Digital natives, digital immigrants.* http://www.marcprensky.com/writing/Prensky%20-%20Digital%20Natives,%20Digital%20Immigrants%20-%20Part1.pdf

Richardson, W. (2006). *Blogs, Wikis, Podcasts, and Other Powerful Web Tools for Classrooms.* Thousand Oaks, CA: Corwin.

Steptoe, S. (2006). *Building a new student in Michigan.* Retrieved June 21, 2007, from http://www.time.com/time/nation/article/0,8599,1568853,00.html

Youth Voices From Coast to Coast: NYC and Utah, Blogging and Podcasting from New York City and Utah Writing Project Classroom. Retrieved April 21, 2007, from http://blogs.writingproject.org/blogwrite265

Bridging to the College Years

The three chapters in this part are primarily based in college classrooms. In Chapter 9, Mya Poe and Julianne Radkowski Opperman shift to a writing-in-the-disciplines focus, showing how they teach students to use technology for scientific inquiry and writing, drawing on both graphic and alphabetic modes. Describing a college course in Quantitative Physics and a ninth grade Foundations of Science course, they show how technology can be applied for similar purposes at both educational levels.

Peter Kittle, in Chapter 10, describes a college course he teaches for prospective K–12 language arts teachers in which he asks students to reflect on their own learning through multimodal documents that combine aspects of story telling and analysis. And in Chapter 11, Alanna Frost, Julie A. Myatt, and Stephen Smith describe their experiences as they taught multimodal composing for the first time in their college writing courses. They reflect on their own changing understanding of what these texts entail and how the texts can best be evaluated.

CHAPTER 9

Scientific Writing and Technological Change

Teaching the New Story of Scientific Inquiry

MYA POE
JULIANNE RADKOWSKI OPPERMAN

The professional writing of science is a dynamic process that changes quickly with technological change (Gross, Harmon, & Reidy, 2002). In the last 30 years, technological innovations, such as new capabilities in image capture and processing, new tools for large data set analysis, and online, interactive applications for delivering information, have changed how contemporary science and thus scientific communication is created and delivered (Bazerman, 1988; Berkenkotter, 2007; Gross, 1990).

With the transcription of scientific discoveries into research articles and other texts that are shared by the research community, scientific advances build upon or diverge from the work of previous scientists when such texts (and thus discoveries) are taken up and cited (repeated as the standard "lore" of the discipline) (Latour & Woolgar, 1979; Sandoval, 2005). Technological innovations, consequently, have not just shaped how scientific discoveries are made (such as genome sequencing) but also how scientific discoveries are communicated (e-mail and personal multimedia devices).

From our perspective, there are three notable ways that scientific communication has changed with technological advances:

- *The development of faster, more accurate automatic laboratory equipment.* Observing, measuring, collecting, and analyzing raw data are facilitated by computer-aided operation of more advanced equipment that immediately process the raw information and produce graphically enhanced compilations of the data.
- *Vast scientific publication databases.* Prior to the 1980s, a research project's literature search would require access to a science library with printed journals and books; now extensive quantities of scientific publications are available online. Science Citation Index (SCI) alone includes more than 6,000 journals (Garfield, 1996).
- *Digital peer review and electronic submission of research.* Through electronic channels, results of research can be shared with individuals almost instantly. Organizations such as the National Institutes of Health now have completely electronic submissions and reviews of grant proposals, and journal editors can now submit manuscripts easily to reviewers almost anywhere in the world.

Given these new challenges brought on by technological advancement, we find that teaching scientific communication today means attending to the visual, mathematical, written, and even oral components of scientific communication in ways that allow students to critically assimilate these modalities into their own expression of scientific thought (Kress & van Leeuwen, 2001). The National Science Foundation (NSF), the National Academy of Science, and other organizations have long recognized the importance of communication education in the sciences and have encouraged changes in the way that student scientists are educated. With the emphasis on standards-based education in the United States, scientific societies have also articulated goals for the learning of scientific communication. For example, the American Association for the Advancement of Science (AAAS) Benchmarks for Science Literacy (1993) prescribe that students be able to "choose appropriate communication methods for critically analyzing data" (pp. 12D, 12E).

Our teaching experiences with technology have also reinforced our belief that students must learn scientific communication in the context of scientific inquiry and that scientific communication must be taught as an interactive, process-oriented approach with opportunities for revision and peer review (Bazerman & Russell, 1985). Only through immersion in the practice of science do students learn the new tools of scientific research in producing scientific genres.

In this chapter, we explain several major ways that scientific writing has changed given technological advances. We then explain how we have attempted to address these changes in our teaching of scientific writing, for Julianne at the high school level (Greely High School, Maine) and for Mya at the college level (Massachusetts Institute of Technology, Massachusetts). At each site, we incorporate technology into our teaching as we lead students through the scientific research process. In this chapter, we focus on four areas that we have specifically integrated technology into our teaching—proposal writing, literature reviews, *storying* research findings, and peer review.

CONTEXTS

Greely High School, Cumberland, Maine

Greely High School, Cumberland, Maine, is a 4-year secondary school located in a suburb of Portland, Maine. The student population includes approximately 700 college preparatory students in grades 9 through 12. All students are enrolled in a Foundations of Science course in ninth grade that includes basic physics, chemistry, and environmental topics. Two more years of science are required (GHS Course Guide, 2007). Students of all abilities are encouraged to explore science through inquiry. To this end, all ninth grade students participate in the Greeley High School Science Fair as a common assessment. The Science Fair is an academic competition in which "students methodically plan, conduct, analyze data from, and communicate results of in-depth scientific investigations, including experiments guided by a testable hypothesis" (Maine Department of Education Regulation, 2007, p. 7).

At GHS the effort to teach writing in the secondary science classroom arose from a need to increase the depth of understanding students obtain in the high school laboratory. School district data indicated GHS students were less proficient in writing and science than peer populations (Galin, personal e-mail, March 2008). After the New England Association of Schools and Colleges Accreditation (2006) process noted this problem, the GHS mission statement was revised: "Students at GHS will: think critically, write effectively, deliver effective oral presentations" (GHS Mission Statement, 2007). In addition to revising its mission, the GHS school administration adopted a multi-disciplinary approach to the teaching of writing. Since 2006 the science department has evaluated student writing in science by focusing on writing related to laboratory work, in particular the Science Fair.

Massachusetts Institute of Technology, Cambridge, Massachusetts

The Massachusetts Institute of Technology (MIT) is a 4-year, doctoral granting university in Cambridge, Massachusetts. The student population includes approximately 4,000 undergraduate students and approximately 6,000 graduate students. All undergraduate students are required to take a core set of six classes in math, biology, chemistry, and physics as well as laboratory-based classes in which students have "a substantial role in planning the design of the experiment, selecting the measurement technique, and determining the procedure to be used for validation of the data" (MIT Course Catalogue, 2007). Undergraduates are required to take four "communication intensive" (CI) courses—courses that integrate "substantial instruction and practice in writing and speaking"—during their 4 years at the Institute (About the Requirement, n.d.). Quantitative Physiology, the course profiled in this chapter, is one of these CI courses in the Department of Electrical and Computer Engineering. In Quantitative Physiology, students learn "principles of mass transport and electrical signal generation for biological membranes, cells, and tissues" (MIT Subject Listing and Schedule, Fall 2007). Writing is associated with two projects: an experimental project in a wet lab and a theoretical study using computer simulation. Students work in pairs to complete these projects.

Although MIT has a long tradition of teaching technical and scientific writing, the current Communication Requirement was the result of alumni feedback (Russell, 2002). While alumni felt that they had received an outstanding technical education, they needed more training in writing and speaking to succeed in their professional careers. In response, in 1997 MIT initiated multiyear curricular pilots involving communication education (About the Requirement, n.d.). These pilot programs became the basis for the communication intensive curriculum in effect since 2000 at MIT.

PROPOSAL DESIGN: USING WORDS AND GRAPHICS TO SHAPE THE STUDY

Professional scientists recognize the importance of providing a clear focus and rationale for any proposed research (Myers, 1985). At both the high school level and college level, solid scientific proposals provide a rationale for the student's research question as well as a proposed methodology gleaned from the literature. Requiring students to develop well-defined research projects is not new to the teaching of scientific communication, but new technologies now allow us to give students more rapid, asynchronous feedback so we can track and archive student progress throughout their research.

Greely High School

With guidance from teachers and mentors GHS science students choose their science fair projects based on their individual familiarity or interest in a particular topic. Students determine what measurements or observations they are going to make in their research.

Traditionally, students have worked alone or in personal conference with their teacher to talk through their ideas for the project. While the teacher can provide more expertise individually, this method of developing ideas does not foster the collaborative nature of science practice, and it does not recognize the potential for novel input from student peers. Technology provides a way to foster the scientific thought that the science fair seeks to promote.

As students design their project, they present their proposals to the entire class using PowerPoint visuals. The GHS process now mimics the informal review process within a research group that often precedes submitting a formal grant proposal. Students unfold their research plan one piece at a time.

When students present their initial goal, the following class discussion usually encourages them to produce a clearer statement of the goal of the study. As each student presents, the other students gain expertise in evaluating project goals and hypotheses. Feedback to the student researcher is provided orally and in writing, so students can use that feedback to improve their work.

Figure 9.1 shows the preliminary proposal presented by Becca, one of 22 students in a ninth-grade science class. The student used the feedback session to refine the study on the degradation of milk.

After students have defined the goal of their research they determine how best to record the data so it can be analyzed. With a succinct hypothesis, students identify variables, establish controls, and determine sample size. Identifying scientific parameters is one of the most important aspects of the project. They present this information to the class in a data chart using MS PowerPoint (see Table 9.1 for Becca's data chart).

Class discussion helps students determine if their experimental design will produce data that are scientifically coherent. Sharing multiple examples of the scientific parameters also clarifies the character of these parameters for all students.

Along with their data chart, students also produce a schematic diagram of their experimental procedure (see Figure 9.2). A schematic of the procedure on one PPT slide provides an outline of the procedure and can be used to augment the final paper and presentation.

These opportunities for high school students to collaborate at the proposal stage establish what high quality data collection looks like and what statistical analysis will be required. Multiple opportunities to share their work with others and receive comments, also, improve student understanding of the scientific process as well as the writing process (Bransford, Brown, & Cocking, 2000). Each student researcher can pinpoint the critical elements of his or her experiment to produce a complete, cohesive proposal.

Figure 9.1. Becca's High School Project Preliminary Proposal Using PowerPoint Slides.

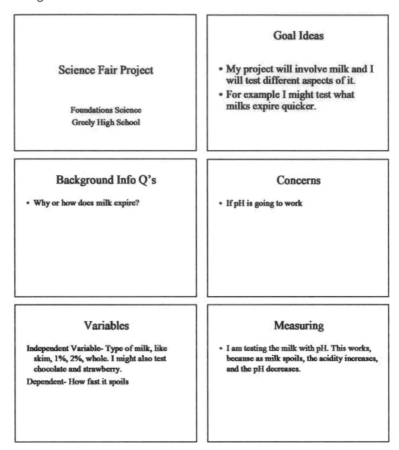

Massachusetts Institute of Technology

The process we use at MIT is similar to the process used at GHS. Like high school students, college students need support in developing meaningful hypotheses, statements, and focused projects. In Quantitative Physiology we allow students to choose a topic for their assigned experimental project based on their own interest. The faculty discuss the project's goals in class, and demonstrate how to develop a hypothesis statement for a topic. The faculty model the thought process for students by working through a series of sample proposal topics in class. Students then work in pairs to develop a formal proposal for their project.

Table 9.1. Data Chart for Becca's Milk Study. The Data Chart Gives Students a "Draft" Explanation of Their Variable, Controls, and Trials.

Milk Type/pH	Day 1	Day 2	Day 3	Day 4
Skim				
1%				
2%				
Whole				

Students submit their proposals electronically through the course Web site. The faculty and the teaching assistants download the proposals online. Projecting them onto a screen, they discuss the pros and cons of student proposals. These critiques are then returned via e-mail directly to the students. Approximately, 75 percent of students' proposals are initially rejected because the students' research approach is too broad or their methodology is unfocused. Students revise and resubmit their proposals until their research approach is approved. The class Web site submission application

Figure 9.2. Becca's Schematic Diagram Showing Her Graphic Representation of the Procedure for an Inquiry into the Spoiling of Milk Through the Production of Lactic Acid.

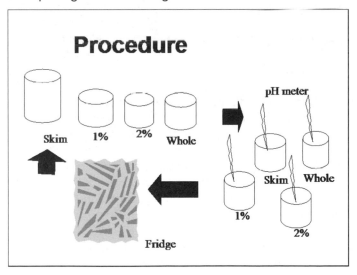

tracks when students upload their revised proposals and keeps an archive of comments.

This process of electronic submission and revision for the proposal process enables students to modify their proposals through a series of guided "conversations" with the teaching assistants. This allows the TAs to become familiar with student projects and can help the students more readily in the laboratory. The online submission process allows teaching assistants, technical faculty, and communications staff involved in the class to listen in on the feedback between TAs and students and provides a portfolio of student work along with the feedback that they receive at each stage of revision.

LITERATURE SURVEY: READING SCIENCE TO WRITE SCIENCE

In professional scientific practice, reviews of the literature are important mechanisms to show that a researcher has done his or her due diligence in keeping up-to-date with current trends (Hyland, 2004; Latour, 1987). Professional scientists are masters at navigating the vast research databases that are now available to find the most relevant, timely articles for their particular area of research. Typically, however, the common resources read by students are citation-free textbooks. Textbooks perform a useful function in that they provide what the current scientific community considers "facts" necessary for basic comprehension of scientific discoveries (Kuhn, 1970). Yet, textbooks do not help students understand the broader context in which scientific practice occurs, and they do not teach students how to use citations in scientific writing. Only by reading current scientific research do students learn the conversation in which research discoveries and failures are accepted.

Greely High School

At the high school level, we work with students to develop the reading skills necessary to understand basic concepts described in scientific research. The librarian at GHS provides a lesson for students on how to

> use internet search engines and procedures for conducting a Boolean search
> analyze a general internet Web site for content
> use various databases for specific topic searches, and
> identify sources of journal articles.

We then select and read a scientific journal article in class, showing students what they will find in the writing and where they will find it. Using a projected image, critical statements can be identified and marked, labels on graphics can be explained, and convoluted sentences clarified.

By involving high school students in searching for and reading scientific literature, we scaffold learning at the college level by helping students learn to use those sources more strategically in their writing. This process helps us achieve the larger goal of getting students to internalize that good scientific research stands on the shoulders of previous research and that sound proposals are strengthened by supportive background information and previously tested experimental methods.

Massachusetts Institute of Technology

At the university level, we also help students locate research articles in databases, but we expand the kinds of databases that students are expected to use to include patents and grant databases in addition to standard article databases like PubMed or Web of Science. These databases increase the kinds of information that students can find and provide more tools for tracking scientific research, for example, the cited reference search in Web of Science that allows researchers to see where else an article has been cited. We also encourage students to cite these articles in their research by pointing to the importance of citations in providing a compelling rationale for their research and showing students how to cite strategically. A *strategic* citation might be one that backs up a tenuous claim about a research finding or supports the use of a particular method. Finally, we help students learn to use EndNote or other citation management tools. These tools allow students to build a personal database of articles they use in their own research, which will allow them to work more efficiently later when they need to recheck a fact in an article or change citation style.

At the college level, the goal of teaching literature reviews with technology is getting students to use a wider array of databases available for research and getting students to start managing their searches. By using technology to access and analyze current scientific literature, our goal is to have students model the professional practices of working scientists and ultimately avoid problems like unintentional plagiarism (Benos et al., 2005).

EXPERIMENTATION: "STORYING" WITH DATA

The language of argument is central to the activity of professional science (Latour, 1987; Locke, 1992). Scientists talk about *convincing data, showing due diligence* as a researcher, and making a *compelling* argument for the *significance* of a research study. In fact, the language of argument pervades almost every aspect of scientific research, beginning with the selection of research topic, formation of hypothesis, and design of experiential protocol. In the experimental stage, data must be organized, categorized, selected, and analyzed. The teacher's challenge is helping student researchers understand what relationships are revealed in the experimental data. While technology allows students to easily generate plots of their findings, often those plots are poor representations of their work (Tufte, 2001). We use the process of visual storyboarding to help students think about the arguments they are making with their data and build the story of their scientific article around those data. Our choice of the term *story* rather than *argument* was deliberate. In choosing to call our approach storyboarding rather than argument and evidence, we sought to encourage students to think about the overall arc of scientific findings and not just a single point in time. In a compelling scientific argument, there is an overarching story or narrative to the research that ties together the research question, methods, results, and interpretation of the findings.

Greely High School

At GHS, the storyboard is an evolving series of student presentation slides (see Figure 9.3). Research slides describe the objectives, hypothesis, variables and constants, experimental design, procedure, data charts, graphic analysis, and results. The storyboard becomes the basis for a science fair presentation board, research paper, and abstract.

When students present their data plots (for example, pH Data slide and Average slide in Fig. 9.3), we discuss the selection of data display that best represents their work—scatter plot, bar graph, or linear regression. For example, if a student has epidemiological data, a bar graph might be best used; if a data relationship might result in a mathematical representation, then a scatter plot with a linear regression would most easily express this outcome. Upon choosing a graphic design students create a design framework with labels and units. This step tests the students' depth of understanding of the study. Sometimes students do not understand the concept of isolating a variable and have erroneous preconceptions about the outcome of their experiment. Other students may not understand exactly what they are trying to test.

The high school storyboard ultimately makes the process of scientific research manageable for students. It is only five or six slides, not an entire lab report. Establishing a graphic representation helps students discern the behavior (increasing, decreasing, or fluctuating patterns) of the phenomenon during the experimentation. Designing these figures early in the process permits us to assist the student in using technological tools, such as statistical software and plotting programs, to best represent their findings.

Figure 9.3. Becca's Storyboard. While her project was her own, Becca had a group of five friends and classmates who helped collect data and commented on the results. Using Excel statistics functions, she and her friends averaged data, determined standard deviations and performed T-Tests and ANOVA tests as appropriate.

Hypothesis

If skim, 1%, 2%, and whole milk are poured into cups and their pH is measured everyday for a number of days, then skim milk will spoil the fastest, because of the fat content.

Procedure

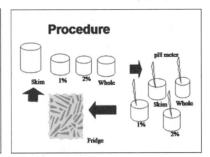

pH DATA

Milk #5	Day 1	Day 2	Day 3	Day 4	Day 5
Skim	6.76	6.88	6.95	6.94	6.94
1%	6.7	6.67	6.9	6.66	6.3
2%	6.73	6.76	6.79	6.83	5.96
Whole	6.85	6.86	6.92	6.72	6.59

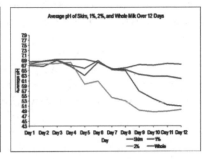

Summary

This experiment was to see which kind of milk spoils the fastest out of skim, 1%, 2%, and whole. It will help determine what milk is the best to be stored for a period of time, and it will help determine if the freshness of a type of milk is in question. The tested hypothesis was that there would be a difference in the changes of pH from milk to milk, and the skim milk would spoil the fastest. The way it was tested was each day the pH was recorded for each sample of milk for twelve days. The results were not as expected because even though there were differences in the change in pH, but the 2% had the greatest change, which was 1.78, while the skim milk only had a change of .02. However, after factoring in the standard deviation, there is chance that the whole milk could have also spoiled the fastest, because its change was 1.92, and the 2% was 1.84 with the standard deviation. An ANOVA test was then done, and it was determined that the probability of the null hypothesis was less than 1% (p=0.000478). So with that and the calculations it was concluded that the 2% and whole milk spoil the fastest.

Massachusetts Institute of Technology

At MIT, the storyboarding process is used to help students focus on their data findings while in the process of conducting research. We want students to understand the following:

1. Professional scientists think about communicating their findings throughout the data gathering process.
2. Each figure in a report tells its own story: while there are "correct" conventions for presenting data, different kinds of visual presentations also lead readers to interpret data in particular ways.
3. In sum, the figures in a report tell a narrative of the research that can be conveyed as a story.

Pacing this story of scientific findings is important if readers are to be convinced of the conclusions drawn from the data. Scientific readers want to see how the researcher moved from raw data to analysis of that data to regression trends.

Figure 9.4 shows a sample storyboard used in class to demonstrate a model for a microfluidics experiment in which students studied the properties of diffusion in a microfluidics chamber. The top left figure is an image taken by a Camscope program of the blue dye mixing with a clear dye (that is, a photo of the raw data). The bottom left image is of this diffusion process quantified over a series of images taken over time (that is, raw data chart of quantified information). The top right and bottom right images are plotting analyses of raw data, showing trends. This storyboard illustrates how to move readers from raw data to regression analysis through a series of steps that gives readers confidence that data is not being fabricated or manipulated unethically.

In a class workshop on scientific writing, we explain that as a researcher gathers data, he or she begins to define the principal results of the experiment, which can be summarized through key figures. Given the limited scope of the projects in Quantitative Physiology, we suggest that those principal results can be refined into five or six specific figures. We stress to students that often researchers cannot present every finding within the limited space of a research article. Like in essay writing, writers must develop a focus for their writing and eliminate tangents.

In our workshop, we show several various plots and ask students to read these plots. Our goal is to illustrate to students that different kinds of data displays can be interpreted differently by readers. This process also helps students generate text about a figure, for example, what is being shown in a figure belongs in the Results section of the report, while how those data were

Figure 9.4. Sample College Storyboard. (Courtesy of Dennis Freeman)

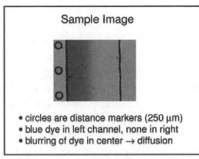

Sample Image

- circles are distance markers (250 μm)
- blue dye in left channel, none in right
- blurring of dye in center → diffusion

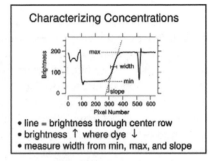

Characterizing Concentrations

- line = brightness through center row
- brightness ↑ where dye ↓
- measure width from min, max, and slope

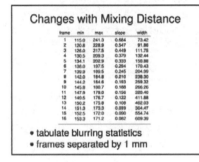

Changes with Mixing Distance

frame	min	max	slope	width
1	115.0	241.3	0.684	73.42
2	120.8	228.9	0.547	91.86
3	126.0	217.5	0.449	111.75
4	130.5	209.3	0.379	132.44
5	134.1	202.9	0.333	150.88
6	138.0	197.5	0.294	170.43
7	129.9	189.5	0.245	204.99
8	142.0	184.8	0.210	238.30
9	144.2	184.6	0.183	259.32
10	145.8	180.7	0.168	266.26
11	147.9	179.0	0.156	320.40
12	149.5	176.7	0.122	411.88
13	150.2	175.8	0.108	462.03
14	151.3	173.3	0.099	304.47
15	152.5	172.0	0.090	554.74
16	153.3	171.2	0.082	609.39

- tabulate blurring statistics
- frames separated by 1 mm

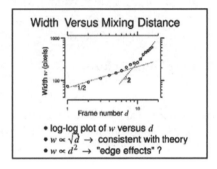

Width Versus Mixing Distance

- log-log plot of w versus d
- $w \propto \sqrt{d}$ → consistent with theory
- $w \propto d^2$ → "edge effects" ?

collected belongs in the Methods section. We also ask students to evaluate various combinations of figures that have been combined into a storyboard, such as the example shown in Figure 9.4. By evaluating a series of figures together, students assess the overall quality and believability of the "story" conveyed about a particular research project.

Following the workshop, students work in pairs to draft their own storyboards. While the initial storyboard may be a series of hand-drawn sketches, students generate plots in MatLab or Excel for their next drafts. Students write descriptions and captions for each figure with transitions between figures and then convert this text into a research article format. These drafts are then shared with peers and faculty for feedback.

Used in this manner, the college-level storyboard is the primary bridge between the research and writing efforts. The storyboard of figures helps ensure that students have a coherent narrative of their study that runs from the Introduction through the Methods, Results, and Discussion sections.

COLLABORATION: PEER REVIEW
USING TECHNOLOGY

Science is intensely collaborative, characterized by the candid sharing of ideas. In the peer review process, scientists "insist that the critical assumptions behind any line of reasoning be made explicit so that the validity of the position being taken—whether one's own or that of others—can be judged" (American Association for the Advancement of Science, 1993, p. 300). The peer reviewer's report is ultimately, "an assessment of the persuasiveness of a submitted paper" (Gross, 1990, p. 129). Conversations between scientists are facilitated by technology, making feedback on the content and clarity of scientific writing rapid, whether the individuals are in the same room or on the other side of the globe. Today's student is comfortable with casual conversations via the internet or text messaging but needs support in learning how to use technology for peer review in ways that model professional practice.

Greely High School

At GHS, as each frame of the storyboard is created—goals and objectives, hypotheses, experimental design, results, conclusions and implications—students share their work with each other. One or two slides at a time the student scientist describes his or her research, and the class critically reviews the work. The continuous presentation in class of each phase of the project to classmates and the immediate oral feedback helps students hone their presentation skills.

Feedback is modeled on the actual judging formats used at both local and state science fairs. Although the peer review is not graded, we guide the quality of the interaction with questions that promote critical thinking and can assess the students' understanding of underlying scientific principles. It is not just the presenter who learns from the feedback; each student in the room takes away a deeper understanding of the content and process of science and communication. Students have said about the process: "The written comments told me what I had to work on," and "It was easier to do after I saw someone else do it."

Massachusetts Institute of Technology

Peer review is also an important part of teaching scientific writing at college, so students gain experience reviewing drafts as professional scientists would in both process and substance. Students review each other's work in pairs. We give them guidelines for their response, and we require that students meet with their reviewers in person.

After students upload PDF copies of their papers to the class Web site, we send those files electronically to student reviewers. In our comments and the peer review guidelines, we specifically point students to the visual elements of their peer's report, and we reward students for commenting on those "high level" (i.e., narrative of the data) aspects of the report draft, as indicated by the following:

Grading rubric for critique of peer report

A: Several helpful high-level suggestions (e.g., suggesting major restructuring, new figures, . . .) plus probing questions (could your result be caused by . . . ?) plus appropriate low-level comments (e.g., on grammar or graphics).

B: At least one helpful high-level suggestion or probing question plus appropriate low-level comments.

C: Helpful low-level comments.

D: Few helpful comments.

While professional scientists are not "graded" on their peer reviews, it is expected that reviewers comment on "big picture" issues, not solely on sentence-level issues. Our Grading Rubric attempts to move students toward these "big picture" comments by asking them to suggest major revisions or ask probing questions. (We realize that student research is limited within the scope of a five-week project, so criteria like "significance" are not appropriate here.)

To build community in the class, students not only comment electronically but also meet with authors in person during a "writing clinic," a decidedly low-tech face-to-face forum. The personal interaction ensures that peer readers have carefully considered their advice to the authors and that their comments carry a professional tone. After one of the writing clinics, one student told us:

> One of the things I realized from the peer review especially is that there are many ways to take data and analyze data, so its important to justify to the reader why you took a specific approach and why you think its valid—particularly because it might not seem that obvious to someone else. Also, data presentation matters—both in terms of tables vs. figures and text description in Results. Our first draft, we primarily just [threw] the data at the reader. In the final we tried hard to present it more pointedly. (Maia)

Through this combination of electronic feedback and face-to-face feedback, we teach students to use technology to model professional practice without losing sight of the community of researchers in which they work. By linking new technology for peer review with face-to-face communication, we ultimately want students to keep real readers in mind as they write and review work electronically.

ASSESSING THE NEW STORY
OF SCIENTIFIC INQUIRY

We have found that by changing our teaching practices to include technology in scientific writing instruction we can better link the scientific research process with the exposition of scientific findings, provide students with a forum for giving and receiving substantial feedback, and more quickly identify high-level misunderstandings in student research.

Greeley High School

The months of preparation result in a tri-fold poster display of the student's project at the Greeley High School Science Fair, a judged presentation of the student work ending with an evening public display. Judges listen to a 5-minute oral explanation of the experiment and results after which they can quiz the student on any aspect of the project. Twenty-five students are selected to attend the more rigorous State Science Fair at the University of Maine, Orono. The criteria used to assess students' science fair projects are based on the Maine State Science and Technology Fair (2008) Judging Criteria, partially excerpted below:

Personal Achievement (27 points)

- Does the project clearly indicate in-depth scientific research?

Presentation (27 points)

- Does the presentation follow a logical sequence according to the scientific method?
- Does the presentation clearly show understanding of background material and involve detailed explanations?

Scientific Methodology (46 points)

- Does the project clearly define the problem and state a hypothesis that can be tested?

- Does the project clearly indicate the procedure used, the data collected, and the interpretation of data?
- Does the project indicate all important sources of error?
- Does the project indicate a reference list (literature that is cited), bibliography (literature that is read but not cited), and acknowledgements (any persons or institutions that help the student with the project)?

Prior to using PowerPoint-enabled storyboards, students' Science Fair presentation boards were often unorganized and more artistic than scientific. Storyboarding has helped students focus on the narrative of their work, resulting in coherent, cohesive display of their research. Students using the storyboarding process are confident, articulate, knowledgeable, and prepared for the Science Fair. As one student said, "[Science Fair judging] was a lot easier than I thought it would be. I think [the judges] understood it. They asked a lot of questions." The judges of the Science Fair (members of the school faculty and community) have commented on the quality of the scientific thought and presentations of the students, particularly those students who have had past difficulty producing work. Judges have said, "The students' data were easily understood and they could explain them;" and "Their graphs and data were properly labeled."

Massachusetts Institute of Technology

At MIT, we evaluate students' final papers based on the seven criteria of the grading sheet, as follows:

Grading Sheet Criteria for Microfluidics Project Report (2007)

- First draft (20%)
- Peer Review (10%)
- Clarity and Conciseness of Exposition (20%)
- Experimental Design / Method (10%)
- Storyboarding (Selection of data) / Figures / Captions / General Clarity (10%)
- Data Analysis / Results and Discussion (20%)
- Overall Quality / Significance / Exceptional Effort (10%)

Some of these criteria map onto our earlier evaluations of student writing and guidelines for peer review. Other criteria focus on things that are central to the evaluation of professional work, such as significance and experimental design. Although writing faculty typically comment on the first half of the criteria and technical faculty comment on the second half, it is not uncommon for both groups to comment on all criteria. Such commenting has led to more dialog among writing and technical faculty (as well as teaching assistants) about the quality of the papers and our goals for student learning.

Since developing the storyboard approach in the early 2000s, we have modified the grading criteria and peer review guides to focus more on storyboarding. For example, beginning in 2007, 10% of the final project grade was based on the quality of the storyboard (previously, selection of figures was included under a criterion called "Report Structure," which was simply too ambiguous.)

With the increased attention in the past 8 years on storyboarding, students submit better drafts of their first projects, which then allow them to make more progress on their work before submitting a final article for grading. Our qualitative analysis suggests that students need multiple opportunities to use storyboarding to become proficient at the concept, but once they begin to understand how to tell a story with their data, the payoff is rapid. In using the storyboard approach through a second iteration, students seem to develop a deeper understanding of its use. By the second project, students are producing better representations of their data, and because we now have a shared language about storyboarding, we can encourage even deeper revision of their work. As the course professor explained:

> [Storyboarding] lets you write at a higher level. It's too tempting when you jump straight into the figures to hone the figures before you've thought about how important they are to the whole presentation. It's easy to fall into the trap of polishing something that ultimately should be discarded. But you then have such a, you're so wedded to it that it's difficult to discard. I think what [storyboarding] allows you to do is structure the whole talk or paper at a more global level before you've become wed to the particular plots. (Freeman, 2007)

Students' reception of our approach has been positive. At the end of semester we ask students to assess the course curriculum (see Table 9.2). Approximately 95% of students who returned course surveys in 2004 said that we should *not* eliminate the revision process. Similar findings are reported in 2005–2007.

At the university level, Quantitative Physiology has become a model communication intensive course. As departments look for novel ways to integrate writing and speaking into disciplinary courses, Quantitative Physiology provides one model of how this integration may be done effectively. The Writing across the Curriculum program at MIT has also looked to Quantitative Physiology as a way to "theme" communication intensive courses so that students do not receive the same kind of communication instruction in every CI class. We are beginning to explore how students leave Quantitative Physiology and use the storyboarding in their other classes. More important, Quantitative

Table 9.2. Summary of MIT Student Surveys for the Quantitative Physiology Course, 2004. Left column displays suggestions and the right columns show the number of students that strongly agree (YES), mildly agree (yes), mildly disagree (no), strongly disagree (NO), or were ambivalent (?).

	NO	no	?	yes	YES
Should reduce emphasis on writing and speaking in this class	11	13	7	6	2
Should eliminate first drafts of written reports	22	16	2	0	0
Emphasis on writing detracted from technical content	8	15	9	7	1
Should eliminate lectures on writing & speaking	10	17	4	4	5
Projects should be done individually rather than with partners	24	12	3	1	0
First project reinforced the technical content of the class	5	8	9	13	5
Second project reinforced the technical content of the class	1	1	2	21	15

Physiology is the "gold standard" for collaboration between technical faculty and writing faculty with writing faculty sharing in the design of course assignments and assessments. This close collaboration, which has led to multiple conference presentations and a proceedings paper, shows other MIT faculty that writing instruction need not be relegated to stand-alone technical writing classes.

CONCLUSIONS

Changes to science due to technological advances have brought a number of exciting and challenging opportunities in the teaching of scientific writing. The impact of technological change on science has made us keenly aware of how communication practices change over time and that communication instruction must be continually updated to keep instructional methods abreast with those changes. While technological change may not have altered our definition of scientific writing, which has always been highly visual, it has changed how we teach writing. Technological change has given us the opportunity to bring science and writing closer by opening new ways of thinking about composing and new opportunities to integrate the composing process throughout the process of scientific research. Technology has allowed us to build off writing-across-the-curriculum models of instruction to include multimodal ways of teaching and learning. New ways of composing facilitated by technology include storyboarding and other data-driven ways of beginning the writing process. The ability to quickly share information electronically means that we have more flexibility and creativity in peer review methods. Ultimately, technology has helped us minimize the challenges of technological change in science and capitalize on its promises and, in the process, put success with science and scientific writing within the reach of all students.

The outcome of these changes has been to make us better teachers of writing. Our two years of conversations and experimenting about how to integrate technology more effectively to teach scientific writing have taught us to look beyond texts or genres of science to the activity of professional practice as it has been affected by technological change. Without talking about the difficulties of student scientific papers brought on by technological change, we would have likely not found a shared goal for our teaching. The payoff of all this activity for us has been to redefine old notions of teaching writing for ourselves and our colleagues.

REFERENCES

American Association for the Advancement of Science. (1993). *Project 2061. Benchmarks for science literacy.* Washington, DC: Author.

Bazerman, C. (Ed.). (1988). *Shaping written knowledge: the genre and activity of the experimental article in science.* Madison: University of Wisconsin Press.

Bazerman, C., & Russell, D. (Eds.). (1985). *Landmark essays on writing across the curriculum.* Mahwah, NJ: Erlbaum.

Benos, D. J., Fabres, J., Farmer, J., Gutierrez, J., Hennessy, K., Kosek, D., Lee, J. H., Olteanu, D., Russell, T., Shaikh, F., & Wang, K. (2005). Ethics and scientific publication, *Advanced Physiology Education, 29,* 59–74.

Berkenkotter, C. (2007). *Multimedia genres and cognitive change.* Paper presented at the 4th International Symposium on Genre Studies. Tubarao, Santa Catarina, Brazil.

Bransford, J., Brown, A., & Cocking, R. (Eds.). (2000). *How people learn: Brain, mind, experience, and school.* Washington, DC: National Academy Press.

Garfield, E. (1996, September 2). The significant scientific literature appears in a small core of journals. *The Scientist, 10*(17), 13.

Greely High School. *Course Guide.* (2007). Retrieved February 1, 2008, from http://greely.msad51.org/Pages/MSAD51_GHSGuidance/Coursecatalog/

Greely High School. *Mission Statement.* (2007, October 31). Retrieved February 1, 2008, from http://greely.msad51.org/Pages/MSAD51_GHSInfo/mission/

Gross, A. (1990). *The rhetoric of science.* Cambridge, MA: Harvard University Press.

Gross, A., Harmon, J., & Reidy. M. (2002). *Communicating science: The scientific article from the 17th century to the present.* Oxford: Oxford University Press.

Hyland, K. (2004). *Disciplinary discourses: social interactions in academic writing.* Ann Arbor: University of Michigan Press.

Kress, G., & van Leeuwen, T. (2001). *Multimodal discourse: The modes and media of contemporary communication.* London: Edward Arnold.

Kuhn, T. (1970). *The Structure of scientific revolutions (3rd ed.).* Chicago, IL: University of Chicago Press. (Original work published 1962)

Latour, B. (1987). *Science in action: How to follow scientists and engineers through society.* Cambridge, MA: Harvard University Press.

Latour, B., & Woolgar, S. (1979). *Laboratory life: The social construction of scientific facts.* Los Angeles, CA: Sage.

Locke, D. (1992). *Science as writing.* New Haven, CT: Yale University Press.

Maine Department of Education Regulation. (2007). *Learning results: Parameters for essential instruction science and technology,* section B1 performance indicators 9-diploma. Retrieved May 14, 2008, from http://mainegov-images.informe.org/education/lres/pei/sci_tech102207.pdf

Maine State Science and Technology Fair Bulletin. (2008). Retrieved May 11, 2008, from http://www.mpa.cc/pdf/scienceb.pdf

Massachusetts Institute of Technology Course Catalogue 2007–2008. (2007). *General institute requirements.* Retrieved June 1, 2007, from http://web.mit.edu/catalogue/overv.chap3-gir.shtml

Massachusetts Institute of Technology Subject Listing and Schedule. (2007, Fall). 6.021J Quantitative physiology: cells and tissues. Retrieved June 1, 2007, from http://student.mit.edu/catalog/m6a.html

Massachusetts Institute of Technology Undergraduate Communication requirement. *About the Requirement.* (n.d.). Retrieved February 1, 2008, from, http://web.mit.edu/commreq/background.html/

Myers, G. (1985). The social construction of two biologists' proposals. In C. Bazerman & D. Russell (Eds.), *Landmark essays on writing across the curriculum.* Mahwah, NJ: Erlbaum.

New England Association of Schools and Colleges (2006, October 29–November 1). Report of the Visiting Committee, Greely High School, Cumberland, Maine.

Russell, D. (2002). *Writing in the academic disciplines: A curricular history (2nd ed.).* Carbondale: Southern Illinois University Press. (Original work published 1991)

Sandoval, W. (2005). The quality of students' use of evidence in written scientific explanations. *Cognition and instruction, 23*(1), 23–55.

Tufte, E. (2001). *The visual display of quantitative information* (Reprint ed.), Sheshire, CT: Graphics Press. (Original work published 1984)

CHAPTER 10

Student Engagement and Multimodality

Collaboration, Schema, Identity

PETER KITTLE

FAST-FORWARD

A few times each year, my e-mail in-box starts filling with requests from students who would like me to write recommendation letters for them. These generally coincide with approaching deadlines for applications to graduate school or teaching credential programs, and the e-mails take a fairly standardized form. After a general salutation (a casual "Hi Peter" from some, a more formal "Dear Professor Kittle" from others), and before the ubiquitous request for the letter itself, the writers provide a brief reminder to me about who they are and how I know them: "I was in your writing class during fall semester last year." I usually smile inwardly as I read these explanations, simply because the students' assumption that I wouldn't remember them is generally flawed; it's pretty rare that I don't immediately recognize not only the student, but also the course, semester, and even classroom. It doesn't hurt that most students making these requests have taken courses from me when they were nearing graduation, so I don't often have to stretch my memory beyond a couple semesters worth of students.

I mention all of this merely because students from a particular class I teach have begun to include a new element into these letters. Along with the "I was in your ENGL 333 section . . . ," the writers from this class have begun situating themselves in terms of the work they completed within that class. So their letters include statements like "I did the digital documentary on the learning strategies I used to master the guitar," or "I made the multimodal project on learning how to live in a new city." The first time I received an e-mail containing this extra bit of information, I chuckled a bit, because as soon as I saw the student's name on the e-mail, I immediately thought of the very project she referenced in her e-mail. But then a second student made a request, and included again a reference to a class project I'd thought of immediately upon seeing her name. By the time a few more had shown up, a pattern was becoming visible: my students and I were identifying the same multimodal projects as touchstones for identity within the course. This gave me pause. I wondered: why were students suddenly referring to particular course projects in these requests? Why did I associate those students with the very same projects, even before reading the e-mails containing those references? I have come to believe that the nature of a particular assignment completed in the class had a lasting impact on both the students and me, and I will investigate that impact in the following pages.

REWIND

The students referenced above all took English 333, Advanced Composition for Future Teachers, during spring semester of 2007. The class was offered at California State University, Chico, where I teach in the English Education program. This course is a required, upper division, writing-intensive class required of two distinct populations: future elementary school teachers, and future secondary English teachers. In most sections of the course, the former population outnumbers the latter by about 5 to 1.

Given the population of pre-service teachers, the course has traditionally focused on issues related to education, and genres often encountered by teachers in their professional lives. Assignments commonly given in the course include literacy narratives, memoranda to administrators and/or school board members, guest opinion columns for newspapers or professional publications, and lesson units focused on writing. Several instructors employ an ongoing inquiry into the teaching of writing in a twofold effort to enact best practices in teaching composition, while simultaneously increasing students' knowledge of how writing is effectively taught and learned.

When I taught ENGL 333 in terms prior to spring 2007, I began the semester with a literacy narrative assignment. Literacy narratives, advocated widely by Wendy Bishop (2004) in *On Writing* and elsewhere, ask students to examine and reflect upon the ways they learned to read and write; in my class, we also framed that learning within a framework of literacy theory. We would read several examples of thoughtful literacy narratives—the opening chapter of Mike Rose's (1990) *Lives on the Boundary*, for instance—and inductively define characteristics of the literacy narrative as a genre. We would also read at least one theoretical piece focused on literacy and/or learning—Deborah Brandt's (1998) seminal *Sponsors of Literacy* worked well—to use as a lens through which the literacy narrative would find focus. The student work produced in response to this assignment was, in general, quite engaging, with a few outstanding pieces produced each semester. Yet I began to rethink the assignment as a result of my interactions with several ongoing professional events and networks.

In 2003 I was appointed to the post of Technology Liaison for the Northern California Writing Project (NCWP), and that appointment connected me with hundreds of National Writing Project (NWP) teachers interested in using technology to teach writing. I had been an early adopter of technology for teaching, beginning in the late 1980s when I taught high school English in Kelso, Washington. Asked to advise the school's newspaper, I agreed, on condition that we be given access to Macintosh computers and a then new page layout program called PageMaker. To this day, I apparently enthuse regularly about the technology I use in my classes; I was rewarded with my appointment to the NCWP technology position.

As a member of the NWP's Technology Liaison network, I attended an NWP-sponsored institute called Technology Matters in the summer of 2004. There, I met many others whose technology know-how and classroom implementations put my own efforts to shame. In the following 3 summers, I was asked to be part of the subsequent Technology Matters facilitation teams. Each experience fortified my knowledge of technology use in the classroom, and put me in contact with ever-increasing numbers of tech-savvy teachers. I began to see possibilities for revamping elements of my classes to take advantage of the emerging technologies available to educators.

It became apparent to me that ENGL 333, with its focus on the teaching of writing and a population of pre-service teachers, was the right place to begin infusing this new technology. My interactions with NWP colleagues—many of whom have authored chapters in this book—who were successfully implementing Weblogs, wikis, podcasting, vodcasting, and other technologies in their classrooms made me realize the potential of technology to revitalize the writing curricula across grade levels and disciplines. Future teachers of writing, I reasoned, would be well served by not just exposure to, but immersion in, new communicative technologies.

PLAY

Making curricular change is never as simple a process as it seems when in the planning stages. I had decided to make a couple of significant modifications to the course's assignments, as well as to the ways those assignments could be completed. My plan was to insert so-called Web 2.0 technologies into what had been the literacy narrative assignment. *Web 2.0* is a descriptor for Internet-based technologies that invite Web users not just to consume, but also contribute to and/or produce online texts. Educational technologist David Warlick (2008) identifies three attributes of such online technologies that particularly render them apt for classroom use: rich and interactive information, collaboration, and contributive expression.

To make these adjustments to the course, I revamped the readings and activities associated with the literacy narrative. A new text was required for the course: James Paul Gee's (2003) *What Video Games Have to Teach Us About Language and Literacy.* Gee's argument, drawing on the work of Lave and Wenger (1991), posits that video games create environments constructed specifically to scaffold players' learning. Gee is particularly attentive to the notion of multimodality, noting the ways that different media (written, audio, and visual texts, for instance) require different—and sometimes competing—literacies to decode. The intermingling of modalities requires increasingly dexterous literacy on the part of the reader. The book identifies more than 30 learning principles evident in the multimodal environments of video games, tying those principles to real-world learning strategies.

The role Gee's book played in the class curriculum was to help students think through and understand their own learning processes. While we were reading Gee, I asked students to apply the learning principles from the text to topics or activities that they were currently learning outside of a formal school setting. Students recorded their thoughts and reflections in personal Weblogs, which in turn became a resource for a larger composition: the multimodal learning document. Their assignment was to craft a multimodal document that represented their own learning, and articulated that learning to one or more of the principles identified in Gee's book.

What I've been describing so far corresponds to the planning I had done for the curricular changes. However, the implementation was far less straightforward. It played out something like this:

Me: So, instead of writing a traditional essay on Gee, we're going to create digital documents that show how his ideas play out in our own learning. You know, so we can use, as writers, some of those multimodal attributes Gee is always talking about.
Students: . . .
Me: Any questions?
Students: . . .
Me: No?
Students: Um, we don't know how to make a multimodal document.
Me: Nothing to worry about. We're going to learn how.

Students: Okaaayy. . . . But we don't really know what one is, either.
Me: I can show you that, too.
Students: Uh-huh . . . if you say so . . .
Me: Don't worry! It'll be great! We'll play around and figure it out as
    we go.
Students: Yeah . . . sounds, uh, great . . .

I can't fault the students for their lack of enthusiasm (nor would it be accurate to lump all of the students together, as the response was in fact varied). It became clear rather quickly, however, that we needed models so that, as had happened with literacy narratives in prior classes, we could inductively determine the genre features of a multimodal document.

But first, a few words about the term *multimodal document*. When I first envisioned this project, I was using as a baseline the work termed *digital storytelling*. The Center for Digital Storytelling (2008), in Berkeley, CA, identifies this genre as using the "tools of digital media to craft, record, share, and value the stories of individuals and communities," noting in particular "its emphasis on personal voice." I wholeheartedly wanted these attributes to be part of my students' projects. But I also knew that storytelling has been a fraught term in academic circles, often used pejoratively. Charles Tilly (2003), in *Stories, Identities, and Political Change* notes that while stories "do crucial work in patching social life together," many of the "strongest insights" offered by academic research "do not take the form of stories, and often undermine the stories people tell" (p. 26). I wanted my students' projects to use the attributes of digital storytelling to help them craft engaging work, but I did not want them to simply rely on their stories to make seemingly self-evident points. Rather, I wanted their projects to tell a compelling story while using rigorous academic thinking as a lens for helping their audiences understand the significance of the points made by those stories. I wanted, in short, for the projects to fit under the label of "analytical writing," as defined by George Gadda and William Walsh (1988): "writing whose primary purpose is to define the significance of [its] subject matter for readers" (p. 4).

This, to me, necessitated a label other than digital stories, even if the final projects appeared, on the surface, to be closely related to that genre. When I first introduced the assignment to the class, I used the term *digital document*; I wanted to foreground the notion that the story they would tell *documents* a particular learning theory in a real-life scenario. As we worked on the project, and simultaneously saw the term *multimodal* used repeatedly in James Gee's book, students suggested that multimodal was perhaps a better descriptor for their projects.

Regardless of the label given to the work, we viewed many different examples in our effort to define its attributes. Of those models, the one that students found most compelling was made by Jason Shiroff (2008) of the Denver

Writing Project. Called "Daddy Duty," Shiroff's three-and-a half-minute video details his learning process as he takes over the primary caregiver role for his infant daughter during the summer. Combining still images, music, video footage, and voice narration, the document captures his trepidations, false steps, and gradual mastery of childcare. After watching Shiroff's piece several times, the class generated a list of attributes of effective multimodal documents. We determined that such documents:

- Include a compelling narration of a story;
- Provide a meaningful context for understanding the story being told;
- Use images to capture and/or expand upon emotions found in the narrative;
- Employ music and other sound effects to reinforce ideas;
- Invite thoughtful reflection from their audience(s).

We also examined the structure of Shiroff's piece, using a backward storyboarding technique. I asked students in small groups to look through different sections of "Daddy Duty," and identify the functions of the audio and visual attributes Shiroff included in his document. We first considered, together, the opening, during which soft guitar music plays as a white backdrop dotted with colored stars slowly spins over the title of the piece. As the narrative begins, an image of Shiroff's baby daughter appears, zooming slowly in on her face. During discussion, students noted that the backdrop looks like a baby's blanket, and the music has a lullaby-like quality; both of these attributes, they concluded, have the effect of evoking the subject of the document before a word of the narrative has even been heard. The effect of our discussions on the structural functions of the multimodal document was that students began to read multimodal texts from the perspective of a composer, not simply a consumer.

PAUSE

I should stop here and mention that I was doing something fairly risky. I had very little experience with multimodal composition myself at this point. Like many people—and perhaps parents in particular—I had access to lots of video and still photos that documented aspects of my life; however, I had done little to organize, reflect upon, or (re)present that collection of media to an audience. Two NWP Technology Liaisons, Kevin Hodgson from Western Massachusetts WP and Bonnie Kaplan from Hudson Valley WP, had proposed a *Collaborative ABC Movie Project* (2008) using short videos of the sort I envisioned for my students, and I (foolishly? gallantly?) volunteered to contribute to the project. This was not prior to, but concurrent with, my students' learning. The bottom line is that there was little expertise in the room when our class met, and any that I possessed I had generally acquired mere days, if not hours, prior to my putting it on display.

Although by turns terrifying and exhilarating, this learn-as-you-go strategy actually paid off well, pedagogically. I was able to share my own frustrations, sticking points, and successes with the class, almost as they occurred. I used Google Docs, an online word processing and sharing service, to compose the narrative of my multimodal project, and made that available to students. I even included many of the starts and stops I had made, with commentary to make visible my thinking as I was editing the piece (see Figure 10.1). Students recognized the processes involved in composing such a document and were somewhat comforted that the same issues that they faced were also impacting their teacher.

RECORD

By the time we had studied various multimodal documents, the students were more than able to think conceptually about the work I had assigned them. However, they still retained something of a deer-in-the-headlights demeanor when it came to the nuts and bolts of putting together a multimodal document. I was bombarded with questions each class meeting:

Figure 10.1. Google Docs Shared Document Draft of Multimodal Document

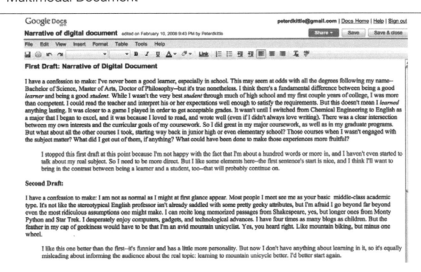

- Where do I get pictures?
- How do I record my voice?
- Are there free video clips I can use?
- What if I don't have a camera/video camera/modern computer/voice recorder?

These were important questions. We had access as a class to a computer lab nearly each day we met, although it was stunningly outdated. Students learned (and taught each other) how to capture pictures, video, and audio with their cell phones, and then transfer them to computer files. Online resources were investigated, tested, and shared among all classmates. All the while, I was colearning with the students. Each day was chaotic, with sometimes manic, oft-times panicked students rushing about the lab, uncovering new problems and discovering novel solutions. Eventually, students worked out the particular issues related to creating their projects, and put together rough cuts for viewing and peer response. Revision and editing took a rather organic form, with students gladly watching each others' projects as they developed, offering continual feedback and soliciting opinions from various class members during the course of any typical day.

When students had finally reached a point when the projects were ready for submission—about 4 weeks after I had initially planned the due date, simply because the projects took longer to complete than I had anticipated—they insisted on having a viewing day. I brought a laptop and projector into our classroom, and students immediately began volunteering to show their final projects. Of the 31 students enrolled, 19 went public with their work during that 80-minute class before we ran out of time, and each project shown was greeted with enthusiasm. Questions popped up about craft ("How did you do *that*?" was commonly heard), and the subject matter of the projects—everything from learning healthy eating habits to mastering kayaking—served to build community among class members.

FREEZE FRAME

Once students had finished and submitted their projects, I found myself facing the problem of assessment. The multimodal documents differed significantly from any prior student work I had ever graded. Believing in the efficacy of the class's collaborations on the project thus far, I asked for input on a rubric for evaluating their final projects. After looking at some samples from other assignments, we identified 6 areas for evaluation: topic and ideas, narration, multimodal attributes, creativity, audience, and multimodal effects/technical aspects (see Figure 10.2). These areas were more aligned with prior

Figure 10.2. Evaluation Rubric

Category of Evaluation	Your Score/ Points Possible
Topic and Ideas: • Relates to personal learning and learning strategies, not "how to" • Connects to Gee's ideas, either directly or indirectly • Demonstrates complex understanding of learning	/25
Narration: • Narrative progresses naturally from start to end • Thought processes are made clear through narration • Project's narrative makes sense to intended audience	/15
Multimodal Attributes: • Use of multimodal elements (text, pictures, videos, audio effects) enhances effects of project on audience	/20
Creativity: • Project demonstrates creativity in representing ideas to audience	/10
Audience: • Project attempts to engage audience through presentation	/10
Multimodal Effects (technical aspects): • Narration and visual elements complement each other • Project uses smooth transitions • Visual elements are clear and effective • Audio effects are easily audible and enhance project	/20
Total	*/100*

evaluation criteria than I had anticipated. The content of the projects would be evaluated in essentially the same way as a written piece, as would the attention to audience. The narration category roughly equated to organizational issues, and multimodal effects (technical aspects) paralleled presentation issues (surface errors and the like). This left two areas—creativity and multimodal attributes—that coincided most closely with craft and/or style in an essay. The students described these as the spots in the projects where their choices as composers were most evident, and where their individuality was on display. These were also the two areas I anticipated being most difficult to assess uniformly. I found in practice, however, that it was relatively clear to evaluate. As I *read* the projects (*viewed* seems too passive to accurately represent the level of engagement involved), I would often be struck by the inclusion of an image or sound effect that seemed the perfect complement for the narration. This melding of multimodal traits—words, images, sounds—ably demonstrated each student's individual style and mastery of craft.

As I assessed the projects, I found that my students as a whole had demonstrated their ability to evaluate ideas and issues carefully, think in complex and abstract ways, shape and organize material effectively, skillfully integrate material from research, and follow appropriate conventions and rules—all of which align with attributes outlined by Patrick Sullivan (2006) as essential to college writing. But, as is common when using any rubric, the articulated criteria failed to fully capture all aspects of students' projects. I decided to add comments to supplement the rubric's feedback. These took the form of MP3 audio files I recorded immediately after reading each project, so that a little multimodality was part of the assessment as well as the assignment.

Before moving on to some conclusions about the project as a whole, I would like to stop for a moment and examine more closely four particular cases from the class that provide a rich representation of the work of their classmates. Although the written syntheses I provide of the multimodal documents are no substitute for seeing the actual projects, I hope to convey the tenor of the student work sufficiently to demonstrate the ways that they engaged the course's academic content. When appropriate, I have included the students' thoughts as recorded on their public Weblogs; all quotations are unedited.

Case 1: Tracee

Tracee's project focused on her quest to learn to play the guitar. In a mid-project blog entry, she described her processes as she worked on composing the multimodal document:

> So far I have some pictures, a narrative, and an idea in mind. I am doing mine on learning how to play the guitar, so I found a bunch of images relating to that. My next step was to decide how to put it all together. I was not sure where to even start with that. I knew that I could throw some images into moviemaker, but that would not be the best way to go about doing it. I then realized that I needed to write a narrative to help with the process. As I was writing, a lot of different ideas came to mind . . . all of a sudden I had images I knew I was going to ask my parents back home to send me and where they were going to correspond to my narrative. I found that writing the narrative first was the best way, for me, to get started on this process and get something accomplished. My next difficulty is becoming friendly with the technical aspect of moviemaker, and once I get that done I will be on my way.

Tracee's final project situated her desire to learn the guitar within the context of leaving the musical culture of her family when she moved away to college. She wanted a way to keep alive her tradition of singing to the guitar, even when her guitar-playing father was 500 miles away. The document itself began with video footage of her family singing on their patio, and ended with her own performance of a self-accompanied song. In between, she described how she was mastering the new *semiotic domain*—Gee's (2003) term for meaning-making systems associated with a particular cultural practice—related to learning to play the guitar. In her end-of-semester blog post, she highlighted the multimodal document:

> This was by far the coolest writing class I have ever taken. I loved how technology was incorporated into the class and I loved how new ways of doing papers was experimented with (if I could make a video instead of writing a paper for every class in the future, I would do it in an instant). Even though it started out as a struggle, I am so glad that I had the opportunity to learn how to use Windows Movie Maker; I think that it is definitely something I will use again for various purposes.

Case 2: Caitlin

Like Tracee, Caitlin focused on learning a musical instrument, but with a slightly different emphasis. Her multimodal document, "Harmonica: Pocket-Sized Soul," features a playfulness centered on the notion of her developing identity as a harmonica player. "Prepare for the insight and experience of a musical genius," she intones, over a picture of herself making a goofy face. "Oh, I'm kidding," she continues, as the image transitions to a picture of raised hands at an outdoor concert. "But who knows. Maybe one day." Later, she documents visiting a music store and exploring the various accoutrements of the instrument, and in a blog entry reflecting on the project, ties this to Gee's notions of identity:

> In the section where I get carried away with the thoughts of a career in Harmonica playing, with special accessories and my own tour bus, I was dealing with the Identity Principle of Gee's book. I was playing with identity, creating a fantasy about what I would do. Eventually, I slowed the process of daydreaming as I reflected on the reality of my identity, and how I would first have to learn the instrument, then begin to try to live out the dream. I have to understand my potential identity in baby steps, starting with my understanding of the instrument.

Caitlin's project as a whole, and her reflection on it, showcase the ways that the multimodal document as a genre invite creativity and voice while maintaining a rigorous engagement with academic ideas.

Case 3: Elyse

As a second semester junior, Elyse was noticing how much more stressful her life as a student was becoming, and she decided to focus her multimodal document on something she was learning in order to reduce her stress: yoga. In a mid-project blog posting, she noted that her method was to begin with storyboarding and gathering materials: "I had drawn a storyboard in my notebook and I knew which images I wanted to use *and* which songs . . . I found it surprisingly easy to put the images I wanted along with music and fun transitions."

Her choices came together nicely in the final product, which opened to an image of Elyse grimacing, eyes closed, hands on head, with the opening strands of the Queen/David Bowie collaboration "Under Pressure" playing in the background. As the topic transitioned from life's stressors to Elyse's solution—yoga—the background switched to a quiet, soothing, acoustic music with an Asian flavor. Trying to reach an audience of peers, she makes clear in her post-project blog entry that she cares deeply for the subject matter:

> I wanted to relate the benefits of yoga to the life of a college student. I have been soo stressed and it feels like I can never catch up. When I started doing yoga this semester I honestly felt a difference in my over all health. I *believe* in the benefits of yoga and I wanted to make that clear in my movie. Basically I had four aspects of learning that I wanted to address: *what* I'm learning, *why* I'm learning, *how* I'm learning, and if it works. Easier said than done my friend.

Elyse's work on the multimodal project exemplifies two important aspects of composing: the need for a genuine audience, and the significance of personal engagement with the topic. Although she initially felt intimidated by the scope of the project ("Make a movie? are you kidding me??" she blogged), her belief that the outcome would have significance kept her working throughout.

Case 4: Michelle

Initially, Michelle had trouble identifying a topic for her project. An early-semester blog posting had her claiming that "Actually I don't think I've learned much lately, but I have been trying to be a better student, and make time for homework. I have been trying to hang out with others out of my 'comfort zone.'" These ideas proved to be too vague for serious pursuit. Michelle, however, finally discovered that she already had a subject when talking incidentally about her Spring Break plans. She was struggling to raise funds for a return visit to her host family in Costa Rica, where she had been an exchange student, and the need to budget carefully proved to be an engaging focus for her project. In her document, "Spring Break On a College Student's Budget," she identifies three areas of problem spending in her own life: going out to eat, shopping for recreation, and barhopping. She provides a solution to each through short video clips of herself cooking, borrowing clothes from roommates, and entertaining friends at home. The way she represents each of these solutions, however, doesn't minimize the difficulty of implementing them; as she peers into a full refrigerator, she says, "There are so many things I could cook in here, but it's just not that tempting. Does it look tempting to you?" The same sense of ironic (but necessary) compromise appears as she rifles through her friends' closets for clothes and shoes later in the document. In Michelle's end-of-semester blog reflection, she noted the ways that her multimodal document would impact her future as a teacher:

> The Video Doc. is something that i never thought i could pull off. It seemed like such a challenge, i consider myself pretty nifty with computers and the net but this assignment was a big struggle. It showed me that there are many ways in which a student can showing their writing through different outlets. I'd like to be able to do an assignment like this with my own students one day, and although it may seem impossible at the begining it is very do able.

While one strength of Michelle's project was that it situated the abstract idea of budgeting within the actual social practices of college students—in keeping with Gee's notion of pattern-based thinking—its impact on her as a future teacher seems more significant. Rather than thinking of writing as limited to traditional forms, she expresses a desire to stretch her own conceptions of what it means to teach writing.

REVIEW

One of my NCWP colleagues, Amanda Von Kleist (2005), once used "Why Did it Work, and How Can I Do it Again?" as the working title for presentation she gave at our NWP Summer Institute. In reflecting upon the work completed by my students that first semester I taught the multimodal document, the same question arises. My students were uniformly successful in completing the project, taking great pride and feeling personally invested in their work. The quality of the work, too, exceeded that of the literacy narrative assignment the multimodal project replaced. Students effectively integrated personal narrative and academic sources in both assignments, but the multimodal document excelled in terms of the writer's purposeful and effective engagement of the audience. It was clear that, when students' engagement with the work actually differed in the two assignments, the multimodal document more fully represented and captured that engagement.

So what happened that helped the project work, and what role did the infusion of technology play in that success?

- *Collaboration and Decentering.* First, it was clearly a collaborative effort throughout. The students' collective solutions to (often technology centered) problems—aided by my own limited expertise in the creation of such projects—contributed to a decentering of the knowledge in the course. The variety of topics students chose for their projects, in a similar way, made public the array of talents and skills embodied by the collective class population. In short, it seems as though the multimodal project helped enact the kind of critical learning McLaren and da Silva (1993) have argued for in *Decentering Pedagogy.* They argue that learners "gain a greater purchase on social agency through a critical narrativization . . . of their own histories" (p. 52). The increased investment by my students in the course's expertise and direction certainly seems to point toward the efficacy of decentered instruction. This would fall under what Gee (2004) calls the "appreciative system" wherein learners' goals and desires conspire to create a new valuing of events and outcomes (pp. 96–97).
- *Mediating Schema.* While working on the multimodal document project, students tended to have a very clear vision of their desired final projects. Their problems with composing were technical and pragmatic—how to achieve their visions—rather than conceptual or structural. I attribute this at least in part to the students' schema for multimodal texts. Although the particularities of the assigned work differed in many respects from films and television shows, the general tropes of the medium (transitions, narrative flow and pacing, visual impacts, sound effects) carried over into the project. In other words, the students' knowledge of multimodality acts to use Carol D. Lee's (2005) phrase, as a "semiotic mediation" rooted in students' cultural schema. This semiotic mediation—the system of meaning that intervenes between what students know and what they want to achieve—provides schematic cues for learners, helping them see "how to raise appropriate questions,

how to attend to salient parts of the text, how to generate arguments using both textual and real-world knowledge, and how to monitor this understanding" (p. 273).

* *Identity.* Closely related to the role of schema in the students' success is the way that students adopted an identity as a composer (or director, or writer, as these terms were used rather synonymously by students). In past classes, students in the midst of writing more traditional essays often found themselves somewhat lost, feeling neither sure where their compositions were leading, nor how to find (and reach) their destinations. The genre of the multimodal document, coupled with the technology used to produce it, seemed to support students' ability to vest themselves in what Gee (2003) calls a "projective identity" (p. 55). This is the simultaneous creation of a new identity related to a particular project (activity or practice), and the projection of oneself into that identity, a process reinforced when the project's efforts are marked by some degree of success. In subsequent assignments for the class, students asked again and again if they could create multimodal projects. They were anxious to maintain their identities as composers in this new genre.

EJECT

I began this chapter by considering my students' requests for recommendation letters, and how those requests had begun referencing particular projects completed by the students. Obviously, the projects referenced were the multimodal documents. My students' use of those projects in their requests to me serves as an indicator of two important aspects of the project's role in the class. First, students apparently see their multimodal documents as a touchstone of identity; that is, their references suggest that the projects, at least to some degree, are representations of the students themselves. This is indicative of the students' level of engagement and ownership in the project; the work had become inextricably tied to their own sense of identity within the class. Second, the assumption made by students that their projects would successfully identify them—a correct assumption, in this case—points toward a classroom environment that placed considerable "value" on work completed in the class. I put "value" in scare quotes because it seems clear that the value here goes well beyond the grading weight carried by the assignment. This is further indicated by the insistence of the class on holding a viewing day for the projects. While prior classes have also enthusiastically completed assignments, I never fielded unanimous requests to spend a class period with everyone reading aloud their essays (although this may say more about my other assignments than anything else). The class environment, as a whole, benefited from the shared investment all course stakeholders had in the multimodal document.

The technology available to students clearly had a significant role in the success of the multimodal project. Online resources of rich and interactive information like the Internet Archive, Flickr photo hosting and sharing, and the Podsafe music network, provided students with materials for their projects. Programs like Windows Movie Maker and iMovie facilitated students' fashioning their raw materials into finished projects. Online hosting services like YouTube and Blogger allowed students to contribute their expressions to the public. The various technologies, in and of themselves, did not lead to the success of my students' multimodal projects, but the computer-based resources very obviously were essential to facilitating the work. Without the technology, the visions my students had for their projects would not have been realized—and I would never have received those emails saying, "I made the digital document about . . ."

REFERENCES

Bishop, W. (2004). *On writing: A process reader*. Boston: McGraw Hill.

Brandt, D. (1998). Sponsors of literacy. *College composition and communication, 49*(2), 165–185.

Center for Digital Storytelling. (2008). Retrieved June 6, 2008, from http://www .storycenter.org/index1.html/

Gadda, G., & Walsh, W. (1988). Analytical writing in the university. In G. Gadda, F. Peitzman, & W. Walsh (Eds.), *Teaching analytical writing* (pp. 1–22). Los Angeles: California Academic Partnership Program.

Gee, J. P. (2003). *What video games have to teach us about learning and literacy*. New York: Palgrave Macmillan.

Hodgson, K., & Kaplan, B. (Eds.) (2008). *Collaborative ABC movie project*. Retrieved May 18, 2008, from http://dogwritingideas.wikispaces.com/ABC2007

Lave, J., & Wenger, E. (1991). *Situated learning: Legitimate peripheral participation*. New York: Cambridge University Press.

Lee, C. D. (2005). Signifying in the zone of proximal development. In H. Daniels (Ed.), *An introduction to Vygotsky* (pp. 253–284). New York: Routledge.

McLaren, P., & da Silva, T. T. (1993). Decentering pedagogy: Critical literacy, resistance, and the politics of memory. In P. McLaren & P. Leonard (Eds.), *Paulo Freire: A critical encounter* (pp. 47–89). New York: Routledge.

Rose, M. (1990). *Lives on the boundary: A moving account of the struggles and achievements of America's educationally underprepared*. New York: Penguin.

Shiroff, J. (2008). *Daddy duty*. Retrieved May 15, 2008, from http://www.archive .org/details/JasonShiroffDigitalStory/

Sullivan, P. (2006). An essential question: What is "college-level" writing? In

P. Sullivan & H. Tinberg (Eds.), *What is college level writing* (pp. 1–28). Urbana, IL: National Council of Teachers of English.

Tilly, C. (2003). *Stories, identities, and political change.* Lanham, MD: Rowman & Littlefield.

Von Kleist, A. (2005, August). *Why did it work, and how can I do it again?* Working title of paper presented at NWP Summer Institute. Later presented (2005, December) at the Annual Meeting of the National Writing Project as Exploring home and community: Providing opportunities for students to be experts.

Warlick, D. Teacher-crafted educational web environments: ClassWebs. Retrieved April 28, 2008, from http://pinetlibrary.com/page_files/classweb.pdf

CHAPTER 11

Multiple Modes of Production in a College Writing Class

ALANNA FROST
JULIE A. MYATT
STEPHEN SMITH

> We have a moment.
> —Kathleen Blake Yancey, 2004

We, three teachers of first year composition, found ourselves in this moment and decided that we did not want to be left behind. We want to share our participation in what we understand as the irrepressible buzz heard by teachers of writing and described by Yancey's 2004 CCCCs Chair's Address. For us, it was a moment when we could no longer ignore the beckoning of technology in our writing classrooms, when we could no longer look away from YouTube, when we became increasingly curious about our students' elaborately authored Facebook pages and complex text messages. As teachers who collectively have 48 years of experience teaching writing to high school and college students, we have begun to understand, as Yancey (2004) articulates, that "never before has the proliferation of writings outside the academy so counterpointed the composition inside," and that "never before have the technologies of writing contributed so quickly to the creation of new genres" (p. 298). If we are indeed to be charged, as the Council of Writing Program Administrators (2000) directs us, with instructing students to "use conventions of format and structure appropriate to the rhetorical situation," then we know that in this moment, we must begin to utilize composition pedagogies that engage our students in recognizing and applying the rhetorical possibilities of all the technologies available to them. In this moment, we must begin immersing ourselves in what Shipka (2005) calls "students' uptakes of a much wider, richer repertoire of semiotic resources" (p. 279).

We are fortunate that we could turn to scholars and colleagues who recognized this moment and its multiple semiotic resources before we did. We are also fortunate to be working in an academic setting where, though departmental outcomes still refer to the number of pages students should write, our discomfort at the prospect of assigning projects that couldn't be word-count quantified was tempered by administrative support of our exploratory approach to the teaching of writing. Indeed, our department encourages instructor autonomy. Our program director insists that any number of approaches lead to effective writing instruction; and therefore no department syllabus is used, nor is there a common text. This freedom has encouraged us to take risks in our teaching. During the course of the experiment we describe here, the word *composing* itself grew increasingly more important to us. Clearly we continue to deal in written texts, but what we teach students is how to get their ideas across, to make meaning, to say what it is they want to say regardless of the medium they choose. Moving away from the word *writing* allows us to stop privileging print and thus stop limiting our—and our students'—communicative abilities. Our students' multimodal compositions, whether the product of scissor and glue technology or digital sound and image, reflect ever-changing technologies and material access to them in a way that has, perhaps, become invisible in word-processing pedagogies. This project allowed us to make these issues more visible to students as they engaged in acts of inquiry and negotiation necessary in defining their rhetorical context and justifying subsequent choices. In this chapter, each of us will individually describe our course projects, and then collectively, we will offer some closing reflections.

ALANNA—DIVING IN

The time had come for me to open up my writing classroom to composing that was multimodal, far different in its forms and communicative potentials than the linear, argumentative, and word-processed essay. Colliding with this realization were my colleagues' similar interests—both my coauthors and several peers who solicited our contribution to their own research project. In the interests of the research project, it was Julie's and my job to give a multimodal assignment to our first year composition class as the first project of the semester (see Appendix A). The timing meant that we would not have time to learn all of the potential technologies our students had to choose from to complete their projects.

> My misconception: I must learn all the software and applications prior to creating assignments that involve said mysterious tools.

A second and appealing requirement of involving the class in this research project was that the students would use the data they had gathered for their multimodal assignments for completion of project two: a traditional essay. While there remained much trepidation (and mystery) surrounding project one—what would our students' work look like? How would we assess projects which varied obviously in content and drastically in appearance?— we felt that the second project was our comfortable backup. We and our students could go out on a limb with multimodality and then return to familiar territory. What was interesting about this sequence was that we could at the same time debate with our students the merits of both multimodal and traditional composing.

Julie and I had already chosen literacy as a theme for the course. In class we read and discussed with our students selections from several rhetoric and composition scholars concerned with challenging cultural, pedagogical, and classroom-specific definitions of literacy. Important to our conversations were Barton and Hamilton's (2000) discussion of "literacy practices," Brandt's (2004) articulation of "literacy sponsors," and DeRosa's (2004) take on first year composition's "literacy narratives." As DeRosa says,

> The . . . definitions of literacy that writers bring with them to first year composition courses reinforce ideas about literacy as a fixed or static construct—a set of skills to be measured in a single writing event/test or acquired in a semester college writing course. (p. 1)

Importantly, we felt a focus on literacy cohered with the multiple literacies with which the class would engage, and because we believed in the pedagogical merits of teaching students about cultural, local, and personal understandings of literacy, we decided to organize the course around encouraging students to interrogate the term. A significant part of that interrogation was incorporated into the very first multimodal project.

Our Students' Assignments

As described on our assignment sheet, students were required to "compose a multimodal profile essay describing and commenting on one individual's experiences with literacy." I discovered early on in the process that the journey between handing out the project assignment instructions and collecting finished projects was remarkably similar to any other writing assignment I had given out.

My misconception: I will need to drastically alter my pedagogy to accommodate multi-modal assignments.

The students did have a different take on the similarity of the projects; many were very uncomfortable with what they felt was unfamiliar territory:

Upon receiving the guidelines for this project I had no clue what I was going to do. I didn't understand what the professor wanted and I couldn't even begin to develop any possible topics. This project put me into a position where I didn't think that I had any control and I didn't really enjoy it.(Ava)

When starting this project, I felt extremely lost and confused. (Molly)

But during the process I was repeatedly surprised at my own ability to put out the fires of panicked students with standard explanations of how to compose. Thus, when students expressed hesitation at getting started because they "didn't know how," I explained that a good place to start, in any research project, is by gathering data. Questions about the amount of details to include sparked class discussions about audience and purpose. Further, there were useful similarities in terminology. The student whose drafted project was a video recording of his interview and which began with the interview itself was told by peers that he needed an introduction. A student who moved too rapidly in her project from visual PowerPoint slides of her participant to written analysis of the woman's reading habits was told that she needed transitions.

Assessment

My fears of assessing the multimodal projects were allayed long before I collected the students' work. Daily class discussion about the students' rhetorical choices, which so closely mirrored discussions of a traditional essay— "I can't decide where to place my main point"—were comforting. The students were graded for the semester on an Excellent, Satisfactory, Unsatisfactory scale, according to the criteria given in the assignment (see Appendix A). Julie and I created a rubric discussing the features of a satisfactory project and the students went over the rubric long before the project was due.

This is not to downplay assessment angst, particularly of such a range of genre and medium. What seemed best to anchor such a new assessment task was the requirement described in the rubric as "effectively employ[ing] the affordances the selected mediums offer." Whether the student had chosen a means that effectively conveyed his or her main point was very obvious. One student, for example, chose to describe his friend's musical literacy by giving me a CD that incorporated text written on the CD itself as well as musical recordings of the music. His work clearly demonstrated an understanding of benefits of the use of music and the limits in his musical choices to completely convey the results of his interview. The student who presented his mother's piano literacy on a playbill received an Excellent in his use of affordance, while the student who used a scrapbook which included many pictures of her friend playing the piano but without an explanation received a lesser score.

I will conclude with my students' assessment of their multimodal assignments, offered in a commentary to "future Alanna students," as I think they sum up what I learned as well:

> This semester we learned how to do multimodal projects. This was my first experience with them and it was terrifying at first. Don't let it freak you out. The hardest part was getting started. A good place to always begin is with a broad thesis and some supporting facts. As you go along and begin your projects your thesis will develop and change into something more complex. I started this class not knowing what a flash drive was and now, at the end, I can make my own movie on the computer. (Molly)

> In this class you will get to create projects using multiple skills, talents and creativity to form coherent arguments, which will be a lot more fun then linear composition and allow you to obtain skills that, may be more applicable to how we communicate our ideas today through a variety of mediums. It is important to remember this course may stretch you to think beyond your typical style of composition which will still require work and planning like all composition, but the process of composing will be more enjoyable and seem less like work (in my opinion). Multimodal compositions are great way to explore your own abilities and adopt others. (Laricia)

JULIE: THE HYBRID ESSAY—USING CRITIQUE AS A BRIDGE TO DESIGN

For the third assignment of the semester, my students were asked to select a popular culture text relying on the combination of word and image (such as a Web page, blog, television news program, graphic novel, and so forth) and to conduct a close reading of it, paying special attention to its design features and speculating as to why the designers made the choices they did (see Appendix B). After analyzing their chosen texts, students were to present their observations in *hybrid essays*, so named in an attempt to emphasize that these otherwise traditional essays should use word and image together with each playing an equal role in informing readers rather than rely on what Kress (1998) has identified as a less rhetorically effective use of illustration, in which "the written text carries all the information, and the image 'repeats' that information" (p. 64).

As one would expect, the texts the students elected to analyze were as varied as the students themselves. One studied a series of frames from the graphic novel *Persepolis 2*; some looked at segments from television programs such as ESPN's SportsCenter, and others looked at pages from Web sites such as The Onion, People.com, MySpace, and BBCNews.

Upon receiving students' drafts for evaluation, I discovered a disconnect between what the assignment required and what students actually did, one which I believe to be the product of their familiarity with assignments that engage popular texts only in terms of discerning their hidden messages or how they try to dupe consumers, not in terms of considering the choices the designers made in creating the texts. One of the most challenging aspects of the assignment is that of ensuring that students present a focused discussion of the text's design features and their possible effects on viewers. For students to satisfactorily complete the assignment, they must recognize design as rhetorical.

Therefore, my goals for the project included having students consider design, to recognize that they're constantly responding to others' design choices in the Web sites they visit, the television programs they watch, and the magazines they read. I wanted them to apply the tools of critique to their own compositions. Helping students understand, for example, that the placement of a picture has rhetorical meaning helps them understand a composer's agency, and thus perhaps helps them see their own.

Another goal for the hybrid essay assignment was to have students consider alphabetic text as not the only means of conveying information. As a graduate student some 2 years before, I was charged with completing a task similar to the one I presented in this assignment, and yet I did not once consider placing illustrations of the text I analyzed into my own essay. Perhaps this omission is the result of coming of age as an English major in a time when words were the privileged mode of composing in our discipline. And yet, despite their familiarity as readers with multimodal texts, I wonder how many of my own students would have thought to include pictures in their essays without being instructed to do so.

In my mind, the hybrid essay bridges the gap between the kinds of compositions students have been called upon to create in school and those they will be charged with creating in the future. What follows is a text excerpt from Kaitlin's hybrid essay. Kaitlin's essay is text heavy, and yet her analysis of The Weather Channel's local forecast is effective largely because of the way she uses image—her essay demands that readers move between her words and the illustrations she's provided:

> The pictures you see correspond with the forecast such as the sun peeking around a large dark cloud for Tuesday, when it is expected to be mostly cloudy. You cannot see in this still photo, but these pictures are animated on the screen so that the rain actually falls from the clouds, and the sun rays extend and contract around the sun. One misleading aspect of the use of these pictures can be seen on the forecast for Thursday. The picture would lead a viewer to expect rain all day due to the large dark cloud and heavy rain, but the forecast is actually only for A.M. showers. This misrepresentation is one chance that is taken when using pictures to support or replace text in such broadcasts as this one. We see that rain is expected in the morning, but what about the rest of the day? In this case of interdependent combination of the two, that picture takes away from the text where the main content may be better understood with text only. "Interdependent combinations [of picture and text] aren't always an equal balance and may fall anywhere on a scale between word specific and picture specific" (McCloud, 2006, p. 712). This is a case of more text specific and the picture is not needed at all.

As Kaitlin's essay demonstrates, students completing the hybrid essays have to consider how to convey meaning to reader/viewers by using both word and image. They are not only writers, but designers whose choices are informed by the insights they gain while critiquing someone else's design choices. Although Kress notes that "The social and political task of the designer is fundamentally different to that of the critic" (p. 78), I propose that providing students with assignments that allow them to critique someone else's design choices while at the same time being mindful of their own will help prepare them for a future in which "the facilities of design rather than those of critique will be essential for equitable participation in social, economic and cultural life" (p. 79).

STEVE: NEGOTIATING THE BRIDGE TO MULTIMODAL COMPOSITION

Julie's metaphor of the hybrid essay as a bridge between writing traditional print essays and composing in multimodal forms reminds me that I have been approaching this bridge for some time. In the fall of 1991 I learned of

Kentucky's writing assessment, the CATS Writing Portfolio, that would be produced throughout Kentucky public schools at the 4th, 8th and 12th grade levels (Kentucky Department of Education, 2006). Over the next 15 years I attended regional training sessions where representatives of the schools were instructed in the development and scoring of the portfolios. One scoring policy we were informed of every year was that only the *writing* was to be scored. Other textual features, like pictures, photos, tables, and graphs, could be present in the text but would not affect the scoring of the portfolio in any way. Such nonprint additions were not considered to be writing per se. This scoring policy remained the same all the way through the academic year, 2005–2006, my last year as a public high school teacher. As the editors of this collection stated in Chapter 1, "For all of these assessments—even Kentucky's—only traditional print-based writings are assessed." Therefore, when one of my students would ask if she could include a graphic novel as her literary entry, I had to tell her that only the words in the speech/thought bubbles and any narration would be scored. The graphic component of the narrative would not affect the score, regardless of how well-drawn the panels were.

Fast forward to the fall of 2006 when, inspired by such scholars as Kress, Shipka, and Yancey, as well as working in collaboration with my coauthors, I decided prior to the coming spring semester at the university—now that I no longer had to comply with the heavy hand of No Child Left Behind high stakes assessment—that I wanted to teach my students multiple modes of composing. However, looking back over my class's portfolios from the last semester, I realize I have not completely crossed over the bridge—yet. How can I tell? Three pervasive features of their texts give it away:

1. The dominance of print in almost all of the work
2. Students' placement of pictures and hyperlinks found on the Internet as valiant but print-based attempts to make their papers multimodal
3. The almost complete lack of other modes, especially video and audio files.

How did this happen? In an effort to understand the pitfalls of good pedagogical intentions, I think it could be helpful for my own and others' future course design efforts to examine how my class did not truly become a class in multimodal composition.

Excited by the affordances but intimidated by the machinery of New Media, I thought I would start on a small scale and focus the course on exploring visual literacy and visual rhetoric, both of which are in strong evidence in my students' portfolios. Technically, the students' discussion of visual texts and their own inclusion of visual elements in their papers did make their compositions multimodal; the papers however, look very similar to the ones from those high school portfolios. One way to understand this lack of transformation is to examine the writing tasks I gave the students. In the assignment descriptions for all four major papers, there is no requirement to use more than two modes and no encouragement to go beyond the requirement. Here are the key passages that would affect the students' choice of modes:

- Paper 1: Form: Most likely a memoir but I am open to other forms if you can explain your plan.
- Paper 2: Your job is to design a multimodal Valentine. You must use at least one other mode besides print to construct an argument.
- Paper 3: You'll then present your observations in a hybrid essay. By hybrid essay I mean that you are to write your observations in an organized essay that includes images in the text to illustrate the various points you wish to make. You'll want to be thoughtful about how to guide your readers through your words and the illustrations you provide them.
- Paper 4: Use more than one mode.

Only the assignment for the first paper even admits the possibility of using other modes but uses the word *form*, very different from *mode*, which is the carrier/conduit of the message. Two of the other three assignments only offer the option of using more than two modes. Because the course was designed around the relationship between images and words, the students naturally chose to stick to images as the other mode—and static images at that, as do Alan Moore (1995) in *The Watchmen* and William Blake (1997) in *Songs of Innocence and Experience*, two central texts in the course. If we adopt Wetherbee Phelps' (1989) Practice–Theory–Practice arc as a model of pedagogical transformation, we can see that my practice was trying to catch up to my theory.

There may be a better reason why transformation did not occur, however, and that would be my failure to make explicit the connection between the course goals and composing in multiple modes. If teaching in a high-stakes testing environment (like Kentucky's CATS Writing Portfolio) for 15 years taught me anything, it taught me that whatever gets assessed is what gets taught by teachers and learned by students, for better or for worse. But I was not confident enough in my teaching of multiple modes to make the connection between the departmental course outcomes and my vision of what the students should be able to accomplish.

I could have drawn on the first section of the departmental outcomes for English 105, which is "Rhetorical Knowledge (responding appropriately to a variety of rhetorical situations)" (University of Louisville Composition Program, n.d.). This outcome, which covers focused purpose, audience analysis, consistent tone, genre adaptation, and evidence, easily lends itself, because of its broad construction of any given rhetorical context, to the teaching of multimodal composing. For example, whether a student decided to embed a video in a written composition as evidence for an argument, or decided to make a video that constructed the same argument with few written words, the composition would still need to meet the outcome's first stated goal: "Focuses on a clear and consistent purpose." If the video was embedded as evidence to support an argument, then the student would need to decide if it "Analyzes and responds to the needs of different audiences" and "Employs a tone consistent with purpose and audience," both of which are also goals from the first outcome. I now realize that I could have taught the use of any mode as a rhetorical decision, not as another or different or superior or new way to make meaning.

While I was struggling to design, teach, and assess assignments that asked students to consider multiple modes, at least one student in my section somehow managed to catch enough of a glimpse of what was truly possible. I wish I could recall the conversation verbatim, but what I do remember was that Whitney told me that she was worried that she was not fulfilling the requirements of the third assignment, which was to write a hybrid essay critiquing a pop culture artifact. When I looked at her PowerPoint presentation about the website purepwnage.com/, I realized that she knew how to compose in a multimodal fashion. There were hyperlinks to supporting Web sites with helpful definitions, there was a professionally vetted essay covering relevant issues, there were MP3 downloads of music from the show, and there were embedded purepwnage videos, all of them meaning-making components in collaboration with important threads of her argument that she was composing.

I wish I could take some of the credit for this composing moment, but I really think all Whitney needed to hear from me was my enthusiastic "Yes! Keep doing what you're doing." Whitney was clearly not intimidated by the machinery of New Media. She wanted to make sure, though, that she had not abandoned the assignment requirements. Granted, the videos, the Web sites, even the PowerPoint template design, were not Whitney's original work, but Whitney had made a strong move toward her emerging identity as a multimodal composer. She had begun to see herself as a bricoleur, a builder of messages in multiple modes, and not just a composer-in-print.

Perhaps I overstate the case, but Whitney's (and my) "Aha!" moment convinced me that I needed to do more than teach a bimodal course based upon print and the visual. Now that the new semester is under way, and I have the benefits of teaching the course again and being in closer collaboration with Alanna and Julie, I have been revising the course material and assignments to stress all modes as equally as possible. One way I see this happening is through a closer inquiry into all semiotic domains of meaning (Gee, 2003) so that we can move beyond our greatest strength and greatest weakness—a reliance upon print media to make meaning.

CONCLUSIONS

This chapter is intended to convey our experience with multimodal composing in a way that alleviates anxiety about such works. However, we had anxieties of our own: opening our classrooms to technologies that our students know more about than we do; and assessing these assignments that at first appeared so very different from those we had encountered previously. These issues, combined with our excitement about working with new media forms, at times caused us to place more emphasis on technology and clouded our stance on assessment. Our crisis of confidence frustrated both us and our students, often leading to exchanges where they would ask questions not unlike those teachers of traditional text-based assignments would hear. Our responses of "it depends" sounded to our students like nonanswers because we failed to make evident the connection between their projects and principles of rhetoric. To remedy this in future semesters, we have endeavored to make rhetoric more present in our discussions of students' composing choices, responding to their inquiries with questions of our own:

Student: Do our pictures need captions?
Teacher: Will your *audience* expect captions?
Student: Do we have to cite our sources?
Teacher: How would neglecting to include sources affect your *ethos*?
Student: Can I make a MySpace page for my project?
Teacher: What's your *purpose*, or what are you trying to accomplish, and how would a MySpace page allow you to do that?

These kinds of dialogues lead to discussions about the assignment criteria. In this way, we and our students could translate our past composing experiences to the multimodal assignment at hand, seeing connections between the assignment requirements and what we knew of composing generally. Borton and Huot (2007) assert the importance of "a rhetorical understanding of composition" as the groundwork for "all composing tasks, including multimodal projects" (p. 99). Though these multimodal projects are in many ways different from what we and our students are accustomed to, we found that these assignments allowed us to take into consideration our students' composing choices in ways we might not with traditional print essays. Though we believe that students will become more proficient communicators if they have basic rhetorical principles guiding their composing choices, we must make them aware of this as well, helping them understand that they don't have to seek the teacher's approval but rather must determine for themselves whether a given technique is appropriate for that composing context.

And so we begin the moment again in a new semester. Alanna is repeating the assignments from last semester and feeling much more confident, telling her students that they can and will get through this very first multimodal assignment. Julie has reordered her assignments so that the hybrid essay comes first, followed by the traditional profile essay and then its multimodal companion piece. To her, it makes sense to start with the hybrid essay, as it does have as one component the kind of writing students are used to doing for school (though she believes that there is a case to be made for starting with an assignment that completely disrupts students' notions about what college writing—or simply writing—is). Steve has begun the semester with an inquiry into multiple semiotic domains, not just the visual one, in the hope that his students will think more critically about the rhetorical options afforded by the mode they choose as they begin to compose.

Finally, we'd like to offer some suggestions for those considering teaching multimodal compositions in the future:

- Think about the goals you possess for student writing and how the language you use is a reflection of them. Making a small move like using the word *compose* instead of *write* can empower students to think of themselves as multimodal composers, as individuals who have a variety of rhetorical choices at their disposal.
- Know that it's okay if you're not familiar with all the technologies out there; many of our students are more familiar with them than we are, and we found that our students were often able to help each other work through technology-related problems.
- Know that high tech isn't necessarily better. Some of the best projects we received involved simple cutting and pasting of clip art, magazine photos, and so forth.
- Know that your expertise about writing still applies. You should rely on that knowledge when responding to students' projects.
- Provide students with a list of evaluation criteria as early as possible so they'll know what your goals for the project are. You want your list to be broad enough that they will still apply to the varied modes your students will use.
- Stress to your students that technology doesn't trump thought—that they are still charged with making meaning, not just with creating a flashy presentation.
- Encourage students to be creative where their ideas and technology meet—and be willing to be flexible about the quality of their images.

Several of Julie's students captured images of television programs by taking digital photos of them and then uploading those into their hybrid essays.

- Help your students understand their work as rhetorical, as an opportunity to consider how best to address their situation and audience using the most appropriate modes, regardless of what they may be.

ACKNOWLEDGMENTS

Alanna and Julie: Thanks to Kara Poe Alexander, Sonya Borton, Elizabeth Powell, and Rene Prys for inviting us to participate in their study and for giving us the idea for the multimodal profile assignment.

Julie: Thanks to Bronwyn Williams, who introduced me to the assignment that I adapted into the hybrid essay.

All: Thanks to our students, who worked so hard on these composing projects.

APPENDIX A: PROJECT I—MULTIMODAL PROFILE ESSAY

Brief Description

For this assignment you will compose a multimodal profile essay describing and commenting on one individual's experiences with literacy.

Expanded Description

For our purposes, a multimodal essay is one that combines two or more mediums of composing, such as audio, video, photography, printed text, magazine cutouts, a hypertext web document, a Web site, a poster board, video game, etc. One of the goals of this assignment is to allow you to explore different modes of composing.

We're taking literacy as our focus this semester, considering what constitutes literacy, how one becomes literate, how our notion of literacy changes over time and with the introduction of new technologies, etc. In this multimodal profile, you should focus on the individual's experiences as a literate person. You may also choose to focus on one particular literacy event in the person's life. Ideally, the interpretations you present in your multimodal essay will be informed by assigned readings and class discussions.

This assignment requires field research, meaning that you will have to go out and research your subject, much like a reporter on an assignment. You will observe, interview, and take notes on your subject, and then compile this information you gather to form a multimodal essay that both informs and engages readers. The person you profile should be someone you have access to on a semiregular basis since you will be visiting/seeing/interviewing your subject several times. Regardless of whom you choose to profile, you will need to incorporate observation and interviews into your multimodal essay.

Requirements

Your multimodal essay should:

- Employ the affordances (capabilities) of the medium you're using in effective rhetorical ways;
- Be characterized by careful design that helps to convey meaning;
- Add informational value to our discussion of literacy issues/themes;
- Be instructive, that is, inventive, creative, insightful;
- Do more than simply inform the audience; it should also help readers/viewers reflect on and gain insight into the subject;
- Cite any source you use, whether an image, an interview, a magazine ad, or an audio, video, TV clip.

I'm not setting a required length for this project. As you decide on an appropriate length, you need to consider rhetorical elements (audience, purpose, situation, genre, context) that will affect the outcome of your project, and then choose a length that works for those purposes and reasons. If you have questions about whether your project is sufficient lengthwise, ask me and we can work something out together. Remember, you'll be handing this project in to me, so make sure it's in a format I can access.

Criteria for Evaluation

For this assignment, Satisfactory projects will:

- Include only those details relevant to a discussion of the person's experiences as a literate person;
- Effectively incorporate field research (observation and interview) and synthesize information rather than present a straight reporting of facts;
- Reveal the writer's attitude toward the subject, offering an interpretation of it;
- Effectively employ the affordances the selected mediums offer;
- Contain evidence of careful planning and an attempt to present information vividly.

Unsatisfactory projects will fall short of these minimum requirements; Excellent projects will exceed them.

APPENDIX B: PROJECT 3—HYBRID ESSAY
ANALYSIS OF A POP CULTURE TEXT

Brief Description

This assignment asks you to analyze a popular culture genre or form in terms of how it might be relevant to the theories of literacy and new technologies we've been discussing this semester.

Expanded Description

For this project you want to select a popular culture text that relies on the combination of word and image (possibilities include but are not limited to: Web sites, television news programs, comic books or graphic novels, magazine articles, textbooks, owner's manuals, zines, blogs, and so forth). You are then to conduct a close reading of the text, paying special attention to its features and how they work together or perhaps fail to do so, as the case may be; asking questions about why the designers chose to combine word and image in the ways that they did; positing an intended reader for the text, and so forth.

You'll then present your observations in a hybrid essay. By hybrid essay I mean that you are to write your observations in an organized essay that includes images of the text to illustrate the various points you wish to make. You'll want to be thoughtful about how to guide your readers through your words and the illustrations you provide them. Consider what kinds of signposts or directions you'll need to provide readers with so they'll know when they can expect to see or when they should pause to review the images. You may decide to use captions or headings, or perhaps you'd prefer to give readers instructions in the body of your essay. The choice is yours; just make sure readers can follow your instructions. Questions to consider:

- In what ways and to what ends does the text rely on word and image?
- What assumptions does this text make about reader/viewers and their abilities to decode its features?
- Who might be the intended audience of such a text? Another way you might approach this question is to consider what segment of the population you think would be able to navigate this text with the most ease. What tools do they have at their disposal that others don't?
- What other kinds of popular culture texts or practices might have influenced this particular genre?
- Does the text privilege one feature over another? What leads you to this conclusion, and what might this reveal about the designer's (and perhaps even societal) beliefs about word and image?

Sources

You are expected to connect your ideas with some of the readings we have done this semester. You may also refer to outside sources you find helpful to the ideas you're exploring. If you're looking for ideas about sources, let me know; I may be able to help. Sources should be cited in Modern Language Association (MLA) format, including parenthetical citations and a Works Cited page.

Physical Features

Your 6 to 9 page double-spaced essay should be formatted in a standard 12-point font and contain an original title.

REFERENCES

Barton, D. & Hamilton, M. (2000). Literacy Practices. In D. Barton, M. Hamilton, & R. Ivanic (Eds.), *Situated literacies: Reading and writing in context.* (pp. 7–15). London: Routledge.

Blake, W. (1967). *Songs of innocence and experience.* Oxford: Oxford University Press.

Borton, S., & Huot, B. (2007). Responding and assessing. In C. L. Selfe (Ed.), *Multimodal composition: Resources for teachers* (pp. 99–111). Creskill, NJ: Hampton Press.

Brandt, D. (2004). Sponsors of literacy. *College Composition and Communication, 49,* 165–85.

Council of Writing Program Administrators. *WPA Outcomes statement for first-year composition.* (2000, April). Retrieved March 13, 2008, from http://www.wpacouncil.org/positions/outcomes.html

DeRosa, S. (2004). Literacy narratives as genres of possibility: Students' voices, reflective writing, and rhetorical awareness. *Ethos.* Retrieved December 10, 2006, from http://www.pserie.psu.edu/academic/lrc/ethos/teach/DeRosa%20Article.pdf

Gee, J. (2003). *What video games have to teach us about learning and literacy.* New York: Palgrave Macmillan.

Kentucky Department of Education. (2006). *Kentucky writing handbook: Helping students develop as proficient writers and learners.* Kentucky Department of Education, Frankfort, KY.

Kress, G. (1998). Visual and verbal modes of representation in electronically mediated communication: the potentials of new forms of text. In I. Snyder (Ed.), *Page to screen: Taking literacy into the electronic era* (pp. 53–79). London: Routledge.

McCloud, S. (2006). Show and tell. In D. McQuade and C. McQuade (Eds,), *Seeing and Writing 3* (pp. 695–718). Boston: Bedford/St. Martin's.

Moore, A. (1995). *The watchmen.* New York: DC Comics.

Phelps, L. W. (1989). Images of student writing: The deep structure of teacher response. In C. Anson (Ed.), *Writing and response: Theory, practice, and research* (pp. 37–67). Urbana, IL: NCTE.

Satrapi, M. (2005). *Persepolis 2: The story of a return.* New York: Pantheon.

Shipka, J. (2005). A multimodal task-based framework for composing. *College Composition and Communication, 57,* 277–306.

University of Louisville Composition Program. (n.d.). *Outcomes for English 105.* Retrieved March 13, 2008, from the University of Louisville Composition Program Web site: http://louisville.edu/english/composition-program.url/105–outcomes.html

Yancey, K. B. (2004). Made not only in words: Composition in a new key. *College Composition and Communication, 56,* 297–328.

CHAPTER 12

Technology, Change, and Assessment

What We Have Learned

ANNE HERRINGTON
KEVIN HODGSON
CHARLES MORAN

As we, the three editors, read through the chapters that were written for this book, we found what we had expected and hoped for: teachers working creatively with an expanded sense of what *writing* is becoming as it has accommodated emerging technologies. We also found a great deal that we had not expected. In this closing chapter, we draw together these reflections, using three key words from the title of the book: technology, change, and assessment, as our structure. We begin with what we expected, and what surprised us, in the teachers' use of *technology*, and then move to expectations and surprises in the kinds of *change* we saw happening, and conclude with what we'd expected, and what we found, in the area of *assessment*.

TECHNOLOGY

When we issued our call for proposals, we had hoped that our book would, through the classrooms depicted in the chapters, expand our sense of what the word writing might include in this new century. We were not disappointed in this expectation. Alanna Frost and her colleagues, in Chapter 11, argue that they, and we, should replace the word *writing* with the word *composing*, agreeing with Gunther Kress (1999) that the activity of *design* needs to move to the center of our pedagogy. So it is that in this chapter, and in all the others, our understanding of writing as the production of linear text is expanded to include the writing (or composing, or designing) of texts that might include words, images, sounds, and hyperlinks that connect any and all of the above to other words, images, sounds, and hyperlinks. As described in these chapters, the texts that students produce include multimedia research reports, digital picture books on science subjects, blogs, podcasts, and multimedia interpretations of poems. So it is clear that in these classrooms, as in much of the world beyond these classrooms, writing is moving from letters on the page to something new and different.

We had expected as well that increasing access to the Internet would bring change to the writing classroom, and we were not disappointed in this expectation. Our teacher-authors overwhelmingly relied on the Internet for their students' research. School librarians were often asked to work with students as researchers, but the research that resulted happened almost entirely on the Internet—which might have been accessed in the physical space of the library, but was unlikely to draw on the sources that were physically present on the shelves and tables. In Chapter 2 Marva Solomon's primary students search the Web for information for their Expert Pages, while in Chapter 9 Mya Poe and Julianne Opperman argue that learning to search the Internet and use electronic databases is central to scientific literature reviews for their high school and college-level students. And many teachers in this collection went beyond the information-gathering potentials of the Internet to the interactive potentials of Web 2.0, including in their students' projects Weblogs, Wikis, and social networking generally.

What surprised us was the extent to which paper copy still has power. The focus on paper text varied among the classrooms depicted. In Chapter 4 Kevin Hodgson's sixth-grade students, when they were asked to print out their digital science picture books, were unhappy with the results because, in their eyes, the paper copy was flat, two-dimensional, fixed. Their vision of their digital books was altered when they reverted to the paper format, even though the students began their planning on paper and then shifted to the computers for composition. In Chapter 2 Marva Solomon's rising third graders, on the other hand, were pleased and relieved to have paper copy of their Web pages, wanting the seeming permanence and easy portability that paper provides. This indicates that while a shift is happening, the true digital moment has not yet arrived, and may never fully arrive. We are still, perhaps usefully, grounded in the tangible ways of paper.

CHANGE

This brings us to our second topic, *change*. When we set out on this journey, we expected to find in these chapters a great deal that was new, particularly in the areas of new writing genres and new classroom practices. And when we began to read through the draft chapters as they came to us, initially it did seem as if in these teachers' classrooms new genres were emerging, new texts generated by the convergence of media, texts that participated in and reflected newly recurring social purposes and contexts. We expected, too, that this new writing would call forth new classroom practices. And initially it did seem as if the classrooms we were visiting in these chapters felt somehow different from the classrooms we were used to. But as we read and reread the chapters, we began to see that the changes that were occurring were gradual—that the new rested on a foundation of the old. We were reminded of the debate in the literature of technology: will change be sudden, catastrophic? Or will it be gradual and evolutionary? The change that we found was gradual, as new practices and genres evolved from the old.

It may be that in expecting and in initially finding the new we were influenced by the vocabulary of catastrophic change, a corollary to the technological determinism which is so much a part of the current discourse of technology. According to the technological determinists, the archdeacon of Victor Hugo's *Notre Dame de Paris* is right in his assessment of the powers of a new technology: *"ceci tuera cela"*—this will kill that (p. 211)—the book will kill the cathedral, the computer will kill the book, television will kill film (Duguid, 1996, p. 65; Nunberg, 1996, p. 10). But the cathedral, the book, and film are still alive and well. Technologies do not supersede one another but coexist, combine, and overlap in ways that futurists can't predict. The cathedral, the book, and film have lost ground to the emerging technologies of their time, but they have not disappeared. So it is that instead of finding a great deal that was new in our chapters—sharp breaks with the past—we found, as we should have expected, that we were seeing evolutionary change, incremental and gradual, where the genres and classroom practices of the past provided the foundation for the genres and practices of the present.

We see this evolutionary, gradual change in the progress of the chapter authors' introduction of technology into their curricula. In Chapter 11, Alanna Frost, Julie Myatt, and Steve Smith, who are new to teaching their course, decide to add just a bit of technology to what they have done before. They ask their students to include images in one of their assigned writings. In their next semesters, they tell us at the end of their chapter, they will go beyond this and try to support projects that include sound, video, and hyperlinks. Kevin Hodgson, who has been working with students for just 5 years, was given freedom by his administration to design a writing curriculum from scratch. This freedom gave him the opportunity to think about the convergence of technology and writing in new ways, and so over time his paper-based picture-book curriculum evolved into the digital picture book project he describes in Chapter 4.

Both Glen Bledsoe's technologically sophisticated collaborative digital writing project (Chapter 3) and Jeff Schwartz's equally sophisticated "Poetry Fusion" project (Chapter 6) are the result of years of working with technology in their classrooms, years in which their classroom practices have evolved and changed. We could argue that younger and newer teachers might be quicker to adapt to emerging technologies because they, like their students, are digital natives, whereas older teachers are digital newcomers. But in our chapters veteran teachers like Paul Allison (Chapter 5) and Peter Kittle (Chapter 10) are seeing the possibilities too and are not afraid to move their teaching in new directions.

Genres

The genres we first saw as new when we first read these chapters now seem less new, but rather modifications or combinations of already existing genres. For example, it seemed to us initially that the students' productions in Jeff Schwartz's class fall somewhere outside existing genres. Certainly this is substantial, if not catastrophic, change? Schwartz's students, as you'll remember from Chapter 6, interpret poems through audio podcasts and video. Making a video that represents a poem seems like a breakthrough, and to a degree it is. Certainly interpreting a poem by creating a video or a podcast elicits new kinds of thinking about that poem. But the students' videos and podcasts are works of interpretation, works of literary criticism, albeit in new media. They can also be seen as *homage* to the poems selected, and so they connect with a tradition of poets finding ways to praise others' work in their own poems. They can finally be seen as *imitation*, an exercise that is likely as ancient as poetry itself. So these student projects that seem to be new genres fuse previously separate genres and the human, social activities they accompany: the explication and interpretation of a poem, the praise of a poem, and the construction of a poem in imitation of another. What to call these student writings? A remix of preexisting genres? Jeff appropriately titles his chapter "Poetry Fusion."

Chapter 5 provides another example: the blogs produced by students in Paul Allison's classes seemed initially to us a new genre in that the texts produced are not themselves static, but invite responses from others and include these responses as part of what they are becoming. So they grow into a text written by a community, perhaps something like a meeting of neighbors across a backyard fence, or a meeting of an affinity group—a call-in talk show? a book circle? a New England town meeting?—for a conversation or performance. The genre is there to be built upon: the meeting of a group of people for a discussion around a topic. What the new technologies make possible, however, is freezing the discussion so that the participants can reflect and comment on it, keeping the composition in the moment. A suggestion or a comment from the audience of a blog can lead to a quick edit or change in the composition itself. No erasers needed.

For our last example of evolutionary change, the podcasting that Dawn Reed and Troy Hicks describe in Chapter 8 initially seemed to us to be a radical, technological revision of the traditional stand-and-deliver speech class. As you will remember, Reed and Hicks' students prepare "This I Believe" podcasts modeled on the NPR show of the same name. Their use of the podcast, however, brings their students both forward and backward in technology and time: they are using digital recording technologies, but their speeches are written and revised before they are delivered, and their podcasts seem to us very much like radio essays.

Classroom Practice

The teacher-authors classroom practice described in these chapters has changed through their integration of technology into their curriculum, but, like the apparently new genres we've noted above, the change is real but incremental and builds on past practice.

The widely used set of classroom practices that are collectively called writing workshop continues to be the basis for the writing curricula described in our chapters. Writing workshop is a project-based curriculum, based on the work of scholars and teachers in what is often called the *writing process movement* of the 1960s and 1970s and very much in line with the *experiential learning* advocated by John Dewey in the 1930s. Included in this writing curriculum are the recursive elements of the writing process: generating ideas, drafting, getting feedback, revising, and publishing. All of the teachers in this book include some sort of heuristic procedure for generating ideas and planning: Paul Allison's use of freewriting (Chapter 5), Glenn Bledsoe's collaborative brainstorming (Chapter 3), and Poe and Opperman's storyboarding (Chapter 9). Many of these projects include peer response at some stage of the projects' development. All include time for revision; and all conclude with publication.

Although the writing workshop is still there in the background structuring the students' activity, technology has brought important changes in this writing curriculum. Several of the authors mention the ease of revision, the elimination of the copying penalty, as a stimulus to revision. And, once the students' works are online, they are accessible to peers for editing—and now the term *peers* is not geographically constrained. Further, the addition of new technologies to the mix has produced much more diverse projects for publication, including blogs, Web pages, and PowerPoint presentations. A possible downside, as Marva Solomon notes in Chapter 2, is that as the new technologies come into the curriculum, they become themselves a presence that needs to be dealt with: files get lost, servers crash, and students need help with the programs that are being used. But our teachers do not see this as a problem. In fact, used wisely, these moments allow teachers and students to dig deeper into the technology and begin to understand the underlying platforms that can lead to interesting and unintended possibilities. In Chapter 4 for example, as Kevin Hodgson's students ask how to make their characters move or how to layer audio behind a slide, they come to understand that animation and layering of pictures could be a digital substitute for the open-the-flap picture book format. This was not what PowerPoint was intended for, but the students achieved a moment of understanding that technology is a tool they can manipulate, and not the other way around. So talk about technology always seems connected to talk about this new writing—thus, from a writing teacher's perspective, not time entirely lost.

The classrooms we have visited in these chapters seem to us more social and interactive—again a gradual change, an increasing emphasis. This follows our profession's increasing attention to writing as a social and collaborative act, beginning with the work of Ken Bruffee (1984) and Anne Gere (1987). Whereas you might expect the computer-equipped classroom to look like an insurance office, the employees seated and silent in front of their computers, in these classrooms there is discussion among students; sharing of ideas, resources, and knowledge; and in-class communication fostered by the teachers, with the technology as both subject and medium. The chapters in this book together form the best argument that we have seen for the value of face-to-face schooling. In Chapter 3 Glenn Bledsoe puts the idea of collaboration front and center, as his students work together throughout the entire process as a sort of collective writing intelligence. In Chapter 5 Paul Allison's students create social networks and blogs where writing is not written and sent into a void, but is read and responded to by peers from the next classroom or a continent on the other side of the world. In Chapter 8 Dawn Reed and Troy Hicks have their students creating podcasts, not just for the value of voice but also for the sharing of ideas to a potentially global audience. This use of technology for authentic social purposes is an important underpinning to most of the writers of these chapters.

So the change we are seeing in these chapters is real, but it is gradual, incremental, an extension of and addition to what has come before. This observation has important consequences for preservice and inservice teacher training in technology. Given what we have seen in these chapters, we should not expect that new or veteran teachers will instantly adopt a technology-rich set of classroom practices centered on technology. The usual kind of staff development—the one-shot training workshop mandated by the principal or superintendent—will not produce the desired effect, or perhaps any effect at all. Teachers will bring technology into their classroom practice gradually, over time, and at different rates, with long-term help from colleagues and from professional networks like BreadNet and the National Writing Project. And, most important of all, teachers need to be given time to investigate and use technology themselves, personally and professionally, so that they can themselves assess the ways that these tools can enhance a given curricular unit. Technology for its own sake is not what these educators want or need.

ASSESSMENT

So we come to our third topic, *assessment*. When we first conceived of this volume, we thought that assessment might be a difficult topic for our teachers. First, the changes wrought in writing by technology would produce different writing, and that different writing would call for different assessment methods. How would one grade a student's contribution to a class blog? A student's contribution to a collaborative, multimedia project? And second, we anticipated that teachers would find it difficult to satisfy two seemingly incompatible needs: the need to adapt curriculum and classroom practice to the new writing, and the need to prepare students for statewide assessments that tested only the old writing. What we found instead was that teachers were creative and able to adapt their assessment practices to the new writing. They were less able to square what they were doing in multimedia with statewide assessment programs.

Classroom Based Assessment

Regarding classroom-based assessment, we saw what we expected from good teaching: assessment was integrally linked to instruction, arising from learning goals and used to inform teaching. In Chapter 2, one learning goal for Marva Solomon's students in composing their Expert Pages was to synthesize information, and that became one of her criteria for assessment. In Kevin Hodgson's class (Chapter 4), where learning a scientific concept was a goal of the science-based picture book, explaining that concept accurately "with details and examples" was a criterion in the assessment rubric. In Paul Allison's and Glen Bledsoe's classes, since some form of collaboration—either face-to-face or via blogs—was central to their projects, that collaboration figured into their assessments and Allison's students' self-assessments (Chapter 5). In other words, assessment criteria were not generic; they were tailored to the nature and goals of each project. As Bledsoe writes in Chapter 3, "I think of assessment as what teachers do to guide their instruction."

For all of these teachers and the full range of student projects, we also saw traditional rhetorical criteria used for oral and print texts carrying over: indeed, the rhetorical criteria of shaping a text according to audience and purpose were fundamental learning goals and assessment criteria. And, despite the fears of some that popular use of electronic media spells the demise of standards, most of the teacher-designed assessment rubrics included criteria for accurate spelling and grammar, use of detail, and organization. As we expected, these criteria were also supplemented by additional criteria appropriate for bi- and multimodal texts. In some cases, this was a single criterion—for example, for Alanna Frost and Julie Myatt, "employ the affordances (capabilities) of the medium you're using in effective rhetorical ways" (Chapter 11). In others, multiple criteria were presented. For instance, in Chapter 2 Marva Solomon's rubric included a criterion for gathering and synthesizing information from multiple electronic sources and one for combining "multiple digital texts, images, multimedia resources to create a coherent message"—and this, for struggling writers just finishing second grade! For high school students creating blogs (Chapter 5), Paul Allison included multiple specific criteria in his Self-Assessment Matrix, including inserting "snippets" from other blogs and news sources, making intertextual hyperlinks, and including images in one's blog.

State Curriculum Standards and Standardized Assessments

What we see regarding state curriculum standards and state mandated standardized assessments was not quite what we expected. Although the teacher-authors did not see their work as fitting with statewide standardized testing, as we had expected, we discovered that they did see it as matching statewide or national curriculum frameworks. Marva Solomon in Texas, Glen Bledsoe in Oregon, Kevin Hodgson in Massachusetts, Bryan Crandall in Kentucky, and Dawn Reed and Troy Hicks in Michigan point to specific state curriculum standards for English that their students' writing projects addressed, many of them the rhetorical and formal assessment criteria mentioned above. Solomon points also to standards for reading comprehension; Hodgson to standards for science; Bledsoe, Hodgson, and Reed and Hicks to technology criteria. We can't say that these technology standards led these teachers to doing their technology projects, although they might have. Indeed, Glen Bledsoe decides first what feels "powerful" to him and his students and then looks to see how this powerful project can match his state's standards. As he writes, "I believe the purpose of standards is to reflect real-world needs and apply them to student work. If students are creating projects that reflect real-world tasks, then it follows that they will be adhering to standards." In other words, he trusts in his own instincts to develop "real-world tasks" that will satisfy the "real-world needs" reflected in curriculum standards.

Still, whether technology standards provide an impetus for projects or not, they have the power to convey or not convey value and validation for such projects, making it important that these standards be framed in ways that reflect the changes in writing technologies. Glen Bledsoe views the Oregon Technology Common Curriculum Goals as focusing too exclusively on transactional workplace objects: for example, "Access, organize and analyze information to make informed decisions, using one or more technologies." He speculates that creative artists—"the folks at Pixar Studios"—would likely identify a quite different set of skills, reflecting aesthetic and creative uses of sound, image, and text.

Creativity, though, is increasingly seen as a valued skill for all, not just artists. Hodgson notes that the recent report of the International Society for Technology in Education (2007), entitled *National Educational Standards for Students: The Next Generation*, includes "creativity and innovation" as important learning goals for using technology. In its *Framework for 21st Century Learning*, the Partnership for 21st Century Skills (2007) lists "creativity and innovation" as one of the skills that "separates students who are prepared for increasingly complex life and work environments . . . and those who are not." As states develop and revise technology standards and integrate use of technology into standards for English language arts, creative and aesthetic goals should be included alongside the analytic and transactional ones.

Regarding state mandated external assessments for accountability purposes, the best case, and singular case, is Kentucky's portfolio system, for which some of the written work students did for their Senior Boards in Bryan Crandall's class (Chapter 7) could be included for their portfolio, specifically their personal reflection and research paper, both traditional alphabetic texts. Crandall's students' Senior Board presentation with multimodal PowerPoint, however, would not meet portfolio criteria. Further, in Chapter 11 Steve Smith, who also taught in Kentucky, reports that at least until 2005 to 2006, any nonalphabetic print additions to a text (that is, a table or image) were not to be considered by evaluators since they were not writing.

In other cases, the standardized assessments seemed distractions or hindrances. In Chapter 3 Glen Bledsoe writes that while the state of Oregon will allow students to compose their written essay using word processors, they can only use crippled machines that have cut, copy, and paste disabled as well as spell-check and grammar-check. Dawn Reed and Troy Hicks write in Chapter 8 of the pressure exerted by standardized assessments. They note the "acute" misalignment of the state standards—that encourage use of technology—and the Michigan Merit Exam that does not assess technology. They write also of the pressure exerted by this exam "in a high school that is hamstrung by concerns about Adequate Yearly Progress." As they put it, "In short, the test still tests reading, 'riting, and 'rithmetic (as well as science, math, and social studies). In no way does it reflect the types of multimodal composing processes that the Michigan content standards suggest or that, in our experience, podcasting requires." This comment applies to the situation in many states. And, as Reed and Hicks remind us, "what gets measured, gets treasured." What is tested is what one is pressured to teach. We are not implying that testing programs—perhaps with the exception of portfolio assessments—should include new assessments of multimodal compositions, as these new tests are likely to do no better at testing multimodal compositions than they presently do in assessing alphabetic essays. Instead of more or different testing, we need to have appropriate state curriculum standards in place, and then give teachers the responsibility of developing curricula and classroom-based assessments appropriate to the goals of those curricula.

The work of the teachers who contributed to this collection, and the work of their students, validate this recommendation. Far from accommodating and teaching to the test, these teachers continue to give their students what they believe they need, what excites them, what they feel has value and relevance. Our chapter-authors are modeling for their students values that we admire: doing a project for its own sake, for one's own self-satisfaction, and for an audience of peers and significant adults; using one's imagination and intellect to compose texts that engage, inform, and persuade other people. Curricula, packaged scripts, and computer programs that focus too exclusively on teaching to a standardized test—teaching the forms of a five-paragraph print essay—are limiting students' possibilities as writers, failing to help them develop the literacy skills needed for 21st century communication, and giving them the message that the value of their work, and, more broadly, their global competence as composers, is to be assigned by un-named strangers who may determine that more than half of them fall into the category "needs improvement." What we found in the practice of the teachers who have contributed to this collection was uplifting and hopeful: teachers teaching what they believed their students needed to participate fully in the world they were preparing to enter.

REFERENCES

Bruffee, K. (1984). Collaborative learning and the "Conversation of mankind." *College English*, *46*(7), 635–652.

Duguid, P. (1996). Material matters. In Nunberg, G. (Ed.), *The future of the book*. (pp. 63–101). Berkeley: University of California Press.

Gere, A. R. (1987). *Writing groups: History, theory and implications*. Carbondale: Southern Illinois University Press.

Hugo. V. (1832). *Notre Dame de Paris*. Retrieved November 21, 2008 from http: manybooks.net/pages/hugovict1965719657-8/211.html

Kress, G. (1999). English at the crossroads: Rethinking curricula of communication in the context of the turn to the visual. In G. Hawisher & C. Selfe (Eds.), *Passions, pedagogies, and 21st century technologies.* (pp. 66–89). Logan: Utah State University Press.

International Society for Technology in Education. (2007). *National Educational Standards for Students: The Next Generation.* Retrieved May 29, 2008, from http://www.iste.org/inhouse/nets/cnets/students/pdf/NETS_for_Students _2007.pdf

Nunberg, G. (1996). Introduction. In G. Nunberg (Ed.), *The future of the book.* (pp. 9–20). Berkeley: University of California Press. 9–20.

Partnership for 21st Century Skills. (2007). *Framework for 21st Century Learning.* Retrieved June 5, 2008, from http://www.21stcenturyskills.org/index.php? option=com_content&task=view&id=254&Itemid=120

Glossary of Technology Terms

The number in parentheses indicates the chapter in which the term is discussed within the text.

Animated GIF: A standardized photographic image file that allows for simple animation to be embedded within the image itself. (2)

Audacity: A recording software for creating audio files on the computer that is free of charge. (8)

Boolean Search: A mathematical method of searching for information on the Internet by narrowing down the set of data to specific terms. (11)

Chat Programs: A system of synchronous conversations among users of a network. (1)

Digital Platform: The concept of technology tools that are available for creating content, including audio, video, and written documents. (4)

Digital Storytelling: The use of technology to relay a story, often a personal narrative, through the use of audio, video, writing, and other means. (10)

Electronic Portfolios: A collection of work that is organized in a digital format and portfolios may include writing samples, audio files, videos, and other multimedia elements. (1)

Flaming: When a person posts a deliberate message against another person that is hostile or inflammatory, with the intent to provoke the other person. (1)

Flash Drive: A portable media device that uses flash memory to store data files, such as audio, video, and other documents. (4)

Flash Animation: An animated video file that is created with Macromedia's Flash software. (6)

Garageband: A software platform for Apple computers that allows users to create music and podcasts. (6)

Hyperlink: An embedded code that allows a user to move from one Web site to the next through the use of their computer mouse or keyboard. (1)

Hypertext/hypermedia: A form of text that is composed on a computer that allows a user to move to one or more other documents or Web sites from the original document by way of a series of hyperlinks. (1)

iLife: A suite of multimedia software applications for Apple computers that includes iMovie, iWeb, iPhoto and iTunes. (6)

iMovie: A video editing software application for Apple computers. (6)

iPhoto: A photographic imaging software application for Apple computers. (6)

iTunes: A media player software application that allows users to download and listen to music, podcasts, video, and other media content. (6)

iWeb: A software application for Apple computers that allows users to easily create Web pages and publish them to the Internet through Apple's hosting services. (6)

JPEG (Joint Photographic Experts Group): A standardized format for photographic images. (2)

MP3 (Moving Pictures Expert Group): A standard format for compressed audio for the Internet and portable music players. (5)

Multimodal Documents: Computerized texts that are embedded with more than one format of media, including audio, video, and writing. (10)

Networks: A system of interconnected computers that allows users to share information. (1)

Podcast: Digital audio files that are shared from one computer to another via the Internet. (1)

RSS (Really Simple Syndication) Feed: A way for Web sites to syndicate content by sending out updates to users who use a designated RSS reader to automatically collect feeds. (5)

Vodcasting: The distribution of video on the Internet through RSS syndication, in a method that is similar to an audio podcast. (10)

Web 2.0: A trend of the World Wide Web that refers to users of the Internet being able to easily publish original content and use technology for global collaboration. (5)

Web site: A collection of pages and information that is accessible via computer on the Internet. (1)

Weblog (*aka Blogs*): A style of Web site that resembles an online journal, with entries typically posted in reverse chronological order and often centered on a specific topic or interest. (1)

Wiki: A collection of Web pages that can be edited by anyone with access to the site, often as a way to foster collaboration. (1)

Writing Workshop: A philosophy of writing instruction where students explore topics of interest, confer with a teacher and other students, revise their ideas and then publish their work. (2)

Zines: A style of topic-focused, self-published magazine in either traditional paper format or in digital form that is often defined by the personal style of the editor/writer. (9)

Internet Resources

The number in parentheses indicates the chapter in which the term is discussed within the text.

Amazon: (https://www.amazon.com/) A business that specializes in the sale of books and other products exclusively through the Internet. (2)

BBCNews: (http://news.bbc.co.uk/) The online home of the British Broadcasting Corporation news network. (9)

Creative Commons Search (http://search.creativecommons.org) A search engine for materials that are protected by a Creative Commons distribution license. (5)

Edublogs: (http://edublogs.org/) A network of free Weblogs for educators and students. (8)

Everyzing: (http://search.everyzing.com) A search engine that can find multimedia format on the Internet. (5)

Facebook: (http://www.facebook.com/) A social network that allows people to connect with others around similar interests and is geared towards college students and professionals. (9)

Find Articles: (http://findarticles.com) A search engine that accesses articles in the back issues of over 900 magazines, journals, trade publications and newspapers. (5)

FlickrCC: (http://flickrcc.bluemountains.net) A personal Web site that searches through photographs at the Flickr Web site for items that have been designated with a Creative Commons distribution license. (5)

Flickr Creative Commons: (http://flickr.com/creative_commons/by-nc-nd-2.0) A Web site create by Flickr that searches through photographs at the Flickr Web site for items that have been designated with a Creative Commons distribution license. (5)

Google Blog Search: (http://blogsearch.google.com) A search engine that scans through items on indexed Weblogs on the Internet. (5)

Google News: (http://news.google.com) A Web site by Google that collects news feeds from various sources and which can be personalized by the user. (5)

Internet Archive: (http://www.archive.org/index.php) A Web site that collects an archive of Web sites and other media that is posted on the Internet. (10)

KidsClick: (http://www.kidsclick.org/) A directory of Web sites that has been created for children by librarians that can be searched by subject, reading level and degree of picture content. (2)

Morgue File: (http://morguefile.com) A Web site that collects free image (photographic) reference files. (5)

MySpace: (http://www.myspace.com/) A social networking site that is geared toward younger users. (9)

Nettreker: (http://home.nettrekker.com/homeroom/) A search engine for children that offers protection against inappropriate content. (2)

NPR.org: (http://www.npr.org/) The online home of National Public Radio. (8)

OWL: (http://owl.english.purdue.edu/) Officially known as the Purdue Online Writing Lab, or OWL, the site offers access to hundreds of academic resources, including journals and articles. (7)

People.com: (http://www.people.com/people/) A Web site that documents and follows the lives of celebrities. (9)

Podsafe Music Network: (http://music.podshow.com/) A Web site with hundreds of audio files that users can access and use, within copyright guidelines. (8)

PubMed: (http://www.ncbi.nlm.nih.gov/pubmed/) A search engine of the United States Library of Medicine that has access to more than 18 million citations to medical journals. (11)

Rubistar for Teachers (http://rubistar.4teachers.org/index.php) An online site for creating project rubrics for assessment. (7)

Stock.xchng: (http://sxc.hu) A Web site with free stock photographs for use in projects. (5)

Summize: (http://summize.com) A search engine that scans through topics on the Twitter.com social network. (5)

The Onion: (http://www.theonion.com/content/index) An online newspaper that specializes in humor and satire. (9)

Think.com: (http://www.thinkquest.org/en/) An online community that connects schools, teachers, and students from around the world to collaborate on projects through a protected online setting. (2)

Tweet Scan: (http://tweetscan.com) A search engine that scans through topics on the Twitter.com social network. (5)

Twitter: A Web-based application that allows users to send short text messages to friends and others who are part of the user's self-designated network. (5)

United Streaming: (http://streaming.discoveryeducation.com/) A Web-based video distribution portal by Discovery Education that allows educators and students to reuse content for school-based projects. (2)

Yahooligans: (http://kids.yahoo.com/) An Internet search engine run by Yahoo that is designed for young children and has safety measures against inappropriate content embedded into its search engine. (2)

Youth Twitter: (http://youthtwitter.com) A social networking offshoot of Twitter that is designed specifically for students. (5)

Youth Voices: (http://youthvoices.net) A social networking site for students. (5)

YouTube: (http://www.youtube.com/) An online archive of user-created video. (7)

Web of Science: (http://scientific.thomson.com/products/wos/) A Web site that provides users with access to thousands of science-based research journals and articles. (11)

Wikimedia Commons: (http://commons.wikimedia.org/wiki) A searchable database of media files that are designed with the Creative Commons distribution license. (5)

About the Editors and the Contributors

Anne Herrington is Professor of English and Site Director of the Western Massachusetts Writing Project at the University of Massachusetts Amherst. With Charles Moran, she has edited two collections, *Writing, Teaching, and Learning in the Disciplines* (MLA) and *Genre Across the Curriculum* (Utah State UP). With Marcia Curtis, she wrote *Persons in Process: Four Stories of Writing and Personal Development in College* (NCTE). She and Charles Moran have also published shorter pieces evaluating automated essay assessment programs.

Kevin Hodgson is a sixth grade teacher at the William E. Norris Elementary School in Southampton, Massachusetts, and the technology liaison for the Western Massachusetts Writing Project. He received a bachelor's degree in English from Eastern Connecticut State University in 1989, and he has taught sixth grade for 6 years. He is also a member of the New England Association of Teachers of English.

Charles Moran is Emeritus Professor of English at the University of Massachusetts Amherst. With Gail Hawisher, Paul LeBlanc, and Cynthia Selfe he co-authored *Computers and the Teaching of Writing in American Higher Education, 1979–1994* (Ablex). With Anne Herrington, he has co-edited *Genre Across the Curriculum (Utah State UP)* and *Writing, Teaching, and Learning in the Disciplines* (MLA). He was one of the founding directors of the Western Massachusetts Writing Project.

Paul Allison has been teaching since he graduated from Hunter College, CUNY, in 1983. He has been an English, humanities, and technology teacher in several New York City public schools, including University Heights High School in the Bronx, the International High School at LaGuardia Community College in Queens, and East Side Community High School in Manhattan. Currently, with Felicia George, Paul is the NYC Technology Liaison for the National Writing Project.

Glen L. Bledsoe is a fourth grade teacher at Molalla Elementary in Molalla, Oregon. He received his MAT at Willamette University in 1991 after earning his BA in Fine Arts from Indiana University in 1983. He previously taught fifth grade at Keizer Elementary in Keizer, Oregon. He has been the Tech Liaison for the Oregon Writing Project at Willamette University and has worked with the University of Oregon on many technology and writing projects.

Bryan Ripley Crandall is earning a PhD in English Education at Syracuse University. He taught English for 10 years at the J. Graham Brown School in Louisville, Kentucky, and is a member of the Louisville Writing Project, the Bread Loaf School of English and the Critical Friends Network. He has an MAT from the University of Louisville and an MS in Interdisciplinary Science from the Kentucky Institute for Education and Sustainable Development.

Elyse Eidman-Aadahl has been a high school English and journalism teacher, a writing project director, and teacher educator. Currently she directs National Programs and Site Development for the National Writing Project and serves as faculty in the College of Education, University of California, Berkeley. In that capacity she directs the NWP's Technology Initiative and has worked with the National Assessment of Educational Progress (NAEP) in Writing since 1992.

Alanna Frost is an Assistant Professor and the Director of the Writing Center at the University of Alabama in Huntsville. She completed her PhD from the University of Louisville in 2008.

Troy Hicks is an Assistant Professor in Central Michigan University's Department of English Language and Literature and a co-director of the Red Cedar Writing Project at Michigan State University. His research interests include composition, the teaching of writing, and writing with newer literacies and technologies. He is currently co-authoring a book about digital writing in K–12 schools that is being produced in conjunction with the National Writing Project.

Peter Kittle directs the Northern California Writing Project. An Associate Professor of English at California State University, Chico, he received his PhD from the University of Oregon in 1998. Kittle began his professional career in 1987 as a high school teacher of English, speech, drama, and journalism.

Julie Myatt is an Assistant Professor of English at Middle Tennessee State University in Murfreesboro, Tennessee, where she teaches first-year writing and literature courses. She received her PhD from the University of Louisville in 2008.

Mya Poe is Director of Technical Communication at the Massachusetts Institute of Technology (MIT). At MIT she teaches courses in rhetoric, scientific, and technical writing. She received her PhD from the University

Massachusetts. Her research interests include equity in writing assessment, scientific writing systems, and writing across the curriculum. Currently, she is working on a book on scientific writing and an edited collection on racism and writing assessment.

Julianne Radkowski Opperman is a science teacher at Greely High School in Cumberland, Maine. She received her BA in Molecular Biology from Wellesley College and her MS in Nutritional Biochemistry and Metabolism from MIT. Julianne has taught science at the university level and has presented at international science education conferences. She is a visiting scholar at MIT and a member of the science standard setting committee for the Maine High School Assessment.

Dawn Reed is an English teacher at Okemos High School in Okemos, Michigan. She taught at Charlotte High School during the course of this research study. She received her MA in Rhetoric and Writing from Michigan State University in 2008. Her research interests include the writing process, the teaching of writing, and multiliteracies. She is a teacher consultant and program leader with the Red Cedar Writing Project at Michigan State University, and a member of the National Council of Teachers of English.

Jeffrey Schwartz teaches English and film at Greenwich Academy in Connecticut. He is co-author of *Word Processing in a Community of Writers* and co-editor of *Students Teaching, Teachers Learning*. For 30 years he has used computers at *Aspect* magazine, Carnegie-Mellon, Sewickley Academy, Greenwich Academy, and the Bread Loaf School of English, where he was fortunate to be involved in the first years of BreadNet. His best teachers continue to be his students, wife, and son.

Steve Smith teaches as a member of the Term Faculty in the English Composition Program at the University of Louisville. He received his MA in English from Western Kentucky University in 1980 and retired from teaching 7th through 12th grade English, humanities, communications, and creative writing in Kentucky public schools after 28 years of service.

Marva Solomon is a long-time teacher at Menchaca Elementary School in Austin, Texas. She has taught grades one through three with groups of gifted and talented and English Language Learners for 13 years. She was a pioneer in Austin schools as a member of the MAESTRO team, responsible for mentoring teachers toward technology integration in the late 1990s. She is a graduate of Texas Tech University and is now a doctoral candidate in Language and Literacy Studies at the University of Texas at Austin.

Index